John Gould, Silvester Diggles

Companion to Gould's Handbook

Or, synopsis of the birds of Australia. Containing nearly one-third of the whole, or

about 220 examples, for the most part from the original drawings

John Gould, Silvester Diggles

Companion to Gould's Handbook
Or, synopsis of the birds of Australia. Containing nearly one-third of the whole, or about 220 examples, for the most part from the original drawings

ISBN/EAN: 9783337314279

Printed in Europe, USA, Canada, Australia, Japan

Cover: Foto ©Andreas Hilbeck / pixelio.de

More available books at **www.hansebooks.com**

COMPANION

TO

GOULD'S HANDBOOK

OR,

SYNOPSIS

OF THE

BIRDS OF AUSTRALIA.

CONTAINING

NEARLY ONE-THIRD OF THE WHOLE, OR ABOUT 220 EXAMPLES,

FOR THE MOST PART

From the Original Drawings.

BY

SILVESTER DIGGLES.

VOL. I.

IN THIS VOLUME THE FOLLOWING GENERA ARE TREATED OF—

EAGLES, FALCONS, AND HAWKS,
OWLS, GOAT-SUCKERS, AND SWALLOWS,
KINGFISHERS AND SHRIKES,
FLY-CATCHERS, ROBINS, AND WRENS,
LARKS, FINCHES, AND THRUSHES,
BOWER BIRDS AND CROWS,
HONEY-EATERS, CUCKOOS, AND CREEPERS,
ETC., ETC.

BRISBANE:
PRINTED BY THORNE & GREENWELL, EDWARD STREET.

INDEX TO VOL. I.

V.

ORIGINAL PROSPECTUS.

SEEING that the magnificent work of Mr. GOULD, on "The Birds of Australia," so completely supplies every want of the Ornithologist in this particular direction, it may be thought that any other work is superfluous; but copies of Mr. GOULD's Ornithology are so difficult to procure, and their price is so far beyond the means of any but the most wealthy, that the Author of the present publication deems any further reasons for the necessity of a second work unnecessary, as he desires to place within the power of all who wish to obtain it, an accurate and useful book of reference, at as low a cost as will allow of its being published in a creditable manner. In the present work all that is absolutely necessary will be given, and only that omitted which is of minor importance.

The Author's impression is, that, whenever practicable, life size pictures of Birds are most desirable, as tending to convey a more accurate idea than those on a reduced scale, and it will be his aim to represent the majority of the Australian Birds the size of life. The form in which the work will appear (imperial quarto) will, therefore, preclude his giving a complete portrait of many of the larger Birds; but as much of each Bird will be figured as will enable any one to identify the species represented, especially as the accompanying letter-press will describe the Bird in full, with the important addition of careful measurements. From four to six of the smaller Birds (most of which will be complete figures) will appear on one plate, and thus be favorably situated for comparison.

The assistance of several practical Ornithologists has been kindly given, among whom may be named CHARLES COXEN, ESQ., M.L.A., and Mr. ELI WALLER, of Brisbane, from whose fine collection the greater number of the Birds in this work have been figured. Each plate will be colored after the Original Drawings, and the work will be issued in Parts (monthly, if possible), price Ten Shillings. Six Plates will appear in each Part.

It is expected that the number of Parts will not much exceed forty.

The Author would invite the kind attention of all who possess information concerning scarce or local species to the desirability of communicating the same to him, for the purpose of having it embodied in the letterpress. Specimens of Birds, Nests, or Eggs lent to be figured or described will be carefully returned. It is hoped that, in bringing out in Brisbane—the capital of so young a colony—so large and important a work as the present, such assistance and support will be accorded to the Author as will enable him to bring the same to a successful termination. As the immediate expenses are so great, the Author requests that each Part be paid for on delivery.

Intending Subscribers are desired to fill up the form appended, and to return it without delay, as the number of copies issued will be regulated by the number of applications received.

In reference to the above Prospectus, I think it desirable to explain why this work has not been completed. Twenty-one parts only had been issued when the commercial crisis of 1866 caused the withdrawal of so many subscribers that it would have been ruinous to continue it; and thus the assiduous labors of twelve of my best years were in a great degree lost.

Of the first six parts only one hundred copies were struck off; when, finding the circulation increasing, I thought it advisable to have fifty additional plates for the succeeding ones. In the course of time it became necessary to have the first six parts re-drawn to make the sets complete, and this, with a few exceptions, was done on stone principally by myself, the remaining portions of the work being from the pencil of Mr. H. G. EATON, and nearly all are faithful copies from my original drawings. I then made an appeal to the Government for some assistance to enable me to complete this truly colonial work, but, although I offered a handsome inducement,* I was unable to prevail upon the Government to afford me the necessary help, or to render me the material aid I required. A similar appeal to the Board of Education met with no better fate, and thus closed the last chance of my work being successfully terminated.

I am now content to style it "A Synopsis of the Ornithology of Australia; or, Companion to Gould's Letterpress Handbook," which, in my opinion, is in great want of illustrations in order to be properly understood by those who have not means of access to that author's great work on "The Birds of Australia."

Giving, as it does, an assortment of the whole—or, more precisely, of about one-third of the avi-fauna of Australia,—any one possessing "Gould's Handbook" (published in two volumes), will have material in his possession to guide him in the discovery of any bird therein described. In the index will be found, with rare exceptions, the names used in the *folio volumes* of Gould, which are also carefully preserved in his Handbook; and I deem it very inadvisable at present to make such changes in the nomenclature as appear in both the Handbook and the Sydney Museum Catalogues.

The old names, as given by Gould on his folio plates, can never lead to confusion, and will always be quoted as synonyms by naturalists.

A few recently discovered birds will not be found in the Handbook (which was published after I had commenced this work), but such will be found, accurately described, in the short letterpress description appended to every plate in this Synopsis.

No index has hitherto appeared to this book, such being a matter almost impossible before it was finished; but now that the work is as complete as it probably ever will be, the birds figured are alone catalogued, and those required to be known must be sought for in "Gould's Handbook."

My original drawings are contained in four volumes, and are the "Ornithology" as it should have appeared. Scarcely a dozen birds published in Gould's splendid volumes being wanting, and many new birds (about twenty-five in number) have been named and added thereto by myself.

To those gentlemen who have rendered me their assistance by the loan of specimens, or information, I hereby tender my best thanks. Among whom I may mention—besides those noticed in the original Prospectus —Mr. Cockerell, of Brisbane, whose large and valuable collection was of the greatest service, and was the means of furnishing me with a number of new and interesting species; Mr. White, of Reed Beds, near Adelaide, S.A.; Mr. Waterhouse, of the South Australian Museum; the late Mr. Stapleton, of the Northern Territory, S.A.; the late Mr Rawnsley, who kindly lent the unique specimen of his bower bird, which I felt justified in naming after him; Messrs. Krefft, Masters, Ramsay, Gulliver, &c.

My Subscribers will find twenty or more of the sea birds not represented by a single example, as such cannot, in my opinion, be ranked as Australian species, being merely passing visitants met with by accident. The twenty-four birds, described in the latter part of the second volume of "Gould's Handbook," not being Australian, are in no instance represented, but are of great interest to students of natural history, preserving as

---

* This consisted of an offer to provide the public schools of Queensland with a series of uncolored object lessons of the various plates which, from time to time, should be issued until the work was completed, these plates to be drawn on stone, by myself, at the Government Lithographic Office, and accompanied with a letterpress description, for the use of the teachers, also written by myself. This offer the Government thought proper to decline, alleging as a reason that uncolored prints would be unsuitable for use in its schools, ignoring the well-known fact that most of the great illustrated publications in the world are issued with uncolored plates. Apart from this, also, the coloring constituted the chief expense, the skilled labor necessary being almost unattainable,—a fact the Government was, doubtless, perfectly aware of.

they do, records of an ancient neighboring fauna rapidly disappearing, and of which any enlightened government in Australia should preserve all information, at any cost, before they shall be numbered among things of the past, and their fossil remains alone are handed over to the student of paleontology.

During the issue of the work, then entitled the "Ornithology of Australia," it was favorably commented upon as a desirable work by the Australian press, and obtained a prize medal at the Intercolonial Exhibition of Victoria, 1806-7; also another at the Exhibition of Colonial Products, in Brisbane, Queensland, in 1861.

A handsomely-bound copy of the first fifteen parts, with illuminated title and index, was presented by the Government to Prince Alfred on the occasion of his visit to Queensland; and Sir George Bowen, first Governor of Queensland, permitted the work to be dedicated to himself.

The following extract from an article in the *Brisbane Courier*, of April 3, 1875, is inserted with a view of shewing the more liberal treatment accorded to similar works in other colonies :—

BIRDS AND OTHER BIPEDS.— . . . . In New South Wales, for many years past, the public have had the advantage of the illustrations of the "Mammalia of Australia," drawn by Miss Scott and Mrs. Ford, and described by Gerard Krefft. The Government there are alive to the advantages of such object lessons for the children, although uncolored; and did not hesitate to reward the ladies named for their services to the cause of education and art. In Victoria, the works of Professor M'Coy, and others, on natural history, were not brought out unsupported by the Government. And in South Australia, from G. F. Angus downward, her men of talent have met with appreciation and support in the production of similar works.

AQUILA AUDAX
Wedge Tailed Eagle

AQUILA AUDAX.

(Wedge-tailed Eagle.)

MALE.—General plumage, blackish brown; the edges and tips of the wing coverts and upper tail coverts, pale brown; sides and back of the head, clothed with lanceolate feathers of reddish brown; cere and orbits, yellowish white; irides, reddish brown; bill, yellowish horn color, tipped with black; foot, light yellow; claws, black.

The FEMALE has the general plumage of a lighter tint, and the feathers margined in a larger proportion with the rusty red. In the young birds the plumage is very much margined with ferruginous, both on the upper and under surface, and the head and neck are lighter than in the adult birds. The female is larger than the male.

Male.—Expanse, 6 feet 8 inches; length, 35 inches; wing, 24; tail, 18½; bill, 2½; tarsus, 4¾.

This fine and distinct species of eagle is the largest raptorial bird in Australia, in every known portion of which it is to be found. In Tasmania and all the southern parts of the continent it is rather numerous, so much so as to prove a considerable source of annoyance to the squatter, upon whose flocks (more especially at the lambing season) it commits great depredation. In some districts it is more plentiful at one time than at another. Thus Captain Sturt mentions its scarcity about the Depôt, Cooper's Creek, he only having observed two specimens during his six months' detention at that spot. Mr. White, of Adelaide, says he found it very plentiful in all parts of South Australia, especially *towards the north*, having seen sixty or seventy at a time, soaring high in the air, or perched about in the trees. Dense forests and open plains are equally frequented. It is certainly not often seen in Queensland, and becomes more rare to the northward. The flight of this species is soaring and majestic, and performed frequently at an immense elevation, appearing as a small speck in the blue sky. It circles round and round with scarcely a movement of the wings, and from its high position descends with startling rapidity upon its quarry. The natural prey of this powerful eagle consists of large birds and small quadrupeds of the kangaroo tribe; rats also form a principal portion of its food. When it swoops down upon a wallaby the latter seems paralysed, and thus forms an easy prey. Like the vulture, it delights in carrion, and the putrid carcase of a horse or bullock never comes amiss. On such occasions large numbers may be observed enjoying their unclean repast. When gorged almost to suffocation, it resorts to the nearest tree, and perches there until again prepared to renew the feast. When thus engaged it is not difficult to approach, as at other times. It is generally seen in pairs. When found troublesome about stations the aid of poison is usually resorted to as the best mode of getting rid of them. The nest of the Wedge-tailed Eagle is always placed in the fork of a large tree, usually a gum (Mr. White, of Adelaide, saw one built in a pine), not invariably near the top, but always in the most inaccessible position. The nest is flat, and composed of large sticks. The eggs are two in number, stone color, blotched and marked with reddish and yellowish brown. Size, 3 by 2¼ inches.

ICHTHYIÆTUS LEUCOGASTER
White-bellied Sea Eagle

ICHTHYIAËTUS LEUCOGASTER.

(White-bellied Sea Eagle.)

MALE—Head, neck, and all the under surface, white; the tail feathers, for about a-third of their length, terminated by the same color; primaries and base of the tail feathers, blackish brown; the rest of the plumage, grey; bill, bluish horn color, tipped with black; cere and lores, bluish lead color; irides, dark brown; feet, whitish, inclining to yellow; claws, black.

The female is similar to the male, but much larger in size. The young have the head, throat, and back of the neck, buff; back and wings, brown, each feather tipped with whitish buff; abdomen, buff, each feather margined with brown; bill, brown.

Length of female, 32 inches; wing, 22; tail, 10½; bill, 2½; tarsus, 4.

This noble species of eagle is found all round the coasts of Australia and Tasmania, where it frequents bays and inlets of the sea, often ascending the streams running into the same. In such situations its food consists of fish and other marine animals, principally such as have been left dead upon the shore. It is also occasionally met with in the larger rivers of the interior, where its food for the most part consists of waterfowl, especially ducks. It is not known to dive beneath the surface. Mr. Coxen informs me that, in November, 1865, he took from this bird a saw-fish two feet in length, which it had just dragged out from a shallow in Pimpama Creek (near Brisbane). He had an opportunity of witnessing the struggle, which was a severe one. The fish is now in Mr. C.'s collection. The flight of this bird is lofty and soaring, and it delights in describing large circles in the air, the pinions when at full stretch being curved upwards. A pair are generally seen together, their union being probably permanent. The nest is a large flat structure of sticks, and usually placed in the fork of a high gum-tree, near the top, the same being re-visited and repaired from year to year at the time of incubation. On islands where there are no trees suitable, it builds on the flat surface of a rock, the materials used being portions of bushes and low shrubs. The nest seen and described by Captain Cook on Eagle Island in the Great Barrier Reef, and which doubtless belonged to this bird, was 2 feet high, and 26 feet in circumference. The eggs are two in number, white, faintly stained with reddish brown: size, 2 inches 9 lines long, by 2 inches 3 lines broad.

HALIASTUR LEUCOSTERNUS.

(*White-breasted Eagle.*)

Head, neck, chest, and upper part of the abdomen, white; back, wings, lower part of the abdomen, thighs, upper surface of tail, and upper and under tail coverts, rich chestnut red; primaries, tipped with black; tail feathers, tipped with greyish white; bill, yellowish horn color, frequently tinted with rose color on the culmen; both mandibles, tinged with dark grey at the base; irides, yellow; legs and feet light yellow.

Length, 22 inches; wing, 15; tail, 9; bill, 1¾; tarsus, 2.

This truly beautiful raptorial may frequently be seen on the banks of the Brisbane River, and also among the small islands of Moreton Bay, and when seen in its full plumage on a bright sunny day it becomes peculiarly attractive, by the snowy whiteness of its head and neck contrasting with the deep rich coloring of its wings and back; it is also frequently met with in the bays and inlets of our north-eastern coast, and is occasionally met so far south as the Hunter River, but never farther inland than such parts as are under tidal influence; it is not uncommon in the neighborhood of Cape York and Port Essington. Its food consists chiefly of fish, and it exhibits considerable activity in taking its finny prey by dexterously darting on and seizing it with its strongly armed foot while skimming along near the surface of the water. When not on the wing it is generally seen on some tree overhanging the water, and it is to some such place that it retires after capturing its food, to devour it at leisure; but, if disturbed, it experiences no difficulty in doing so while on the wing. It is very nearly allied to two Asiatic species, differing only in a slight marking of the white feathers of the head and neck. Its time of breeding is about the months of October and November, when it usually lays two eggs, marked with many irregular and angular fine streaks and a few small spots of reddish brown, the egg being of a dusky white. The nest, like others of a similar order, is composed of sticks roughly placed together in the fork of a tree, in some secluded spot near the water, and is lined with coarse grass or very fine twigs.

FALCO PEREGRINUS.

(Peregrine Falcon.)

HEAD, cheeks, and back of the neck, black; upper surface, wings, and tail, deep grey, equally banded with darker grey or blackish brown; outer webs of primaries, blackish brown; inner webs, obscurely barred with light buff; throat, whitish, passing into the buffish fawn color of the chest, and becoming of a redder cast on the abdomen; each feather of the throat streaked with a dark brown line down the centre, the tip of each streak being expanded into a spot in the feathers covering the chest; the remaining feathers of the under surface crossed with numerous bars of deep brown; bill, lead color; cere and legs, light yellow; claws, black; irides, dark brown. The sexes are nearly alike in coloring, but in the female the markings are darker and better defined; she is also a good deal larger than the male.

MALE.—Expanse, 34 inches; length, 15; wing, 11¼; tail, 5¾; bill, 1¼; tarsus, 1½.

This noble species of Falcon is distributed over almost every country on the globe, being found from Canada to Cape Horn in America, and throughout the whole of Europe, Asia, and Africa. No bird is more celebrated for its courage, strength, and rapidity, and in the olden time it occupied a first place in the estimation of our ancestors, when the practice of falconry was their favorite pastime. The Australian specimens differ somewhat in color and markings from those of Europe, which has induced Mr. Gould and other authors to separate it as a species, under the name of Falco Melanogenys; but the very slight differences between the British and Australian specimens, attributable, doubtless, to a long residence in this portion of the globe, and beautifully exemplifying the law of variation, scarcely justify us in considering it a different species from the true Peregrine, with which it agrees, both in size, habits, and appearance. There is little doubt that, were sufficient pains taken, it, as well as several other species of Australian Falcons, might be educated to pursue the different kinds of wild animals distributed over this continent. It is known to inhabit every settled portion of this territory, and in all probability is a denizen of the whole, though more commonly met with in the older colonies of New South Wales and South Australia, and always in pairs. The food of the Peregrine Falcon consists of small animals and birds, especially of the duck tribe, whence its name of the "duck hawk" in some parts. It delights in rocky and precipitous localities, and, from its great strength and daring disposition, is able to cope with prey of much greater weight than itself. During Captain Sturt's residence at the "Depôt," one was shot in the act of taking a duck from the water in the "glen;" and Mr. White says he saw it strike and break the wing of a large cormorant, and, in spite of its struggling and cries, conduct it to the water's edge. The sandstone cliffs on the banks of the Murray, and other rocky and inaccessible situations, are chosen for the purpose of nidification. The nest is rather flat, and formed of sticks, generally placed on the edge of a cliff. It has been known, though rarely, to build in trees. The eggs are two in number, of a reddish buff color, thickly blotched and streaked with chestnut brown. Size, 2 inches 1 line, by 1 inch 7½ lines.

FALCO SUBNIGER
Black Falcon

FALCO SUBNIGER.

(Black Falcon.)

THE whole of the plumage, dark sooty brown, the feathers of the upper surface and wings, margined with a lighter tint; chin, whitish; irides, dark brown; bill, lead color; cere, yellow; legs and feet, leaden yellow; claws black.

Expanse of Male, 34 inches; length, 20; wing, 14; tail, 9; bill, 1½; tarsus, 2; mid-toe, 2¼.

The Female is considerably larger, but similar in her coloring.

The information respecting this noble species of Falcon is as yet extremely meagre, and from its excessive rarity, it is likely that a long period may elapse before any definite knowledge is acquired respecting it. It was first recorded by Mr Gould as inhabiting South Australia. Captain Sturt met with it at the Depôt, when two specimens (a male and female) were procured. During his long detention at that memorable spot he only saw two other examples. It has since been obtained by Mr. White and others in South Australia. It has recently been proved that this bird is not so strictly confined to the interior as was at first supposed, from the fact of Mr. Waller, of Brisbane, having shot a fine male near the city. He subsequently saw another under rather curious circumstances. The common Whisking Eagle (Haliaster Sphenurus) was giving chase to the falcon, which presently alighted on the branch of a tree, the other being scared off by Mr. W.'s presence. While making preparation to secure so rare a bird, the attack by the eagle was renewed, when the falcon commenced an ascent into the air in a series of magnificent circles, and disappeared. Its food is supposed to consist of small birds, especially parrakeets, as its presence always causes great alarm and commotion among them.

FALCO FRONTATUS
White breasted Falcon

FALCO FRONTATUS.

(White-fronted Falcon.)

FOREHEAD, whitish; crown, ear coverts, cheeks, and all the upper surface, dark bluish grey; primaries, nearly black, barred with buff in the shape of large oval spots on the inner webs; two middle tail feathers, grey, obscurely barred with black; the remainder are alternately barred with dark grey and chestnut; throat and chest, whitish buff, each feather with a stripe of brown down the centre; abdomen and thighs, bright rufous; bill, lead color; cere and legs, yellow; irides, blackish brown.

Length, 12 inches; wing, 9½; tail, 5½; bill, ⅞; tarsus, 1¾.

This is the smallest of the true falcons found in Australia, and is distributed over the whole of the continent and Tasmania. It much resembles in appearance the European Hobby, and is very daring and courageous. Its favorite resort is the neighborhood of swamps and marshes frequented by snipe, plover, &c., which form its principal prey. Its dart is most unerring, and it seldom misses its victim. Captain Sturt remarks that "it follows the line of migration, and makes sad havoc among the parrakeets and smaller birds. He is generally hid in a tree, and would descend like an arrow when they came to water, frequently carrying off two of the little Amadina Castanotus—one in each talon." The approach of Milvus or Circus is disregarded by the feathered tribes generally, but directly one of these small falcons makes its appearance, all is twitter and commotion.

It builds its nest (which is a rather large but shallow structure, formed of sticks, and lined with strips of bark, grass, &c.) in lofty inaccessible trees. Eggs, from two to three, light buff, blotched and marked all over with dark buff; size, 1 inch 10 lines by 1 inch 4 lines.

IERACIDEA BERIGORA.

(Brown Hawk.)

Crown, reddish brown, with a black line down the centre of each feather; a streak of black from the base of the lower mandible down each side of the check; ear coverts, brown; throat, chest, centre of the abdomen, and under tail coverts, pale buff, each feather having a central line of brown; flanks, reddish brown, marked with whitish spots; thighs, dark brown, marked with reddish spots; back, reddish brown; scapularies, wing coverts, and tail, brown, barred and spotted with reddish brown; primaries, blackish brown, largely spotted with buff on the inner webs; bill, bluish horn color, with the tip black; cere and naked space round the eye, bluish lead color; irides, dark brown; feet, whitish lead color.

Length, 19 inches; wing, 14; tail, 9½; bill, 1; tarsus, 2; longest claw 2½.

This bird is common in Tasmania, New South Wales, and South Australia, becoming rather scarce in the southern portions of Queensland. In Western Australia it is represented by another species very closely allied. The plumage of the Brown Hawk presents considerable variety, no two examples being exactly alike; but the above description will enable an ordinary observer easily to identify the majority of specimens. The one from which the accompanying plate is taken is from the collection of Mr. Waller, of Brisbane, and may be regarded as an exceedingly dark variety, the whole plumage being entirely of a deep brown tint. The bill, cere, orbits, and feet are similar in color to those parts in birds of the ordinary plumage. The other species, I. Occidentalis, is so like the present that the plate in which it is figured will serve to depict the common variety of the present species, with the difference only of the cere being yellow instead of lead color. Its food consists of carrion, small mammalia, and birds, but principally insects, especially caterpillars. At certain seasons the latter pest prevails to such a degree that whole tracts of country are cleared of every blade of grass, when this bird may be observed devouring the larvæ with great greediness. The numerous dead animals which, in times of drought, are to be found throughout the country, also attract this bird in great numbers. In disposition it is not so courageous as many others of the Australian raptorial birds, but it is still sufficiently so to make it at times a nuisance to the breeder of poultry, as it not unfrequently visits the farm yard and carries off chickens and ducklings. Its nest is formed of sticks, lined with shreds of bark, and generally placed near the top of a high gum tree. Eggs, two or three, very variable in appearance; ground color, buffy white, much blotched with reddish brown; length 2 inches 2 lines, by 1 inch 6 lines.

TINNUNCULUS CENCHROIDES.

(Nankeen Kestrel.)

MALE—Forehead, white; head and back of the neck, reddish grey—the shaft of each feather, black; scapularies and wing coverts, cinnamon red, with an elongated black spot near the end of each feather; primaries, secondaries, and greater coverts, dark brown, fringed with white—the basal portions of the inner webs, with dentate blackish markings; face, white; a small patch of dark brown from the gape across the lower portion of the face; chest and flanks, whitish buff, with a streak of brown down the centre of each feather; abdomen and under tail coverts, white; upper tail coverts and tail, grey—a broad band of black near the extremity of the latter, each feather of which is tipped with white, but very slightly in the two central ones.

FEMALE—Upper surface and wings, cinnamon red—more broadly marked with black than in the male; wing coverts, marked with arrow-head shaped spots of black; tail, tipped with white, followed by a broad black band—the remainder, cinnamon red with about ten narrow bars of black; throat, vent, and under tail coverts, white; the rest of the under surface, reddish buff, with a brown stripe down the centre of each feather; cere, orbits, base of under mandible, and feet, yellow; bill, horn color, with the tip black.

Expanse, 20 inches; length, 14½; wing, 9½; tail, 6½; bill, ½; tarsus, 1½.

This beautiful species, which is closely allied to the Falco Tinnunculus, or European Kestrel, is found in various parts of Queensland, New South Wales, South Australia, and Western Australia, but is by no means common in any portion of the continent. In some districts it would appear to be stationary, in others, according to Sturt, following the line of migration taken by the different species of birds which constitute its food. Mice and lizards are also favorite morsels, and are frequently devoured by it when upon the wing. The flight of the Nankeen Kestrel is easy and graceful, frequently at a great elevation, when it may be seen performing large circles in the air with scarcely the slightest motion of wing. It lays its eggs (four in number) in the hole or spout of a gum tree, making no nest, or (according to Mr. White of Reedbeds, near Adelaide,) occasionally using the deserted nest of the Brown Hawk (Ieracidea Berigora). The eggs are freckled all over with blotches and minute dots of rich reddish chestnut on a paler ground, and are 1½ inches in length by 1½ broad. The breeding season is October.

ASTUR NOVÆ HOLLANDIÆ.

(New Holland Goshawk.)

———◆——

All the upper surface, grey ; throat and all the under surface, white, irregularly barred with light grey ; cere, dull orange ; feet, yellow ; bill and claws, black ; irides, yellow or dark brown.

Length of male, 15 inches ; wing, 9¼ ; tail, 7¾ ; bill, 1 ; tarsus, 2¼.

Length of female, 19 inches ; wing, 12 ; tail, 10 ; bill, 1¼ ; tarsus, 2¼.

This elegant species is found in New South Wales and Queensland. It may at times be observed in the open forest country, but its favorite resort is the dense scrubs. Considerable controversy has been awakened as to whether the white Astur (A. N. H. Albino) is or is not a variety of the present species. The measurements of the two are precisely similar ; but the fact that in Tasmania the white one only is to be found would seem to give great weight to the supposition that the latter is certainly a permanent variety, if not a species. I must add, however, that on one occasion I saw a white and a grey bird of this genus (evidently a pair) flying together in company, the smallest, or the male, being the white one. The food of this Astur consists of birds and small mammalia. It occasionally attacks the poultry yard, and carries off young fowls. It makes its nest, composed only of sticks, in trees, forty or fifty feet from the ground. The eggs are two in number ; skin, milk white.

BUTEO MELANOSTERNON
Black-breasted Buzzard.

BUTEO MELANOSTERNON.

(Black-breasted Buzzard.)

———•———

Crown and sides of the head, chin, chest, and middle of the abdomen, deep black, passing into chestnut red on the flanks; thighs and under tail coverts, rufous; back of the head and neck, chestnut red—the centre of each feather, black; shoulders, buff; upper surface, brownish black—each feather margined with chestnut; primaries, white at the base, the remaining portion black; cere, purplish flesh color; irides, light brown; feet, whitish, with a tinge of lilac. The sexes are alike, but the female is the smallest.

Length, 22 inches; wing, 19½; tail, 8½; bill (around the curve of cutting edge), 2; tarsus 2½.

This well marked and elegant bird is the only species at present known of the genus to which it belongs inhabiting Australia, and to which it is also exclusively confined. It is of great rarity, though frequenting parts of the continent far removed from one another, but more particularly in the south and middle portions of this great island continent. No examples have as yet been recorded from the north. It is equally a denizen of the colony of Western Australia and that of New South Wales. The Black-breasted Buzzard flies high, and the strongly contrasted colors of its plumage render it a very conspicuous object as it careers in majestic circles through the air. It feeds upon the various small animals which are so numerously dispersed over the country. Gilbert, when out shooting, records its dexterity in extracting all the interior portions of specimens of small kangaroos, etc., which he temporarily placed in a tuft of grass, tree, or the fork of a branch, intending to resume possession of them on his return, nothing being left but the bare skin, and that to all appearance uninjured.

MILVUS AFFINIS.

(Allied Kite.)

HEAD, neck, shoulders, and upper portion of wings, reddish brown, each feather with a black line down the centre; back, blackish brown, the tip of each feather slightly tinged with brownish buff, the black line down each feather, as in other parts, but less conspicuous; throat, dirty reddish buff; all the under surface dull brown, the centre of each feather being reddish brown, with a well-defined black streak in the middle; greater wing coverts, primaries, and secondaries, brownish black; tail, greyish brown, indistinctly barred with a darker tint; cere, yellow; bill, black; feet, yellowish; claws, black; irides, dark brown. This species varies much, some specimens being of a nearly uniform dull brown excepting the shoulders, which are lighter.

Length, 21 inches; wing, 15½; tail, 10½; bill, 1½; tarsus, 2.

This bird is spread over the whole of the eastern portion of the Australian continent, from Victoria to Port Essington. It visits Port Albany in large flocks, and after a short sojourn suddenly disappears, probably migrating to the southward. Though always a plentiful species, it has been observed to be more so in dry seasons, when it makes its appearance in great numbers about the towns and settlements, but especially preferring the neighborhood of the slaughter-houses and boiling-down establishments, where the ground is literally blackened with its numbers. Its favorite food being offal, as long as any of that is to be obtained it is contented, but it has been known occasionally to carry off chickens. Though its disposition is rather timid than otherwise it has been seen to snatch food from the hands of children, and it may be even rendered familiar to some extent, as it is on various stations, where persons amuse themselves by throwing pieces of meat into the air for it to catch, which it does very dexterously. It may often be seen to pounce down on floating substances in rivers and suddenly dipping its claws in the water to seize the same, which, if suitable for food, is often devoured upon the wing. Small animals swimming never fail to attract its notice, but it does not venture to lift any beyond its strength. Its flight, though sluggish, is easy, graceful, and generally at no great height above the surface of the ground, which it may be observed examining carefully as it glides along. The slightly forked tail is used with great address, and enables the bird to make very sudden turns in its course. Its voice is a loud and shrill whistle.

ELANUS AXILLARIS.

Black-shouldered Kite.

FOREHEAD, cheeks, and under surface, white; back of the neck, back, scapularies, and upper tail coverts, light grey. A large black patch extends from the shoulder over a considerable portion of the wing. Primaries, dark grey; tail, greyish white; mark over the eye, black; irides, reddish orange; bill, black; cere and legs, yellow. The sexes are very much alike, but the female is the largest. The young have the tips of the feathers of the upper surface tinged with brown.

Length of male, 12 inches; wing, 9½; tail, 4½; bill, 1¼; tarsus, 1¼.

This species is widely dispersed, being found from Queensland, on the east, to Swan River, on the west of the Australian continent. It cannot be considered plentiful, seldom more than two being seen at a time. This bird is generally found in open country, and when seen soaring over the inland plains in search of its food, attracts much interest and attention by the gracefulness of its movements. Its food consists of insects and various small animals. In disposition, it may be considered rather timid than otherwise.

CIRCUS JARDINII.

(Jardine's Harrier.)

Crown, cheeks, and ear coverts, dark chestnut, streaked with brown; facial disk, back of the neck, upper part of the back, and chest, grey; lower part of the back and scapularies, the same color, but marked with two spots of white at the tip of most of the feathers; shoulders, under side of wing, abdomen, thighs, and under tail coverts, bright chestnut, spotted with white; primaries, black—the basal portions, buffy brown; secondaries, dark grey, crossed with three narrow bars of dark brown, and broadly tipped with the same color; upper tail coverts, brown, barred and tipped with whitish; tail, barred with whitish grey and blackish brown, the tip being broadest and of the latter color, with a whitish termination; irides, orange in the adult, brown in the young; cere, greenish yellow; bill, blue at the base and black at the tip; legs and foot, yellow; claws, black. The female is larger than the male, and brighter in color.

Expanse, 55 inches; length, 20; wing, 15; tail, 10; tarsus, 3¾.

This very handsome and conspicuous species of Harrier is found pretty generally dispersed, though by no means common, over New South Wales, South Australia, and Queensland, especially in the peninsula of Cape York, where it is a permanent resident, frequenting the open land. Its usual resort is flat country in the vicinity of creeks, where it may be generally seen perched upon a stump or stone, or flying at a short distance from the ground minutely surveying every object beneath in search of its food, which consists of various reptiles, birds, and small mammalia. A nest of this species was found by Mr. White, of Reed Beds, near Adelaide, October 21, 1865. It was large, formed of sticks, and placed in the fork of a stunted Eucalyptus, and contained three young birds thickly covered with grey down, and also one white egg, which was of a rounded form—the size measuring 1¾ inch by 1½ inch.

STRIX CASTANOPS

STRIX CASTANOPS.

(Chestnut-faced Owl.)

FACIAL disk, reddish buff, or chestnut, encircled with black; upper surface, wings, and tail, rufous brown, each feather barred with darker brown; under surface and legs, buffish brown; head and shoulders, minutely spotted with white; sides of the neck, chest, and flanks, spotted with deep brown; bill, yellowish horn color; feet, yellow; irides, deep brown.

Length, 18 inches; wing, 15; tail, 7; bill, 2½; tarsus. 3½.

This large and powerful species is a denizen of the southern portions of Queensland, also of New South Wales and Tasmania. It varies much in color, the above description being of most usual occurrence. Some specimens are much lighter, and have the facial disk and under surface white; the characteristic markings and spots, however, occur in all. Like the other members of the genus *Strix*, the male is smaller than the female. The present species, which is one of the most formidable of the Australian rapaces, is generally to be found in thinly timbered country, near swamps, the borders of scrubs, etc.; during the day it lies concealed in the hollows of trees and other suitable situations, coming forth in the evening to search for its prey, which consists of the various descriptions of small nocturnal mammalia which are so abundant at that time.

STRIX WALLERI.

(Waller's Owl.)

Crows, back, and upper tail coverts, blackish brown intermingled with tawny buff, each feather having a small white spot at the tip; facial disk, buffy white, with a patch of blackish brown in front of the eye; fringe around the disk, bright buff, the shafts of each feather marked with black; wings, blackish brown intermingled with bright tawny of a deeper tint than that of the back, and spotted with white at the tip of each feather; from the shoulder to the body, a broad piece of bright tawny buff speckled with numerous small black spots; primaries and secondaries, bright tawny buff, tipped for a considerable portion of their length with brownish, the larger portion of their inner webs, pure white—the former are barred with four, and the latter with three, bands of blackish brown; scapularies, blackish brown with a spot of white at the tip of each feather; central feathers of tail, beautiful bright buff, with four black bands, the nearest of the lateral feathers partake of the same color, but those edging the tail are much paler, being nearly white and the bands almost obsolete; sides of the neck, chest, and upper portion of the abdomen, buff, becoming gradually paler towards the tail; the whole of the under surface marked with small brown spots near the tip of each feather; thighs, buff externally and white internally; under side of wings, white, slightly mixed with buff, and marked with arrow-head-shaped spots of blackish brown; under surface of quills, white, banded and tipped with dark brown; tarsi, long, rather slender, and feathered for about half their length, the remainder portion being clothed with short hairs; legs and feet, yellowish flesh color; bill, flesh color; irides, dark brown.

The Female is not so bright in color, but in other respects is very similar to the Male.

Length, 16 inches; wing, 13; tail, 5; bill 1½; tarsus, 3¼; middle toe and claw, 2⅓.

This fine new species of Owl is now figured for the first time, and it is with much pleasure I name it after the discoverer, Mr. Eli Waller, of Brisbane, to whose large and valuable collection I am so much indebted for most of my figures, and to whose scientific and extensive practical knowledge of the birds of Australia, and energy and perseverance as a collector, I am happy to bear testimony. It does not often happen in a country so well searched as Australia, since the visit of Mr. Gould in the years 1838, '39, '40, that so important and interesting a bird as the present, is brought to light; and the fact of this new species having been shot in the immediate neighbourhood of Brisbane, may serve to encourage others interested in the study of ornithology (more especially in the newly settled districts, where novelties are mostly to be looked for), to endeavor to add their contributions to the very numerous and interesting fauna of their adopted country. Two specimens (a male and female) are in Mr. Waller's collection.

The figure is very much less than the natural size, as the measurements given above will sufficiently shew. Nothing is as yet known of the habits of this bird, but it doubtless assimilates in every important respect to the family in general. Its nearest ally is Strix Delicatulus, a much smaller species, which, like the present, has the tarsus naked for about half its length, the remainder of the Australian Owls yet known being feathered to the toes.

ATHENE STRENUA
Powerful Owl

ATHENE STRENUA.

(Powerful Owl.)

ADULT.—Facial disk, small, whitish in front, greyish behind; a number of fine black bristles point forwards towards the bill and overlap its base; crown, upper surface, back of the neck, and back, sepia brown, barred with light buffy brown, which shows lighter and more conspicuously on the lower portion of the back; wings and tail, the same, but the bars are wider and better defined, particularly on the greater coverts and tertiaries; throat, white, slightly streaked with brown; chest and under surface, buffy white, broadly banded with transverse angular markings of dark brown; thighs and tarsi, closely banded with brown and white; bill, dark horn color; irides and foot, yellow; claws, brownish horn color. The sexes are alike.

YOUNG.—Upper surface marked as in the adult, but the bars are whiter and more conspicuous; the head and back of the neck, white and downy, with transverse markings of greyish brown; under surface, very downy and white, with a delicate streak of brown down the centre of each feather; facial disk white, streaked with hair like lines of black.

Length, 21 inches; wing. 15; tail, 10½; bill, 2; tarsus, 2½.

This is the largest and most robust species of owl yet discovered in Australia, being only surpassed in size by the two largest of our eagles. Its appearance is fierce and defiant; and its strength is such that animals of considerable size form no small portion of its food, being easily overcome and killed by the powerful weapons with which it is furnished. Like others of the genus to which it belongs, it is in the habit of hunting in the daytime as well as during the night. On one occasion a fine specimen was disturbed by a gentleman of my acquaintance, in Rosenthal scrub, near Warwick, who says; "I was attracted by a strange knocking. On getting within thirty yards of the " place I saw a specimen of the large owl (Athene Strenua) on the branch of a tree devouring an opossum; on becoming aware of my presence " he raised himself to his full height and looked at me with an expression of haughty disdain, conveying at the same time the idea that if I " did not quickly remove he would punish me. When at a distance of ten or twelve yards I threw a stick at him; he took no notice of this; " but when I threw another, which struck him, he flew quietly away, taking his prey with him. I refrained from shooting him, being on the " look out for wallabies at the time." The present species is found in the scrubs and brushes of the dividing range and the country between it and the coast coast, both in New South Wales and Queensland, but is more frequently obtained in the latter, though far from plentiful anywhere.

ATHENE BOOBOOK
Boobook Owl

ATHÉNE BOOBOOK.

(Boobook Owl.)

FACIAL disk, whitish in front, the hinder part, brown ; upper surface, reddish brown ; wing coverts, scapularies, and inner webs of the secondaries, spotted with white ; tail feathers, alternately banded with dark and light brown ; under surface, light reddish brown, with irregular blotches of white ; thighs, tawny buff ; bill, dark horn color ; feet and irides, yellow.

Length, 14 inches ; wing, 10 ; tail, 7¼ ; tarsus, 1¾ ; bill (measured in a straight line), 1¼.

This species is found in the dense scrubs of Queensland, and is also met with in New South Wales and the other Australian Colonies, especially in tea-tree swamps or marshes in the neighborhood of woods. It is partially diurnal in its habits, and flies with great swiftness, feeding as readily upon insects as upon small reptiles, mammals, and birds. The peculiar note which it utters at night resembles the word Boo-book, and somewhat reminds one of that of the English Cuckoo when heard at a distance. By some colonists it is called the Barking-bird, as its note, when heard near at hand, has a considerable resemblance to the bark of a dog—travellers having been diverted from their path at night by its call, under the impression that they were in the neighborhood of some human habitation. When disturbed, it rises swiftly to a considerable height, and makes a sudden descent into any hiding place in the vicinity ; and the similarity of its coloring to the branch it selects is usually so great as to render it a matter of no little difficulty to discover where it has taken refuge.

ÆGOTHELES NOVÆ HOLLANDIÆ
Owlet Night Jar

ÆGOTHELES NOVÆ HOLLANDIÆ.

(Owlet Night Jar.)

FOREHEAD, grey, minutely freckled with dark grey; lores, dark brown; a series of stiff bristles proceed from the front of the eye, those pointing upwards being branched; general color of the upper surface, dark brownish grey, freckled with blackish; collar behind the neck, whitish or rusty brown, each feather bordered and freckled with dark brown; the remainder of the upper surface and wings, brownish grey, banded and freckled with darker; chin, whitish; throat and chest, dark grey, freckled with whitish; abdomen, white in some, buff in others; in some each feather barred near the tip with dark grey; the bases of the feathers are nearly black, and the shafts white; under tail coverts, white; primaries, edged with whitish or reddish buff, and obscurely banded and freckled on the outer webs with dark brown, the remaining parts of those feathers being dark brown; irides, vinous brown; feet, yellow; bill, dark brown.

Length, 9 inches; wing, 5; tail, 4½; tarsus, ?; bill, ½; width of ditto at the gape, 1.

The range of this pretty little Goatsucker is of large extent, being found in all the coast country, from Queensland round southward to Western Australia. It is very variable in color, some specimens being much tinged with rufous; in others the grey predominates. Its range over the northern portions of the continent is not strictly determined, but it is probably represented in the tropical portions by the following species. It is known to exist in Queensland and New South Wales, in all the country between the coast and the dividing range, and in almost every variety of situation. In habit it is quite nocturnal, sleeping in the day time in the holes or spouts of the gum trees, or perched on the branch of a casuarina, and not coming forth until the shades of evening have gathered. Its food consists of insects of all kinds. One that I kept in an open-roofed building for about a fortnight was particularly fond of cockroaches, and hunted about for them with great assiduity. When disturbed it utters a kind of hiss, but its ordinary note when flying about is something like the mew of a kitten. The eggs are four or five in number, very white, and much rounded: size, 1 inch by ⅞; they are deposited in the hole of a tree, no nest being formed.

ÆGOTHELES LEUCOGASTER.

(White-bellied Owlet Night Jar.)

HEAD, black; crown, crescent-shaped mark at the back of the head, and collar surrounding the back of the neck, freckled with grey; back, freckled black and white; wings, brown, crossed by numerous bands of lighter brown, freckled with dark brown; primaries, margined externally with buff, interrupted with blotching of dark brown; tail, dark brown, crossed by numerous broad irregular bands of reddish buff, freckled with dark brown; ear coverts, straw white; chin, abdomen, and under tail coverts, white; breast and sides of the neck, white, crossed by numerous freckled bars of black; irides, dark brown; upper mandible, dark olive brown; lower mandible, white, tipped with black; legs, pale yellow; claws, black.

Length, 9½ inches; wing, 5½; tail, 5; bill, 1; tarsus, 1.

The above description of Mr. Gould's proves the great similarity which exists between the two species; this is, however, a little larger in size. In its habits it altogether resembles the common species. It is plentiful at Port Essington, and will probably be found to range all over the north coast.

PODARGUE PHALÆNOÏDES
Mal. jeunané Podargue

PODARGUS PHALÆNOIDES.

(Moth-plumaged Podargus.)

FOREHEAD, buffish white, immediately in front of which, and overtopping the bill, is a tuft of fine lanceolate feathers of buff banded with black; crown, sides of the neck, back, wings, and tail, rich reddish brown; scapularies and some of the wing coverts, tipped with white; under surface, rufous grey, mottled with whitish buff; most of the feathers of both the upper and under surface, broadly streaked with brownish black, followed by a spot of whitish buff; tail, reddish brown, obscurely barred with black; in addition to the above coloring and markings the whole of the plumage is minutely freckled with grey; irides, orange; bill, greenish horn color; feet, yellow.

Length, 14½ inches; wing, 7; tail, 9½; length of bill, 2; width of ditto at the gape, 1½; tarsus, ⅝; middle toe, 1¾.

The mingled character of the markings and coloring of the Podargi renders the task of description a work of no ordinary difficulty. The same characters will be found to occur again and again in others of the genus, abundantly proving that a correct figure of the natural size is of more worth than any more description, however minute. When it is borne in mind that the birds themselves vary much in color, as in the present instance (many specimens of the P. Phalænoides being more or less of a brownish grey tint), the difficulty of the undertaking is still further increased, and the necessity of a good figure, as well as accurate measurements, still more apparent. This, which is perhaps the smallest of the genus, is confined to the northern portions of the Australian continent. It was obtained in some plenty at Port Essington by Gilbert, and recently from Cape York. The whole of the country round the Gulf of Carpentaria may be presumed to be its habitat. Nothing definite has been recorded concerning its habits, which, without doubt, assimilate to those of its congeners, whose food consists for the most part of insects and annelides.

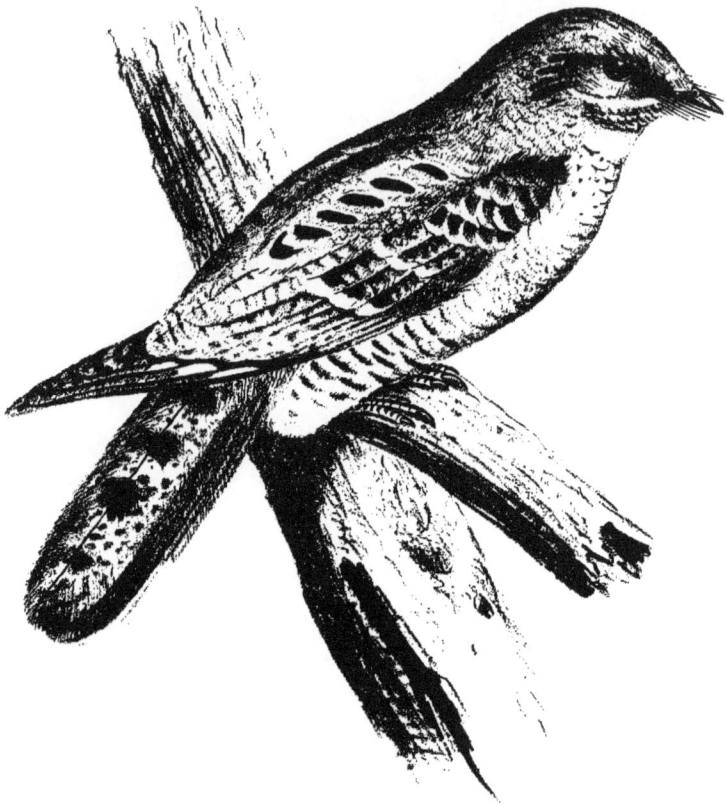

CAPRIMULGUS MACRURUS
Large-tailed Goatsucker

CAPRIMULGUS MACROURUS.

(Large-tailed Goat Sucker.)

GENERAL plumage, grey; crown of the head, a collar of rufous behind the neck, ear coverts, shoulder coverts, and throat, rufous brown, more or less pencilled with black; wing coverts, mingled brownish black and rufous brown, many of the feathers being tipped with white; uppermost tertiaries, light grey, pencilled with brownish black; secondaries, blackish brown, with bright spots of sienna brown; primaries, black, with three white irregular bands on the centre of the three quills next the outermost, which latter has a large white spot on the inner web only; the rest of the primaries are black, mottled with burnt sienna; scapularies, tipped with large oval black spots on their outer webs, each spot bounded by a sharp line of sienna brown; tail, dull brown, indistinctly barred with blackish brown; the two outermost feathers on each side largely tipped with white; a band of buffy white along the gape; a large white patch beneath the throat; the rest of the under surface, reddish buff mingled with grey, and banded and pencilled with black; bill, black; irides, dark brown; feet, brown.

Length, 10 inches; wing, 6¼; tail, 5¾; bill, 1¾; tarsus, ⅝.

This is the only one of the genus yet discovered in Australia. It appears to be confined to the northern portions of the continent: Leichhardt speaks of having met with it in latitude 22° 57', which must for the present be considered its southern limit. What its northern limit may be is probably not yet known, but it is found in various islands of the Malayan Archipelago. At Port Essington it was found by Mr. Gilbert frequenting the open forest, and sometimes in dense thickets, sheltering itself under a bush or tuft of dead leaves on the surface of the ground, in which position it sits so close that it may be almost trodden upon before making any endeavor to escape; but, on taking wing, it flies with amazing swiftness and with a zig-zag motion, suddenly dropping into some near place of concealment. It is said to breed in October.

ACANTHYLIS CAUDACUTA.

(Spine-Tailed Swift.)

Crown of the head, back of the neck, and ear coverts, deep shining green, strongly tinged with brown; lores, deep black; forehead, throat, inner webs of secondaries nearest the back, a patch on the lower part of the flanks, and the under tail coverts, white; wings and tail, deep shining blackish green, with purple reflexions; centre of the back, greyish brown, becoming darker towards the rump; chest and abdomen, brown; bill, black; feet, brown.

Length, to the extremity of tail, 7¼ inches; wing, 8½; tail, 2¼; bill, ⅜; tarsus, ⅜.

Few, if any, of the swallow tribe exceed the present species in size; and probably few other birds in existence can compete with it in rapidity of flight. The immense development of the pectoral muscles and depth of the keel of the breast, at once proclaim its power and endurance. The wings project two inches beyond the tail. So rapid a bird can with the greatest ease traverse the continent of Australia in a short time, a day or two amply sufficing for such a journey. The Spine-tailed Swallow (so called from the prickles at the end of the tail) is found in all parts of Australia (perhaps excepting West Australia). It occasionally visits Tasmania, and is known to migrate to great distances on the continent of Asia. Mr. Jerdon says its breeding place is among the crags and precipices of the Himalayas. When shot it falls very much in advance of the position in which it is struck, the momentum of its rapid flight carrying it to the ground like the stick of a sky rocket. Its arrival is sudden during the months of January and February, after which time it takes its departure to other climes. Its visits to Brisbane are irregular and of short duration.

CYPSELUS AUSTRALIS.

(Australian Swift.)

Throat and rump, white; upper and under surface of the body, brown—the back having a bronzy metallic lustre; each feather of the under surface, margined with white; wings and tail, dark brown; bill and foot, black; irides, very dark brown.

Length, 6¼ inches; wing, 7½; tail, 3½; tarsus, 7-10ths; bill, ⅜.

This species was first discovered by Mr. Gould, on the Upper Hunter River, in 1838. It is found in New South Wales and Queensland, and is, I believe, widely spread over the whole of Australia. The Australian Swift flies high, and performs immense sweeps and circles while seeking its insect food, being frequently in company with the Spine-tailed Swift. Like that bird it performs long and extensive migrations to distant parts of the Asiatic continent. Its visits to the southern portions of Australia are confined to the latter part of summer, and must be considered very irregular, and much dependant on the state of the atmosphere, as in seasons of great dryness it is, perhaps, never seen.

HIRUNDO NECKERA
Wire-tame Swallow

ATTICORA LEUCOSTERNON
White breasted Swallow

HIRUNDO NEOXENA.

(Welcome Swallow.)

FOREHEAD, throat, and chest, rust red; upper surface, deep steel blue; wings and tail, blackish brown—all but the two central feathers of the tail have an oblique mark of white on the inner web; under surface, very pale brown; under tail coverts, tipped with white; irides, dark brown; bill and feet, black.

Length, 5¾ inches; wing, 4½; tail, 3¼; bill, ½; tarsus, ½.

This pretty swallow is found throughout Australia and Tasmania, and also in the islands of the Malayan Archipelago. Its appearance is the harbinger of spring, the time of its visitation depending upon the temperature. Its appearance in Tasmania is much later, and its departure thence earlier, than in the more northern portions of Australia. In New South Wales and Queensland a few may be occasionally observed even in the winter season, but by far the greater number migrate to the north. From the beginning of August to the beginning of May it may be observed busily engaged in the work of incubation, its nest being frequently constructed in situations similar to those of the English swallow, the eaves of houses being favorite spots. The nest is open at the top, and the clay or mud is intermingled with grass to give strength and bind the structure strongly together. It is lined with a layer of grass, and finally with feathers. The eggs, which are of an elongated shape, are generally four in number; color, pinky white, spotted with purplish brown and greyish brown, in many examples forming a zone at the larger end: size, 9 by 6 lines.

HIRUNDO PRETENSIS.

(Torres Straits Swallow.)

THROAT, rusty red, bounded below by an indistinct band of dull bluish black; under surface, white; tail, forked—all but the two middle feathers with a spot of white on the inner web; crown of the head, brownish black, with steel reflexions; back and upper tail coverts, glossy steel bluish black; wings, black, glossed with green; bill and feet, black.

Length, 5 inches; wing, 4½; tail, 2½; bill, from gape to tip, 7/16; breadth at base, 5/16; tarsus, ½.

The above description by Mr. Gould is taken from a specimen received by him from Mr. Raynor, Surgeon of H.M.S. Herald, who shot it on the northern shore of Australia. It was somewhat immature, and the tail feathers perhaps not fully developed. It bore a strong resemblance to the H. Rustica of Europe. Mr. Gould believes it to be an inhabitant of Java, having in his possession a fully adult specimen from that island, which he believes is identical with the present species.

ATTICORA LEUCOSTERNON.

(White-breasted Swallow.)

CROWN of the head, light brown, surrounded by a ring of white; lores, black; a broad band, commencing at the eye and passing round the back of the neck, brown; centre of the back, throat, chest, and under surface of the shoulder, white; wings and tail, brownish black; rump, upper tail coverts, abdomen, and under tail coverts, black; irides, dark reddish brown; bill, blackish brown; feet, greenish grey.

Length, 5¾ inches; wing, 4; tail, 3½; bill, 3/16; tarsus, ½.

This species is widely distributed, ranging from Western Australia to very nearly the eastern coast. It has been obtained on the Namoi by Mr. Coxen, in South Australia by Mr. White, and in Western Australia by Mr. Gilbert. The latter of these ornithologists asserts that it often chooses the deserted retreat of a small burrowing animal (Perameles Lagotis) in which to deposit its eggs, and probably to retire for the night; it also constructs its own burrow, and it is not at all unlikely that the same suffices for the incubation of several broods simultaneously, as more than one pair have been seen to issue from the same hole. The tunnel is about a yard long, and enlarged into a chamber at the extremity, which is lined with leaves of the Acacia and grass. As many as nine eggs have been found in one nest: they are white, and long in proportion to the width. The flight of this species is high and sustained, and it is consequently difficult to procure. It seldom remains long in one locality, and may be sometimes seen, though but for a short time, mingling in the flocks of other swallows.

EURYSTOMUS AUSTRALIS
Australian Roller

EURYSTOMUS AUSTRALIS.

(Australian Roller.)

CROWN of the head and cheeks, brown; lores, dark brown; back and scapularies, light greenish brown; edge of shoulder, brown; upper portion of wings and upper tail coverts, shining bluish green, washed with brown; greater coverts and tertiaries, bright bluish green; feathers of the spurious wing and secondaries, intense indigo blue on the outer webs, edged with lighter—the inner webs, blackish brown; bases of primaries, deep rich indigo blue. Commencing on the inner web of the first primary, and extending across the next five, is a patch of light shining whitish green, which on the fourth quill is 1½ inch in length. On the seventh quill is a small rudimentary patch of the same color. The remaining portions of the primaries are blue, merging into black on the tips and inner webs; base of tail, bright green, passing into indigo and tipped with black; throat, purplish blue; chest, light green, washed with brown; under surface of wing, abdomen, and ventral coverts, light green, with a slight admixture of brown; bill and feet, orange red—the upper mandible tipped with black.

Length, 10½ inches; wing, 7½; tail, 4; bill, 1½; tarsus, ⅞.

This handsome bird is migratory in its habits, visiting the southern parts of Queensland, and also the colony of New South Wales, in the spring, for the purpose of incubation, and retiring northward for the winter. It is to be met with most frequently early in the morning and in the evening, being generally seen perched at a great height on the naked branch of a gum-tree, where it sits watching for its insect food, which it captures for the most part upon the wing. Its flight is rather labored, and of an undulating character, at which time the beautiful silvery blue patch upon the wing being opened to its full extent, shows conspicuously, and is supposed to have given rise to the colonial name of the bird—"Dollar Bird," from the fancied resemblance in size and shape to that well-known coin. Its note is harsh and guttural, and usually uttered when on the wing. The time of incubation is from the early part of September to the latter part of November, and the eggs are deposited in the hole of a gum-tree; they are three in number, pearly white, much pointed at the smaller end: size, 1 inch 5 lines by 1 inch 2 lines.

DACELO GIGANTEA.

(Laughing Jackass, or Great Brown Kingfisher.)

FOREHEAD, buffish brown, each feather marked with a broad black line down the centre. The feathers of the crown are formed into a crest, the fronting and uppermost portion of which consists of black, and the hinder and side portions from above the eye of white feathers. Ear coverts and a patch behind the neck, black; neck and all the under surface, white; back and shoulders, blackish brown, the tips of the feathers being lighter; primaries and secondaries, black, the former white at their bases, and the latter tinged near the extremity of the outer webs with greenish grey, and slightly tipped with white; wing coverts, black, tipped with very light shining verditer blue; upper tail coverts, light verditer blue; tail feathers, reddish chestnut, the two central ones being slightly tipped with white, and the remainder for a considerable portion of their length are white, all being crossed with distinct bars of black, which are broadest in the middle feathers and the upper parts of the others, becoming reduced to mere lines on the white tips of the lateral feathers; upper mandible, black; under mandible, dirty yellowish white, with a large patch of brown near the head; irides, very dark brown; feet, blackish green.

Length, 19½ inches; wing, 9; tail, 7½; bill, 3; tarsus, 1; middle toe, 1⅜.

This, the most common of the three species known to inhabit Australia, is found in South Australia, Victoria, New South Wales, and the southern parts of Queensland. It generally frequents open timbered country or cleared land in the neighborhood of stations, farms, or where timber is being burned off, when snakes, lizards, locusts, &c., offer it an ample repast. Should it meet with a reptile with which it is unable individually to cope, its loud cries soon bring others to its assistance. In dealing with a snake, its custom is to seize the reptile, ascend a short distance in the air and drop it, immediately following and repeating the process a number of times, until its victim, stunned and bewildered, falls an easy prey to its voracious enemy, who, first battering it from side to side, finishes by swallowing it entire. Snakes two feet long have been taken out of the stomach, a fact which should lead persons to afford so useful an animal all possible protection. It is usually seen perching on a dead branch almost motionless, or merely moving its head from side to side, as it intently scans the ground from its elevated position. The popular name by which this bird is universally known is derived from the circumstance that it imitates in no small degree a loud boisterous laugh, which is continued for some time, and accompanied with an upward jerking motion of the tail. The nest is situated in the hole of a tree. The eggs, two in number, are pearl white, and about the size of a pigeon's.

DACELO LEACHII.

(Leach's Kingfisher.)

MALE.—Head and back of the neck, white, streaked with brown; sides of the neck and under surface, white, crossed by numerous narrow irregular bars of brown, which become broader and more marked on the flanks; back, dark brown; wing coverts and rump, bright shining verditer blue; centre of wing, deep blue; primaries, blue on the outer, and black on the inner, webs; the basal portions of the same, white; tail, deep blue, all but the two central feathers irregularly barred near their extremities, and largely tipped with white; bill, blackish brown on the upper, and buff on the lower, mandible; irides, dark brown; feet, olive.

FEMALE.—Is similarly colored to the male, though not so brightly, with the exception of the tail, which is chestnut brown, barred with bluish black.

Length, 10¼ inches; wing, 8½; tail, 5¼; bill, 4; tarsus, 1.

This large and powerful species of Kingfisher is found throughout the whole of Queensland, being as plentiful at Rockhampton as D. Gigantea is to the south. It occurs, though by no means abundantly, in the neighborhood of Brisbane and Ipswich, and in its habits is similar to the common species. It feeds on reptiles, centipedes, and insects, and dives under the water for fish, which are carried to the nearest log, beaten to death, and devoured entire. It is sometimes destructive among young chickens, watching its opportunity and quietly dropping on its prey, carrying it off without the noise and disturbance caused by the swoop of a hawk, and consequently escaping without detection or suspicion. From its great size and strength, this Dacelo is able to encounter snakes of considerable size; and the indiscriminate slaughter of so useful a bird ought on every occasion to be strongly condemned. Its note differs from that of Gigantea in being more harsh and not lengthened into the peculiar laugh of that bird. It builds its nest in the hollow branch of a tree, the same being formed of strips of dry bark and similar materials. Eggs—two, white, and nearly round.

HALCYON SANCTUS.

(Sacred Halcyon.)

CROWN, back, wings, and tail, blueish green; a line of buff from the base of the bill to a little behind the eye; lores and ear coverts, black; throat, white; collar round the neck and all the under surface, buff, blending into white towards the throat; bill, black, except the base of the under mandible, which is flesh color; feet, dark flesh color; irides, dark brown.

Length, 8½ inches; wing, 3½; tail, 2½; bill, 1½; tarsus, ⅝.

This species has an extensive range, being found in all the known parts of Australia, but not in Tasmania. In the south it is only to be seen in the spring and summer seasons, migrating to the north for the autumn and winter. Its general resort is fresh water streams, but it may sometimes be observed in thick brushes and scrubs, and—what in a bird of its habits might be thought curious—even at considerable distance from water. It preys upon insects of all kinds; also on lizards and very small snakes. In saline marshes it feeds largely upon small crabs and other crustacea. It often sits for hours upon a naked branch, until a favorable opportunity occurs for darting upon its prey. It makes no nest, but merely deposits its eggs on the soil in the hole of a tree, or in the deserted nests of the white ant; they are in number four or five, white, 1 inch 1 line long, by 10 lines broad. The plumage of both sexes is alike. The young bird has the breast marked with brown bands.

HALCYON McLEAYII.

(McLeay's Halcyon.)

LINE under the eye and ear coverts, glossy black; head, occiput, wings, and tail, deep blue; primaries and secondaries, white at the base, showing like a white spot when the wings are open; the remaining portion of the primaries, black, margined externally with blue; a spot of white in front of the eye; collar round the neck and all the under surface, white; back and upper tail coverts, light blue. The female is destitute of the white collar round the neck. Bill, black; the basal portion of the under mandible, fleshy white; legs and feet, greenish grey.

Length, 8 inches; wing, 3½; tail, 2½; bill, 1½; tarsus, ⅝.

This handsome species is found in Queensland and the northern portions of Australia. It is known as the "brush kingfisher," from its being frequently seen in thickly-wooded country. The food consists of insects, generally, but more especially beetles. It differs from the H. Sanctus in being confined to the coast, and it is seldom found inland at a greater distance than 30 miles. It may often be seen in gardens in the neighborhood of Brisbane, and when undisturbed becomes very familiar. Its nest is usually to be found in the tea-tree swamps, or on the banks of creeks; the deserted nest of the white ant is hollowed out for the purposes of incubation, which takes place during the month of November, the eggs being merely deposited on the bare earth or material present. Nests may be often seen bulging out from the sides of ironbark, swamp-oak, and other trees. McLeay's Halcyon is plentiful at Cape York in the winter and spring, but migrates to the southward during the hotter months of the year. The eggs, four or five in number, are much rounded in form, and pearly white—11x10 lines.

The note of this species is shrill, and resembles the words "poo poo."

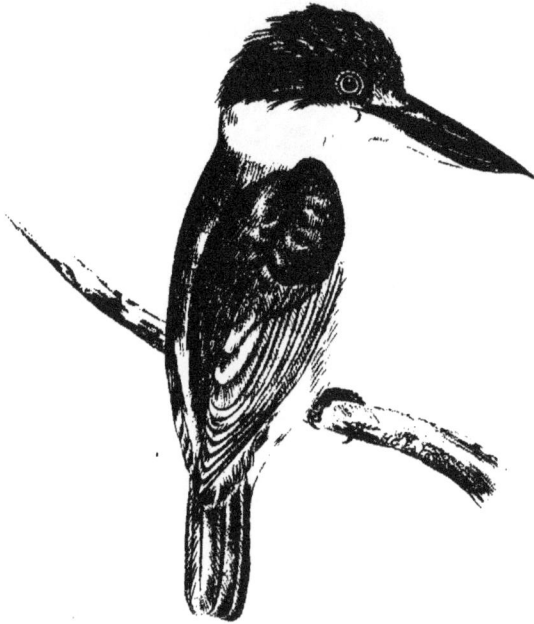

HALCYON PYRRHOPYGIA.

(Red-backed Kingfisher.)

CROWN of the head, dull green, strinted with white; a stripe from the base of the bill, which encircles the eye, and is continued round the back of the neck, black; throat, spot beneath the eye, collar round the neck, and all the under surface, white, the latter sometimes washed with buff; upper part of back, dark green; scapularies, the same, intermingled with a few white streaks; wings, bluish green; secondaries, tipped with white; tail, bluish green; middle of the back, white, followed by chestnut on the lower portion and tail coverts; upper mandible, black; under mandible, fleshy white, tipped with black; irides, blackish brown; feet, dark grey.

Length, 8¼ inches; wing, 4; tail, 2¾; bill, 1½; tarsus, ¾.

This species is very rare in some localities, and rather plentiful in others, and seems to be more confined to the interior portions of Australia, having a wide range from the east to the west. Like its congener, H. M'Leàyi, it may be found at long distances from water, but at other times watching for its prey on the banks of rivers and creeks, generally selecting a dead branch on which to perch. It differs considerably in size, some specimens being much larger than others. The measurements as above were taken from a beautiful specimen shot at Oxley Creek, near Brisbane, in 1864, which is now in Mr. Waller's collection. With this exception, there is no record of its having been found on the eastern waters.

HALCYON SORDIDUS.

(Sordid Kingfisher.)

HEAD, back, scapularies, wing coverts, and upper portion of wings, brownish oil green; quills, greenish blue; tertiaries, verditer blue on the outer webs, blending with oil green on the inner; a small patch at the base of the upper mandible; collar round the back of the neck and all the under surface, buffy white; tail, greenish blue, appearing distinctly barred in certain lights; upper tail coverts, bright verditer blue; upper mandible, black; lower mandible, flesh color, tipped with black; irides, black.

Length, 9¼ inches; wing, 4; tail, 2¾; bill, 2½; tarsus, ¾.

This species of Kingfisher seems to be confined to the northern portion of the east coast. It is not uncommon in the neighborhood of Brisbane, where it has been obtained among the mangroves of Moreton Bay; it is also plentiful as we proceed northwards. Its true habitat is mangrove swamps and inlets of the sea; and its food consists of small crustacea, the fry of fish, and marine insects.

TANYSIPTERA SYLVIA.

(White-tailed Tanysiptera)

CROWN of the head and wings, intense ultramarine blue; a patch of black extends from behind the eye, and is continued round the back of the neck, and shades the scapularies near the middle of the back; centre of the back, pure white, which is continued down to the rump and the whole length of the two long central tail feathers; the remaining feathers of the tail are blue, and are shorter as they recede from the centre; under surface, bright tawny buff; irides, black; bill and feet, scarlet. The female has the central tail feathers shorter, and the colors less brilliant than the male.

YOUNG.—Forehead, blackish, edged with rufous buff, passing into light blue on the crown and occiput; a broad stripe of black behind the eye passes round the neck, and mingles with the feathers of the upper part of the back; a small patch of white is on the centre of the back and upper tail coverts; wings, light dull blue, each feather broadly tipped with rufous buff; outer edges of primaries, dull blue towards the base; inner webs, brownish black, except the bases, which are pure white; tail, light dull blue; the inner webs of the two central tail feathers, white; throat, whitish; sides of the neck, chest, and abdomen, rufous buff; cheeks, striated with blackish brown; the chest has lunate marks of the same color; bill, brownish horn color, lighter beneath; feet, reddish flesh color.

Length, 12 inches; wing, 3½; central feathers of tail, 7; longest of the others, 3; bill, 1½; tarsus, ½.

This beautiful species of Kingfisher is only obtained in the peninsular of Cape York. It is a migratory bird, and makes its appearance at the setting in of the N.W. monsoon, in the month of November, and departs in March to its northern habitat, the island of New Guinea. It is somewhat plentiful near Port Albany, but, from the shyness of its disposition, is not easily obtained. It frequents the dense scrubs and brushes, particularly the open spots, and may generally be observed sitting on a creeper or dead branch watching for insects, and uttering its peculiar cry, which is a harsh shrill whistle twice or thrice repeated, resembling the syllables "wheet wheet," at which time it raises its tail perpendicularly with a jerk. Like many other species of kingfisher, it has the peculiar habit of incubating in the clay-built structures of the white ant, not being very particular whether the same be on a tree or on the ground, but very frequently at the foot of a rotten stump, where these nests often occur. A hole is made completely through from side to side, and a small excavation or hollow in the middle serves for the reception of the eggs, no nest being made. The eggs are three, and sometimes four, in number, nearly round, and of a pure white. The newly-fledged young make their appearance early in January, and do not acquire the long tail feathers until after the first moult.

1. ARTAMUS SORDIDUS   2. A. SUPERCILIOSUS   3. A. LEUCOPYGIALIS
   Wood Swallow   White eyebrowed W. Swallow   White rumped W. Swallow

ARTAMUS SORDIDUS.

(Wood Swallow.)

HEAD, neck, and body, dark sooty brown; wings, deep bluish black; the outer edges of the second, third, and fourth primaries, white; the two central feathers of the tail, bluish black—the remainder, the same, but largely tipped with white; irides, dark brown; bill, blue, tipped with black; feet, lead color. The sexes are alike.

Length, 7 inches; wing, 5; tail, 3; bill, ¾; tarsus, ½.

This species of Wood Swallow is found in the southern parts of Queensland, but is not very common, being found much more plentifully in New South Wales and the southern portions of the continent. It also occurs in Western Australia. In Tasmania it is a migratory bird, arriving in October, and after rearing several broods returns to the north. It delights in thinly timbered country, cleared land in the neighbourhood of farms, etc. Its flight is sailing and circular in direction, and it often takes its stand on a bare twig from which it darts forth to capture any insect which may be passing and then returns to the same spot. The singular habit of clustering together like a swarm of bees, for the purpose of roosting, belongs to this and others of the same genus. Several of the birds suspend themselves to a branch of a tree, others then attach themselves until a mass of forty or fifty are collected together. They are also in the habit of huddling together on the tops of stumps with their heads turned inwards. The nest of A. Sordidus is exceedingly neat and compact, rather shallow, formed of fine twigs, and lined with fibrous roots. It selects a variety of situations for the purpose of building, as the fork of a tree, a leafy branch, or a cleft in the bark. The usual number of eggs is four; they are very variable in their markings, and of a dull white, spotted and dashed with umber brown; size 11 by 8 lines.

ARTAMUS SUPERCILIOSUS.

(White-eyebrowed Wood Swallow.)

MALE.—Lores, space around the eye, and ear coverts, deep black; chin, greyish black, passing into blackish grey on the chest; crown, greyish black; a long white stripe over the eye, widest behind; upper surface, wings, and tail, sooty grey; tail, tipped with white; under surface of body, deep chestnut; under surface of wing, white; bill, blue, tipped with black; irides, brownish black; feet, deep leaden grey.

FEMALE.—In most respects similar to the male, but the stripe over the eye is very indistinct; the throat is grey and the under surface much lighter; the ear coverts also are not black.

Length, 7 inches; wing, 4½; tail, 3½; bill, 1; tarsus, ¾.

The south and south-eastern portions of Australia are frequented by this species, which is not so common as the former. In its general habits it resembles A. Sordidus, and is frequently found with it in company, but is more shy and not so easily approached. The nest is very similar to that of the species above referred to. The eggs are dull buffy white, spotted with umber brown and light grey, forming a zone at the larger end; size 11 by 8½ lines.

ARTAMUS LEUCOPYGIALIS.

(White-rumped Wood Swallow.)

HEAD, throat, and back, grey; tail and primaries, black, tinged with grey; rump, chest, and under surface, white; irides, brown; bill, blue, slightly tipped with black; feet, greenish grey. The sexes are alike. The young are mottled with brown.

Length, 7 inches; wing 5½; tail, 2½; bill, ¾; tarsus, ½.

Every colony of Australia, excepting Western Australia and Tasmania, is inhabited by this bird. The southern portions of the continent are visited by it in the summer time, during which period two broods are reared. It is partial to well watered country, and chooses the vicinity of rivers and streams for its abiding place. It makes its nest in the various trees which line the banks; on the Brisbane River, even building in the mangrove. Though in the habit usually of building for itself a nest of grass and fibrous materials, it sometimes contents itself by appropriating the deserted nest of other birds, which it furnishes to its liking by a new lining of fine grass and root fibres. The eggs are three in number; color, fleshy white, minutely marked with reddish brown and grey; size, 10 by 7½ lines. The actions and habits of this species are very similar to those of A. Sordidus; it clusters in a similar manner, and its flight is graceful and elegant—a succession of quick vibrations, followed by a long soaring flight with wings extended. It sometimes flies very high.

P.RUBRICATUS
Red-lored Pardalote

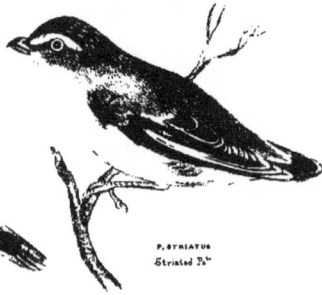

P.STRIATUS
Striated Pt.

P.AFFINIS
Allied Pt.

P.MELANOCEPHALUS
Black-headed Pt.

PARDALOTUS RUBRICATUS.

(Red-lored Pardalote.)

FOREHEAD, crossed by a narrow band of dirty white; crown and back of the head, deep black, each feather spotted with white near the tip; back of the neck, back, wing coverts, and rump, brownish grey; wings, dark brown, margined with pale brown; spurious wing, a small portion of the base of the primaries, and outer margins of secondaries, rich orange; lores, bright reddish orange; above and behind the eye, a stripe of buff; upper tail coverts, bright olive green; tail, deep blackish brown, tipped with white; throat and abdomen, greyish white; chest, bright yellow; upper mandible and legs, brown; under mandible, greyish white; irides, greenish yellow.

Length, 4 inches; wing, 2¼; tail, 1¼; bill, ⅜; tarsus, ⅔.

This rare species is found in the interior, in the neighborhood of Cooper's Creek. Mr. White, of Reed Beds, near Adelaide, says: "It is not scarce, and, like others of its genus, is ever engaged creeping about amongst the foliage of the trees (chiefly stunted Eucalypti) in search of insects, and making a snapping noise with its bill. It is not shy, and its note is a short whistle, rapidly repeated. The sexes are nearly alike in color and size. I believe it burrows in banks of earth, as several specimens I shot had their nostrils and bills plastered with red earth.

PARDALOTUS STRIATUS.

(Striated Pardalote.)

FOREHEAD and crown, black—the latter, striped with white; a stripe, commencing at the base of the upper mandible, and passing over the eye backwards to the occiput, is bright yellow in front and white behind; back, brownish olive, tinged with grey; rump and upper tail coverts, yellowish brown; wings, black; the external edges of from the third to the seventh primaries, white; the bases and tips are also white; secondaries, margined with white and reddish brown; spurious wing, tipped with scarlet; tail, black, tipped with white; sides of the face and neck, grey; throat and upper part of the chest, yellow; centre of the abdomen, white; flanks and under tail coverts, brownish buff, the former tinged with yellow; irides, brownish red; bill, yellowish white, margined above and tipped with greyish brown; feet, greenish grey.

Length, 3½ inches; wing, 2¼; tail, 1¼; bill, ⅜; tarsus, ⅔.

This pretty species is not uncommon in New South Wales, South Australia, and Western Australia. It frequents the higher branches of gum trees in search of its insect food, after which it darts with great swiftness, and utters a short chirp, repeated several times. Though stated by Mr. Gould to build in the holes of trees, it is also known to burrow like others of the genus. Mr. Stapleton, of Mount Gambier, informs me that in that neighborhood caves or subsidences of the earth are common, and that such situations are resorted to by hundreds of these birds for the purpose of breeding, their holes being made in the soft soil forming the upper stratum of these openings; they also take possession of holes or crevices in the walls of stone houses for the same purpose. The nest is always beautifully lined with shreds of dried grasses and fibrous roots. Eggs, four, fleshy white; size, 9 by 7 lines.

PARDALOTUS AFFINIS.

(Allied Pardalote.)

GENERAL plumage as in Pardalotus Striatus, but may be distinguished from that species by the tips of the spurious wing being yellow, and the margin of the third primary alone being white. The rest of the plumage as in the former species

Length, 3½ inches; wing, 2¾; tail, 1¼; bill, ⅜; tarsus, ⅔.

This, which is one of the commonest birds in Tasmania, is also found throughout the southern and eastern colonies of Australia. It is ever on the move, and displays great elegance and dexterity in its movements. Its food consists of insects, buds, and seeds. It breeds twice in the year; the nest is round, and domed like a wren's, and fixed in the hole of a tree; it is formed of grass, and lined with feathers. Eggs, three to five in number, and white; size, 9 by 7 lines.

[OVER.

PARDALOTUS MELANOCEPHALUS.

(Black-headed Pardalote.)

———◆———

CROWN, lores, and ear coverts, black; a stripe from the nostrils over and behind the eye, orange in front and white behind; sides of face and neck, white; back of neck and back, olive grey; upper tail coverts, buff; tail, black, slightly tipped with white; wings, black; spurious wing, tipped with crimson; primaries, from the third to the seventh, white; centre of throat, breast, and abdomen, bright yellow; under tail coverts, buff; bill, black; feet, brown; irides, brown.

Length, 4½ inches; wing, 2¼; tail, 1½; bill, ⅜; tarsus, ⅞.

This very distinct species is plentiful in Queensland, being common in the neighborhood of Brisbane. It frequents trees, and is a very silent bird, its note consisting of a mere twitter. Its ordinary place of nidification is the bank of a dry watercourse, into which it excavates a tunnel, at the end of which is the nest, formed of tea-tree bark. The eggs are from four to six in number, white; size, 9 by 7 lines. This bird has sometimes been caged. One in the possession of a friend lived in captivity two years, and became very tame, taking insects from the hand, but was fed principally upon bread and sugar.

———————————————

PARDALOTUS UROPYGIALIS.

(Yellow-rumped Pardalote.)

———◆———

CROWN of the head, stripe before and behind the eye, black; lores, rich orange; a mark from above the eye to the occiput, chest, and centre of the abdomen, white; throat and cheeks, delicate crocus yellow; rump and upper tail coverts, sulphur yellow; back, olive grey; wings, black; the external webs of the second and five following primaries, white at the base; spurious wing, tipped with scarlet; tail, black—the three outer feathers tipped with white; bill, black; feet, lead color.

Length, 3½ inches; wing, 2¼; tail, 1; bill, ¼; tarsus, ⅞.

This rare species has only been obtained on the north-west coast. Nothing as yet is recorded concerning it.

CRACTICUS NIGROGULARIS   CRACTICUS DESTRUCTOR
Blackthroated Crow Shrike   Butcher Bird

CRACTICUS NIGROGULARIS.

(Black-throated Crow Shrike.)

Head, neck, chest, middle of the back, and two central feathers of the tail, black; wings, black, except the shoulder, spurious wing, and a white longitudinal mark down the centre; upper and lower portions of the back and the abdomen, white; lateral tail feathers, black, largely tipped with white; bill, lead color, tipped with black; irides, dark brown; feet, black. The sexes are alike, but the young are brownish in those parts which are black in the adults.

Length, 13½ inches; wing, 7; tail, 6; bill, 1¾; tarsus, 1½.

This rather plentiful species is found in New South Wales and Queensland, and to a considerable distance inland. It generally is met with in pairs; and in those parts of the country known as "apple-tree flats" it is more common than elsewhere. Its powerful hooked bill serves it for tearing to pieces prey which other birds of its size would avoid; small mammalia, birds, and lizards, large grasshoppers, phasmidæ, and other insects serving it for food. The upper part of a gum tree is usually chosen in which to build. The nest, which is rather open and large, is formed of sticks neatly lined with fine fibrous roots. Eggs, four; dark yellowish brown, spotted and clouded with darker markings, and in some cases a few small black spots. Size, 1 inch 3 lines by 11 lines.

CRACTICUS PICATUS.

(Pied Crow Shrike.)

This species is so similar to the former as to need no separate description, but differs in being smaller in size and in having rather more white on the scapularies and wing coverts. The irides are reddish brown, and the feet greenish grey.

Length, 12 inches; wing, 6½; tail, 4⅞; bill, 1¾; tarsus, 1¾.

It inhabits the northern portions of the continent. At Port Essington it is usually seen in small companies of three or four. Its voice is loud and discordant; and being of a shy and retiring disposition, it frequents the denser and more secluded parts of the forest.

CRACTICUS DESTRUCTOR.

(Butcher Bird.)

Crown, back of the neck, face, primaries, and two central tail feathers, black; back and shoulders, light grey; lateral feathers of tail, black, much tipped with white on the inner webs; lores, throat, all the under surface, and a longitudinal mark in the centre of the wing, white; bill, bluish lead color, tipped with black; feet, nearly black; irides, dark reddish brown. The female is not so brightly colored as the male, the dark portions of the plumage assuming a brownish tint.

Length, 11¼ inches; wing, 5½; tail, 4½; bill, 1½; tarsus, 1¼.

The southern and eastern portions of Australia are the habitat of this species, which is one of the most plentiful of the genus to which it belongs. As its name implies, it is in the habit of fixing its prey upon the large thorns with which so many Australian trees and bushes are so plentifully furnished, though it finds no difficulty in disposing of it without such assistance. It is a bird of restless disposition, and the presence of a stranger near its haunts soon elicits a note of alarm or enquiry. It possesses a voice of extraordinary capability and variety, and is often caged and taught to utter articulate sounds. Though ordinarily shy, it at times exhibits much boldness, and pounces upon its prey like a hawk. Its food consists of mice, birds, small reptiles, and insects. Its nest is neatly formed of sticks, and lined with fibrous roots or the fine twigs of the casuarina. Eggs, three; variable—some being dark yellowish brown, marked and blotched obscurely with a darker tint and a few spots like ink, or lighter in the ground color and the markings inclining to red. Size, 1 inch 3 lines by 11 lines.

GRAUCALUS MENTALIS.

(*Varied Graucalus.*)

ADULT.—Lores, deep black; upper surface and wings, dark slatey grey, becoming lighter on the upper tail coverts; primaries and secondaries, slatey black, narrowly edged with greyish white; tertiaries, black, broadly edged with grey; tail, black, all but the central feathers, largely tipped with white; throat, chest, and upper part of abdomen, grey; lower portion of abdomen, under tail coverts, and under surface of wing, white; bill, black; irides and feet, dark brown.

The young birds differ much in appearance according to age. Shortly after leaving the nest the throat, chest, and back of the neck are jet black, and the chest and abdomen, greyish white, marked with arrow-shaped spots of black. Others are met with in a further advanced state of plumage, partaking more or less of approach to the character of that of the adult.

Length, 10¼ inches; wing, 5¾; tail, 5; bill, 1¼; tarsus, ¾.

This species is found in the northern portion of the colony of New South Wales and the southern parts of Queensland, becoming rare towards the north. Its principal food consists of insects.

GRAUCALUS HYPOLEUCUS.

(*White-bellied Graucalus.*)

LORES, black; crown and upper surface, dark grey; primaries and tail, black; secondaries and tertiaries, edged with greyish white; throat and under surface, white; chest washed with grey; irides and bill, blackish brown; feet black. The females and young have the lores a dull brown color.

Length, 9¾ inches; wing, 5¼; tail, 4½; bill, 1¼; tarsus, ¾.

It is found abundantly in Northern Australia, seldom being seen so far to the south as Brisbane. A single specimen was shot near Sydney, by Mr. Waller, some years ago. Throughout the Coburg Peninsula it is very common as well as very tame and familiar, associating in small companies of ten or twelve. When the settlement at Port Essington was in existence it was always to be seen flitting about the trees surrounding the houses. Its food consists of insects of various kinds. In its habits and notes it approximates closely to the other species of the genus, and is readily distinguished from them by the lighter color of its breast and abdomen.

PACHYCEPHALA GUTTERALIS.

(Gutteral Pachycephala.)

Male—Crown of the head, lores, line beneath the eye, ear coverts, and a crescent-shaped mark from the latter across the breast, deep black; throat, white; back of the neck, a narrow line behind the black band, and all the under surface, bright yellow; back and upper tail coverts, yellowish olive; wing coverts, blackish brown, margined with yellowish olive; primaries and secondaries, blackish brown, margined with greyish olive; tail, grey at the base, passing into black, and tipped with grey; irides, red; bill and feet, brownish black.

Female—Head, all the upper surface, and tail, olive brown; primaries and secondaries, brown—the former margined with grey, the latter with yellowish olive; throat, pale brown, freckled with white; abdomen, pale brown; ventral feathers, yellow; under tail coverts, white; bill and feet, blackish brown.

Length, 7¼ inches; wing, 3⅞; tail, 3½; bill, ¾; tarsus, ¾.

This species seems pretty generally distributed, being found in Queensland, New South Wales, South Australia, and West Australia. It may be obtained more plentifully in scrubs than in other situations, though also frequenting thickly-timbered country. It is rather shy, and seldom permits a near approach. The powerful note which it utters often betrays its presence, the same being a loud whistle repeated a few times, and ending suddenly with a sound not unlike the crack of a whip. Food, insects.

PACHYCEPHALA GLAUCURA.

(Grey-tailed Pachycephala.)

This species is so similar to the former in size and color as to need no separate figure or description. The difference consists in the tail of the male being wholly grey, the yellow portions paler, and the margins of the primaries and secondaries being of a whiter tint. In the female, the edges of the primaries and secondaries are greyish brown, and the under tail coverts are buffy white.

Length, 7½ inches; wing, 3⅞; tail, 3½; bill, ¾; tarsus, ⅞.

This species is confined to Tasmania. Its habits are similar to those of the other members of the family.

PACHYCEPHALA MELANURA.

(Black-tailed Pachycephala.)

This species is also closely allied to *P. Gutteralis*, differing only from that species in the greater richness of its coloring, and in having the tail wholly black. The wings are black; the coverts margined with yellowish olive, the primaries and secondaries with yellowish grey; bill and feet, black; irides, brownish red. A figure is unnecessary.

Length, 6 inches; bill, ⅞; wing, 3¼; tail, 2½; tarsus, ⅞.

This species is found in the northern portions of Australia, and some of the Malayan Islands.

The friends of the Darwinian theory will recognize some further evidence in favor of their views in the close relationship between the three species above described. In the case of that inhabiting the northern position, the colors are most brilliant and intense; in that of Tasmania the opposite character prevails; while, in the species occupying the central situation, the characteristics of both are combined.

PACHYCEPHALA PECTORALIS.

(Banded Thick-head.)

Male—Throat, white, encircled by a broad band of black, which, commencing at the base of the bill, surrounds the eye and crosses the sides of the neck and breast; forehead, crown, and upper surface, dark grey; wings and tail, blackish brown, the feathers being margined with grey; sides of the breast and flanks, grey; centre of the chest, abdomen, and under tail coverts, rich reddish brown; irides, red; bill, black; legs and feet, blackish olive.

Female—Head and upper surface, brownish grey; wings and tail, dark brown, margined on the outer webs with brownish grey; throat, dull white, passing into the tawny buff of the under surface, which is distinctly striped with dark brown; irides and bill, brown; feet, lead color.

Length, 6¾ inches; wing, 3¾; tail, 3¼; bill, ¾; tarsus, ¾.

This species is extensively distributed, being found in Queensland, New South Wales, and the southern and western portions of Australia. It delights in the topmost branches of trees in thinly-wooded country, where its lively and cheering song may be heard during the spring and summer seasons; its note is a long-continued gliding whistle, ending with a smack, which is the characteristic of that of most of the members of this genus. The nest is cup-shaped, constructed with small twigs, and is so loose and thin that the eggs are visible from beneath; the eggs, three in number, are olive, with a zone of brown spots and blotches at the larger end.

PACHYCEPHALA FALCATA.

(Lunated Pachycephala.)

This species is very closely allied to the former, but differs in having no black round the eyes or on the ear coverts. Its note is not so long and sustained as that of the former species, but in its general habits it is similar. Its habitat is the north coast (Port Essington, &c.)

Length, 7 inches; wing, 4¼; tail, 2¼; bill, ½; tarsus, ½. A figure is unnecessary.

COLLURICINCLA HARMONICA.

(Harmonious Shrike Thrush.)

HEAD, brownish grey, with an indistinct line of brown down the centre of each feather; back and shoulders, dark grey, with a tinge of olive; wings, slaty black margined with grey; rump and tail, grey—the shafts of the latter, dark brown; under surface, light grey, blending into white on the vent and under tail coverts; throat, whitish; irides, dark brown; bill, blackish brown; feet, dark greenish grey. The sexes are nearly alike.

Length, 9½ inches; wing, 4⅞; tail 4; bill, 1; tarsus, 1¼.

This plentiful species is found in all the eastern portions of Australia, and round the southern coast to South Australia, frequenting all descriptions of country whether of the coast or the interior, being equally at home among the mangrove swamps bordering the rivers, the thickly timbered forest, or woodland. Its food consists of insects, and its habits are active and interesting. It prospers well in an aviary, and speedily becomes familiar. It has a powerful voice, and its notes, though not so much varied as those of the European Thrush, are very melodious, and generally uttered while in pursuit of food. It builds in a variety of situations, and often in the branch of a tree at no great height from the ground. The nest is a slightly made and cup-shaped structure, formed externally of strips of bark, leaves, &c., and lined with fibrous roots or wool. Eggs, three or four, pearly bluish white, blotched with chestnut and dull bluish grey; 1 inch 2 lines long, by 10 lines broad.

COLLURICINCLA RUFIGASTER.

(Rusty Breasted Shrike Thrush.)

ALL the head, upper surface, and tail, dark olive brown; an obscure band of buff across the rump; inner webs of primaries and secondaries, blackish brown—lighter at the edges; chin, whitish; chest, abdomen, and under tail coverts, rufous buff; feathers of chest obscurely streaked with greyish brown; irides, hazel; foot, fleshy brown; bill, dark brown on the upper, and fleshy brown on the lower, mandible.

Length, 7½ inches; wing, 4; tail, 3¼; bill, 1; tarsus, 1¼.

It can scarcely be doubted that the present species and the one named C. Parvula are merely varieties of one and the same bird, and the suspicion expressed by Mr. Gould on this point is quite sufficient to induce me to adopt that supposition, and the more especially as the name "Parvula" is required for a still smaller species recently discovered at Cape York. This plainly colored bird is at times pretty plentiful in the haunts it is in the habit of frequenting. The brushes of the Clarence, Richmond, Brisbane, and other rivers of the east coast, to Port Essington in the north, may be mentioned as situations where this species has been obtained. Its voice is loud and musical, and it is usually to be seen on the limbs and branches of trees searching for insects, and at all times in active motion. The cup shaped nest is rather ingeniously hidden in a tuft of leaves partly interwoven into the rather loose outer substance of the nest by means of fine grasses and twigs, of which also the main body is composed. Horse hair or wool is also appropriated when at hand. Eggs, three, white speckled with rather large reddish brown spots, which are sometimes more numerous, and form a zone at the broad end. Size, a little smaller than those of the former species, being about 1 inch long by 9 lines broad. The breeding season is November.

COLLURICINCLA PARVULA.

(Little Shrike Thrush.)

UPPER surface, wings, and tail, brownish olive; under surface, dull buff; throat, whitish; secondaries and tertiaries, brown.

Length, 6½ inches; wing, 3⅞; tail, 3¼; tarsus, ⅞; bill, ⅞.

The above description, taken from the only specimen I have ever seen of this, the smallest species of the genus, applies to a specimen which was shot at Cape York, and I regret to say was destroyed with other rare and valuable specimens on board the ill fated ship "Fiery Star," on her passage to England, April 19, 1865. I did not figure it on account of its similarity to C. Rufigaster in everything but size.

OREGICA CRISTATA
Crested Oreoica

DICRURUS BRACTEATUS
Spangled Drongo

OREOÏCA CRISTATA.

(Crested Oreoica.)

MALE.—Feathers from the bill to the eye and throat, pure white, surrounded by the black, which fronts the crest, is continued beneath the eye, and curves round, forming a broad band of black across the chest; hinder part of the crest and sides of the head, grey; upper surface and flanks, light brown; wings, brown, margined with buffish brown; tail, dark brown; centre of abdomen, whitish; vent and under tail coverts, buff; bill, black; irides, orange; feet, brown.

FEMALE.—Not so bright in her markings, the throat being dull white, the face grey, and but a faint approach to a band on the chest; her eyes, also, are hazel, and feet olive brown.

Length, 8¼ inches; wing, 4½; tail, 3½; bill, ⅞; tarsus, ⅞.

This interesting bird is exclusively confined to the southern and middle portions of Australia, being rare in the southern parts of Queensland. It has not been observed in Tasmania, but in Western Australia and New South Wales it is pretty equally dispersed, though common nowhere. It is very terrestrial in its habits, hopping along the ground with considerable swiftness, jerking its tail and throwing forward its crest, and seeming to prefer situations of an open and naked character, and principally in sterile and ridgy country. Its food consists of insects. The note of this bird is very varied. It is said to imitate the notes of other birds; but its own are very remarkable, usually being a succession of notes, or two notes repeated rather slowly, followed by a repetition three times rather quickly, the last note resembling a bell, from its ringing tone. Another sound which it utters has been likened to that emitted by a grindstone wanting oil. The nest is usually placed in the grass tree, and is cup shaped, being formed of fine shreds of bark, and lined with dried grasses. The eggs, generally three in number, vary much, both in color and markings: ground color, bluish white, or bluish green, spotted minutely with black, or blotched and marked with zig zag lines of black. Size, 1 inch 1 line by 9½ lines.

DICRURUS BRACTEATUS.

(Spangled Drongo Shrike.)

GENERAL plumage, deep glossy black; the feathers of the head, with a crescent, and those of the breast, with a spot of metallic green at the tip; wings and tail, much glossed with green; under wing coverts tipped with white; irides, red; bill and feet, blackish brown.

Length, 11¼ inches; wing, 6¼; tail, 5¼; bill, 1¼; tarsus, ⅞.

The Drongo Shrikes are a beautiful genus of birds, characterised by their black plumage and forked tails of only ten feathers, instead of the usual number, twelve. India is the stronghold of the majority of the species. Others are found in Africa and the Malayan Islands. The present species is the only one as yet found in Australia. It is confined to the country along the sea coast, and possesses an extensive range, being found from Moreton Bay to the north-west coast, and, in fact, throughout the whole of the Queensland and North Australian seaboard. At Cape York and Port Essington it is abundant, and generally seen in pairs, but sometimes in flocks of seven or eight. It frequents the scrubs, mangroves, and thickly wooded country. It is active in its habits, and seldom comes to the ground. Its flight, though strong, is not sustained, and its food consists of insects, especially grasshoppers and beetles; it is also known to feed upon wild fruits, a species of lime especially, the interior of which it scoops out, leaving the rind nearly entire. It breeds in October and November. The nest, which is formed of the fine stalks of creeping plants, is shallow in form, and placed near the extremity of a thickly foliaged branch. The young are three or four in number.

R. RUFIFRONS
Rufous fronted Fan-tail

R. ALBISCAPA
White Shafted Fan-tail

R. MOTACILLOIDES
Black Fan-tailed Fly catcher

RHIPIDURA RUFIFRONS.

Rufous-fronted Fan-tail.

Forehead, lower portion of back, upper tail coverts, and basal half of tail feathers, bright rufous; crown of the head, upper part of the back, sides of the neck and wings, light brown; throat and under surface, white, blending into buff on the flanks and ventral portions. On the upper part of the chest is a band of black, beneath which is a series of rather conspicuous black spots. Lower half of tail, dark brown, tipped with white; bill and feet, black; irides, dark brown.

Length, 6 inches; wing, 2¾; tail, 3½; bill, 9-16; tarsus, ⅝.

This species is found in Queensland and New South Wales, round to South Australia, and also in Tasmania. It is not very common anywhere. It is exceedingly active in the pursuit of its insect prey, resorting to the lower bushes of scrubs for that purpose.

RHIPIDURA DRYAS.

This species, if indeed distinct from the above, is found at Port Essington, and probably the northern coast generally. It is very similar in size and appearance to the former, but the tail has more of the rufous tint, and less of the dark brown. A figure is unnecessary.

Length, 5¼ inches; wing, 2½; tail, 3½; bill, 9-16; tarsus, ⅝.

RHIPIDURA ALBISCAPA.

White-shafted Fan-tail.

Head and cheeks, black, with a small patch of white above and behind the eye; neck and back, greyish black; wings, black; coverts, tipped with white; tail, black, all but the two middle feathers margined and tipped with white, and having also white shafts; throat, white, followed by a band of black; belly, white in the male, light buff in the female; bill and feet, black.

Length, 5½ inches; wing, 2⅞; tail, 3⅛; bill, ⅜; tarsus, ⅝.

This widely-distributed species is found in all the Australian colonies, and never fails to attract attention from its lively and playful habits. It is ever on the move in pursuit of insects, which it captures on the wing, and in its flight assumes the most elegant attitudes, spreading out its tail like a fan. It breeds from October to January, building a beautiful nest of a cup-like form, which is most ingeniously attached to a branch. Underneath the nest is a long appendage, which gives the structure somewhat the appearance of a funnel, or wine-glass with the foot broken off; the materials used consist of fine shreds of bark, down, and moss, the whole being matted together with spiders' webs on the outside. The eggs are two in number, white, blotched with olive brown.

RHIPIDURA ISURA.

Northern Fan-tail.

All the upper surface, dull brown; wings and tail, darker brown—the outer pair of tail feathers margined and largely tipped with white; the next feather has an irregular spot of white near the tip, and the next a minute line of white near the tip; chin and under surface, buffy white, with an indistinct dark brown band across the chest; bill and feet, black.

Length, 8 inches; wing, 3¾; tail, 3½; bill, ½; tarsus, ½.

This species can easily be recognized by the square form of its tail. It is more sombre in its coloring than the other members of the family. Locality, Port Essington.

RHIPIDURA PICATA.

Pied Flycatcher.

Crown of the head, back of the neck, back, tail, and wings, brownish black; ear coverts, upper tail coverts, all the under surface, the tips of the coverts and scapularies, and edges of upper tertiaries, white; bill and feet, black.

Length, 5½ inches; wing, 2⅞; tail, 2¾; bill, ½; tarsus, ⅝.

This rare species is found in the northern parts of Queensland, and doubtless approximates in its habits to the other members of the family.

RHIPIDURA MOTACILLOIDES.

Black Fan-tailed Flycatcher.

Upper surface and tail, deep shining black; throat and chest, black; the remainder of the under surface and a streak above the eye, pure white; bill and feet, black; irides, dark brown or black.

Length, 8 inches; wing, 4; tail, 4½; bill, ½; tarsus, 1.

This is a very common and widely-distributed species, being found in all parts of Australia excepting the extreme north. From its tame and familiar disposition, it has been popularly called the shepherd's companion, frequenting farms, stockyards, and all places where cattle and sheep are found. It may often be seen on the backs of domestic animals, busily engaged in capturing and devouring the flies which so much annoy and worry them. It is of a most restless disposition, and is never quiet for one moment. It delights to expand its fan-like tail, and sway itself from side to side as it alights from one of its short jerking flights. It has a variety of notes, but the one which attracts the most notice resembles the sound emitted by a toy watchman's rattle. The season of incubation is October and November. The nest is built on the horizontal branch of a tree, at no great distance from the ground; it is formed of grass intermingled with spiders' webs; eggs, three, greenish white, blotched and spotted with chestnut and blackish brown, especially at the larger end: size, 9½ by 7 lines.

MEGARHYNCHUS · LAVIVENTER
Yellow-breasted Flycatcher

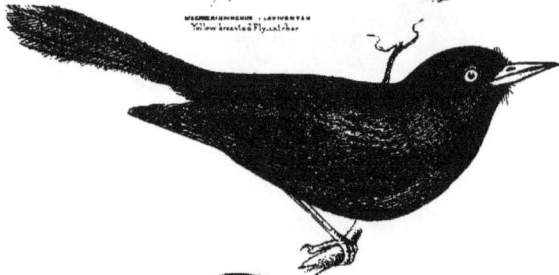

PTEROPTOCHUS NITIDUS
Blue-shining Flycatcher

Pamela

SCIAMA INQUIETA
Restless Flycatcher

MYIAGRA LATIROSTRIS.

(Broad-billed Fly-catcher.)

ALL the upper surface, wings, and tail, dark bluish grey, with a greenish lustre on the head and back of the neck; throat and chest, sandy buff; under surface, white; bill, black; irides, blackish brown; feet, black.

Length, 6 inches; wing, 2⅞; tail, 2⅞; bill, ⅝; tarsus, ⅝.

This species was procured by Mr. Dring on the north coast of Australia, and at Port Essington by Mr. Gilbert. It may be at once discriminated from the other members of the genus by the greater breadth of the bill. Nothing is at present known of its habits or nidification.

MACHÆRIRHYNCHUS FLAVIVENTER.

(Yellow-breasted Fly-catcher.)

CROWN of the head, lores, ear coverts, wings, and tail, black; primaries with a fine edging of white for about half their length; secondaries and tertiaries, broadly margined with white on the external webs; wing coverts, tipped with white; throat white; forehead, a line over and for some distance behind the eye; chest and all the under surface, yellow; all but the central feathers of the tail tipped with white, but most on the lateral feathers; bill, black; irides, brown; feet, dark brown.

Length, 5 inches; wing, 2; tail, 2¼; bill, ⅜; tarsus, ½.

This singular but beautiful little fly-catcher has only been found in the Cape York Peninsula. It frequents the dense scrubs, and is constantly on the move, making short flights after passing insects and returning to the same spot. The short stout bristles proceeding from the base of the bill doubtless assist it in more effectually arresting its struggling prey, and the broad bill must have some special adaptation of which we are not at present aware.

PIEZORHYNCHUS NITIDUS.

(Blue Shining Fly-catcher.)

MALE: Plumage, throughout, glossy greenish black, excepting the tips of the primaries, which are brownish black. Female: crown, lores, ear coverts, back and sides of the neck, glossy greenish black; the remainder of the upper surface wings and tail, rusty brown; under surface, white, washed with rusty on the lower portion of the abdomen; primaries, and central portions of secondaries, nearly black; under tail coverts, reddish buff.

Length, 6¼ inches; wing, 3⅜; tail, 3; bill, ⅝; tarsus, ¾.

This species is found principally at the north. In the peninsula of Cape York it is plentiful, and also at Port Essington. The northern portions of Queensland seem to be its principal habitat. It is a shy bird, and not easily procured, as it frequents dense thickets and mangroves, uttering its cry as it creeps along among the fallen trees. Its note very much resembles the croak of a frog, and, according to Gilbert, is only uttered when feeding on the ground; but when it ascends to the trees, its note is a pleasing succession of sounds resembling the syllables twit-te-twite. The nest is carefully masked so as to resemble the color of the branches on which it builds. It is of a cup shaped form, the outer part being made of stringy bark, bound together with vegetable fibres and cobwebs, and loosely attached are small pieces of bark or lichens, which swing about with every breeze. The interior is lined with a strong, thread-like, fibrous root. The eggs are two in number, of a bluish white color, blotched and spotted with olive and greyish brown, almost forming a zone at the large end; size, 10 by 7 lines.

[OVER.

SEIZURA INQUIETA.

(Restless Fly-catcher.)

CROWN, lores, cheeks, and all the upper surface, bluish black; quills, dark brown; tail, brownish black; under surface, white; irides, dark brown; bill, bluish black; feet, greyish brown.

Length: 8 inches; wing, 4¾; tail, 4½; bill, 1; tarsus, ⅞.

This species is found in most of the colonies. Few situations exist from Queensland to Western Australia where it may not be met with, when the character of the country is suitable to its requirements. The open forest is where it may be most frequently observed, but it is to be found in all situations. Some of its actions are very peculiar: sometimes it will poise itself in the air and remain in the same spot for a short time, and then make a perpendicular descent for the purpose of capturing some insect; or at others it will alight on a stump and commence a series of movements from side to side, describing a semicircle, with its tail expanded all the time; these motions being generally accompanied by the utterance of its singular inharmonious note, which has procured for it the name of "the knife grinder." The breeding season is the spring, viz., from September to November. The nest is cup shaped, and formed of fine grasses, matted together with cobwebs, and lined with fine root fibres and a few feathers. Eggs, from two to three, dull white, spotted with chestnut and greyish brown, and assuming the form of a zone in the centre; size, 9¼ by 7 lines.

ARSES KAUPI.

(Kaup's Flycatcher.)

SMALL spot on the chin, crown of the head, lores, line beneath the eye, ear coverts, broad crescentic band across the back, and a band across the breast, deep shining bluish black; wings and tail, brownish black; throat and a broad band across the back of the neck, white; lower part of the back and abdomen, white—the base of the feathers, black, which, occasionally showing through, give those parts a mottled appearance; bill, bluish horn color, becoming lighter at the tip; feet, black.

Length, 6¼ inches; wing, 5½; tail, 3½; bill, ½; tarsus, ½.

This bird is figured by Mr. Gould from a solitary specimen killed on the north coast of Australia, and by him dedicated to the celebrated ornithologist, Dr. Kaup, of Darmstadt. Mr. Gould remarks that an unwillingness to multiply Genera has induced him to place this species in the genus Arses, the one, in his opinion, to which it is the most nearly related, though showing some alliance to Monarcha. Other species are found in the Aru and neighbouring islands. No information accompanied the specimen.

MYIAGRA PLUMBEA.

(Leaden-colored Flycatcher.)

MALE.—Upper surface, wings, tail, and breast, lead color, glossed with green on the head, neck, and breast, and becoming gradually paler towards the extremity of the body, and on the wings and tail; primaries, slaty black; secondaries, faintly margined with white; under surface of wing, abdomen, and under tail coverts, white; bill, bluish lead color—the tip, black; irides and feet, black.

The FEMALE is paler, less shining, and the throat and chest are reddish buff, gradually fading away into white on the abdomen. The wings also are brown. The young males are similar in appearance to the females.

Length, 6½ inches; wing, 3½; tail, 3; bill, ½; tarsus, ½.

It frequents New South Wales and the southern portions of Queensland in the summer, migrating to the northward for the winter months. Specimens have been obtained at Cape York. Like its congeners its habits are marked by great restlessness and activity, which it exemplifies even in a state of comparative repose, the tail constantly being on the move from side to side. It is usually seen in pairs, and its frequently uttered low whistling note may be often heard in the neighborhood of creeks and woody situations, while engaged in the pursuit of its insect food. It builds a deep cup-shaped nest, which is constructed of mosses and lichens, and lined with feathers, and is usually fixed in the fork or horizontal branch of a tree.

MYIAGRA CONCINNA.

(Pretty Flycatcher.)

THE description of the male of this bird would read exactly similar to that of M. Plumbea, and need not, therefore, be repeated. The female may be easily discriminated from that of the former species by the rusty coloring of the breast not gradually blending with the white of the abdomen, but in being sharply defined. The size will always enable an ornithologist to decide as to the species, it being as follows:—

Length, 6 inches; wing, 2¾; tail, 2½; bill, ½; tarsus, ½.

Habitat, north-west coast.

MYIAGRA NITIDA.

(Shining Flycatcher.)

MALE.—Lores, deep velvety black; upper surface, wings, and tail, rich deep metallic blackish green; primaries, deep brown; throat and breast, similar to the upper surface; the remainder of the under surface, pure white; irides and feet, black; bill, lead color—the tip, black.

FEMALE.—Less brilliant in the coloring of the upper surface; the throat and chest, rich rusty red. The young males are similar to the females in appearance.

Length, 6½ inches; wing, 3½; tail, 3½; bill, ½; tarsus, ½.

This species is found during the summer season in the southern parts of Australia and Tasmania, during which time the work of incubation is performed. The winter is passed in the northern portions of the continent, specimens being pretty common at Cape York at that season. It is a very lively, active, little bird, pursuing its insect food with the greatest pertinacity, the tail being always on the move from side to side. Its nest is usually situated at the extreme end of a dead branch of a tree, at a considerable height from the ground, and is variously constructed, some being formed of light green moss, others of stringy bark thread, but all are lined with the soft hair of the opossum, the downy fibres of the tree fern or delicate blossoms of plants, and decorated on the outside with bits of lichen, the whole being felted together with cobwebs. The eggs are three, rather round, greenish white, spotted and blotched all over with umber brown, yellowish brown, and purplish grey. Size 9 lines by 7 lines.

MONARCHA

M. TRIVIRGATA
Black fronted Fly-catcher

M. LEUCOTIS
White eared Fly-catcher

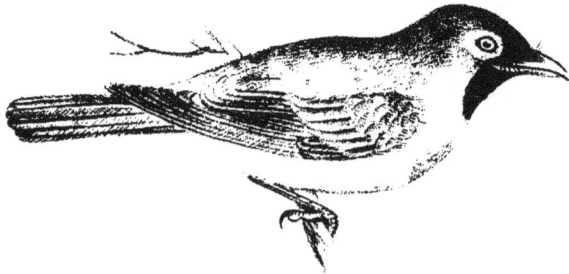

M. CARINATA
Carinated fly catcher

MONARCHA CARINATA.

(Carinated Fly-catcher.)

FOREHEAD, lores, and throat, jet black; all the upper surface, grey; wings and tail, brownish grey; sides of the neck and chest, light grey; abdomen and under tail coverts, rufous; bill, bluish horn color, whitish at the tip; feet, bluish lead color; irides, blackish brown. The sexes are alike.

Length, 7 inches; wing, 3¾; tail, 3¼; bill, ½; tarsus, ¾.

This species is found throughout the whole colony of Queensland, specimens having been obtained at Cape York, and also about Brisbane. Its southern limit is New South Wales, to which country it migrates in the spring, returning northwards in the autumn. It frequents thickly wooded country and scrubs, and in such situations may be observed hopping about the trees in search of its insect food. Its note is a loud and oft repeated whistle. Nothing is at present known of its nest or eggs.

MONARCHA TRIVIRGATA.

(Black-fronted Fly-catcher.)

FOREHEAD, throat, mark round the eye, and the ears, deep black; upper surface, dark grey; tail, black, the three outer feathers tipped with white; cheeks, chest, and flanks, rufous; abdomen and under tail coverts, white; bill, lead color; feet, black; irides, dark brown.

Length, 6¾ inches; wing, 3; tail, 3; bill, ½; tarsus, ¾.

This species is confined to the northern parts of Australia, and is also found in some of the Malayan Islands. Specimens are occasionally met with in the neighborhood of Brisbane at the latter end of summer, when it may be found frequenting the densest scrubs, and, though rarely, thick mangroves. In such situations its loud, harsh, and disagreeable note frequently betrays its presence. It is continually on the move, hopping about from branch to branch, uttering its peculiar cry, as it chases its insect prey through the foliage of the trees. Like the former species, the nest and eggs of this bird are as yet unknown.

MONARCHA LEUCOTIS.

(White-eared Fly-catcher.)

CROWN of the head, back of the neck, back, and six middle tail feathers, black, the three outermost pairs being tipped with white; lores, a broad mark over the eye, ear coverts, and throat, white, surrounded by black on all sides; a broad piece of white down the sides of the neck nearly meets above, and blends below into the grey of the chest; abdomen, grey; tips of wing coverts and secondaries, edges of scapularies and tertiaries, white; primaries and remainder of wings, black. The female differs from the male, and may be easily distinguished by her ear coverts, which are grey.

Length, 5¾ inches; wing, 2¾; tail, 2½; bill, ½; tarsus, ¾.

Cape York, Rockingham Bay (in which two localities it was first procured by Mr. Macgillivray), and the neighborhood of Brisbane, may be mentioned as localities where this species has been taken. From its exceeding rarity in the latter locality it may be presumed that it does not proceed much further to the southward. A male and female were first shot in the neighborhood of Brisbane by Mr. E. Waller, in the month of June, 1861, and another pair at the extreme south of Stradbroke Island, in 1863. Several others have been since obtained by him, one in particular when in company with Charles Coxen, Esq., on the occasion of their visit to Eagle Farm scrub for the purpose of taking the bower of the Regent Bird, then only recently discovered by Mr. Waller. Little or nothing is known of the habits of this species. It has a note not unlike that of Myiagra Plumbea, but, unlike the fly-catchers in general, it does not jerk its tail in the act of giving utterance to the same, but stands perfectly still, and in an upright position, with its throat much inflated. It is generally seen in pairs.

PETROICA FUSCA.

(Dusky Robin.)

Head and all the upper surface, reddish brown, tinged with olive; wings and tail, brown; primaries and secondaries, crossed by a narrow line of white at the base; outer tail feathers, margined and tipped with white; under surface, pale brown, passing into buffy white on the vent and under tail coverts; irides, bill, and feet, blackish brown.

The sexes are alike. The young bird is dark brown above, striated with deep buff; beneath, mottled brown and buffy white.

Length, 6 inches; wing, 3¼; tail, 2¾; bill, ¾; tarsus, 1.

This plain colored species is found only in Tasmania, being very numerous about Hobart Town. It frequents thinly timbered country, thickets, or low grounds covered with stunted bush, and may often be seen perched upon posts or stumps of dead trees. It feeds upon insects of various kinds. Its nest is rather large, cup-shaped, and formed of coarse fibrous roots, small twigs, strings of bark, and grass mixed with wool and moss. Eggs, three or four, light greenish blue, freckled and spotted with minute indistinct markings of brown; size, 10 lines by 7¼ lines.

DRYMODES SUPERCILIARIS.

(Eastern Scrub Robin.)

Upper surface, brown, becoming more of a reddish tinge towards the tail, which is of a still deeper rusty brown tint, the quills being also red; all but the two middle feathers of the tail, tipped with white, the two outermost pairs being black immediately above the white tips; wings, banded with white and black; primaries, black, margined with white on the outer webs, and interrupted near their bases by a broader portion of white, which is continued and runs through the broad inner webs, forming a band; tertiaries, black, fringed with buff; lores and patch above the eye, white; a streak of black runs diagonally backwards from beneath the eye; throat and centre of the abdomen, white; chest and flanks, light brown; bill, black; legs and feet, yellowish flesh color. The sexes are similar in color, but the female is a little smaller than the male.

Length, 8¼ inches; wing, 3⅔; tail, 4; bill, ⅞; tarsus, 1⅜.

This species has as yet been obtained only from Cape York. What may be the southern limit of its habitat has yet to be ascertained. It frequents thin open scrubs, in which situations it may be seen hopping about among the sticks and dead leaves much in the manner of the common English Robin. The nest is fixed in a hole in the ground, into which it fits like an egg in a cup; it is formed of twigs and lined with grass. The eggs are light grey, blotched with brown, particularly at the larger end. Size, 1 inch by 7-10ths.

DRYMODES BRUNNEOPYGIA.

(Scrub Robin.)

Head and all the upper surface, brown, becoming rufous on the upper tail coverts; wings, dark brown, the coverts and primaries edged with dull white; primaries and secondaries, crossed near the base, on their inner webs, with pure white; tail, rich brown—all but the two middle feathers, tipped with white; under surface, greyish brown, passing into buff on the under tail coverts; irides, bill, and feet, blackish brown. The sexes only differ in the female being much smaller than the male.

Length, 8 inches; wing, 3¼; tail, 4½; bill, ⅞; tarsus, 1¼.

This species is found in South and Western Australia, and may be met with in some plenty in the Great Murray Scrub. It is almost always seen on the ground, seldom taking wing, but hides itself when disturbed by hopping among the thick bushes. It has a sharp but monotonous note. Its food consists of insects.

EOPSALTRIA GRISEOGULARIS
Grey breasted Robin.

E. AUSTRALIS
Yellow breasted Robin.

E. CAPITO
Large headed Robin.

E. LEUCOGASTER
White bellied Robin.

EOPSALTRIA AUSTRALIS.

(Yellow-breasted Robin.)

HEAD, cheeks, shoulders, and back, grey; upper tail coverts, bright yellow; tail, blackish brown above, grey beneath—all but the two central feathers slightly tipped with white; wings, black; throat, white; chest and under surface, bright yellow; irides, dark brown; bill and feet, black. The sexes are very similar, but the female is less brightly colored.

Length, 6 inches; wing, 3½; tail, 3; bill, ½; tarsus, ⅞.

This pretty but rather common species is found in New South Wales and Queensland, in various situations, not confining itself to the scrubs alone. It is of a familiar disposition, and its flight consists of short excursions from one tree to another. At sunrise one individual may be heard uttering a note like "chip;" then it repeats the same twice over; after which a regular chorus may be heard on all sides, the note being three times repeated. It breeds about October, and makes its nest of fibrous roots, grass, and strips of bark, very neatly and compactly arranged and matted together with spiders' webs, and attached to the outside are small scraps of bark and lichens. The interior is lined with broad leaves or broad blades of grass. The nest is usually placed in the fork of a tree, and is not easily seen, being wonderfully disguised by its similarity of coloring to the tree itself. The eggs are two in number, bright green, and speckled with reddish brown and dark brown: size, 9 by 7¼ lines.

EOPSALTRIA GRISEOGULARIS.

(Grey-breasted Robin.)

CROWN, back of the neck, and upper part of the back, dark grey; rump, upper tail coverts, and outer edges of the base of the tail feathers, rich yellowish olive; tail, blackish brown, slightly tipped with white in all but the two central feathers; lores and patch beneath the eye, blackish brown; cheeks, lighter, mottled with whitish; throat, white; a broad band of grey across the chest softening into the rich yellow of the remainder of the under surface; under tail coverts paler yellow; quills, deep brown, narrowly edged with light buffy brown; tertiaries, tipped with white; bill and feet, black; irides, dark brown.

Length, 6¼ inches; wing, 3½; tail, 2½; bill, ½; tarsus, ⅞.

This species is nearly allied to the former and inhabits the western and southern portions of the Australian continent. It was formerly supposed to be found only in Western Australia, but Mr. Masters informs me that he shot several specimens at Port Lincoln in South Australia, where it is somewhat rare, but inhabits a very different kind of country to what he found it to do in the more western colony; the specimens obtained in South Australia being found in a dense mangrove swamp, while those shot by him at King George's Sound inhabited the open forest. The nest is of difficult detection and is constructed of similar materials to that of the former species. The eggs are very different, however, being of a wood brown color, obscurely freckled with yellowish red; they are more lengthened in form than those of E. Australis, and are in size 10 by 7⅜ lines.

EOPSALTRIA CAPITO.

(Large-headed Robin.)

UPPER surface, olive green, brownish on the head; wings and tail, greyish brown, faintly margined with olive green; ear coverts, grey; lores, a line beneath the eye, and the throat, greyish white; under surface, light yellow; irides, hazel; bill, black; feet, brownish flesh color.

Length, 4½ inches; wing, 3½; tail, 2½; bill, ½; tarsus, ⅞.

The northern portions of New South Wales and southern portions of Queensland are the habitat of this species, where it frequents the dense tangled scrubs on the banks of the various rivers between the sea and the dividing range. It is far from common. The sexes are much alike, but the female is rather smaller than the male. The nest in the possession of Mr. J. T. Cockerell, of Brisbane, is formed of long thin shreds of bark, the outside of which is coated with fine moss, and matted together with spiders' webs, with a few patches of lichen attached here and there; it is lined internally with dried grasses, and the bottom is covered with leaves from the tea tree. The nest measures 3½ inches in external diameter. Eggs, four in number, beautiful pale green, spotted all over with light greyish brown; being much broken, I regret to say I cannot give their true measurement, but they are probably nearly as large as those of E. Australis.

[OVER.

EOPSALTRIA LEUCOGASTER.

(White-bellied Robin.)

———◆———

Lores, black; a faint stripe of greyish white above the eye; crown and upper surface, dark grey; tail, slate grey, the lateral feathers much tipped with white on the inner webs; primaries, brownish black, with a large patch of white at the base of the inner webs; irides, dark brown; bill, black; feet, brownish black.

Length, 6¼ inches; wing, 3; tail, 2¾; bill, ¾; tarsus, ⅞.

Though stated by Gilbert to be found only in the hilly portions of Western Australia, never being observed between the mountain range and the coast, Mr. Masters, who visited that colony in 1866, says he only met with it in the dense tea-tree flats and swamps near King George's Sound, and never more than a few hundred yards from salt water. During a three weeks' trip through the hilly country he never saw one. Further investigation will perhaps explain the apparent discrepancy between these observations, as it may eventually be found to frequent one or other of those situations at particular seasons of the year. It is very shy, and seeks seclusion on the slightest alarm.

MENURA SUPERBA.

(Lyre Bird.)

MALE.—Upper surface, dark greyish brown; throat and wings, rufous brown; upper tail coverts, tinged with the latter colour; under surface, brownish ash color; upper surface of the two lyre-shaped feathers of the tail, dark greyish brown, partially banded with rufous; under surface of the same feathers, silvery grey, with rufous bands; the extreme margins of the inner webs and the extremities, black; the two next largest feathers are narrow and densely webbed on one side only, except near the tip, which is sparingly furnished with a few rays; the remaining feathers, twelve in number, are thin shafts, sparingly decorated with long filaments on both sides.

The Female is destitute of the long and beautiful tail which adorns her mate, her tail consisting of feathers of the ordinary kind; in other respects she much resembles the Male. Bill, black; orbits, lead color; irides, dark brown; legs and feet, black.

Length, 42 inches; wing, 11; tail, 30; bill, 1¾; tarsus, 5; middle toe, 3¾.

Naturalists have differed very much in opinion as to what family this singular bird belongs; some place it among the gallinaceous class, its large and powerful feet and its general aspect indicating its relationship to the megapodes. As throughout this work I have followed Mr. Gould's arrangement, it will be unnecessary to say anything on these controverted points, except that other naturalists with, what appear to them, reasons equally cogent, have placed the Menura among the family of the Wrens. This remarkable bird is an inhabitant of hilly and mountainous districts in New South Wales, its range extending westward to Port Philip, where it seems to give place to another species somewhat different. The wildest and most inaccessible country, rocky gullies, and precipitous ravines covered with a dense and tangled vegetation, are the situations in which it delights. Its shy and wary habits, added to the natural difficulty of the district it selects as its habitat, entails upon any one anxious to obtain specimens the expenditure of much toil and patience. In the dense brushes of Illawarra it has, perhaps, been obtained most frequently. Its loud and liquid call, or extraordinary imitations of the notes of the various birds frequenting its own neighbourhood, as well as other sounds of more unusual character, as the howling of the dingo, or even the sharpening of a saw, may often be heard in the near proximity of the sportsman, whose only chance of making an approach is at such times, for the moment the bird is silent, the slightest alarm, such as the cracking of a twig, is sufficient to scare it off to a distance. The Menura should be sought for in the winter season, as at that time it is in the full beauty of its plumage. The nest, built upon the ground, is large and deep, formed of sticks, and lined with strips of bark and fibrous roots, and placed in such a situation that, while the bird can see around, it is well screened from the observation of all intruders, and covered at the top with a kind of canopy or dome. Only one egg is laid, the color of which is, doubtless, similar to that of the variety or species found to the westward of Port Philip, viz., purplish grey, with numerous spots and blotches of purplish brown, especially at the larger end; length, 2¼ inches. by 1½ wide.

SPHENOSTOMA CRISTATA
Crested wedge bill

SPHENOSTOMA CRISTATA.

(Crested Wedge Bill.)

———

UPPER surface, brown; under surface, greyish white; wings, dark brown, edged with paler; the fourth and fifth primaries, with white bases; the four central tail feathers, dark brown, barred with darker; the rest, brownish black, much tipped with white; bill, blackish brown; feet, lead color.

Length, 7¼ inches; wing, 3; tail, 4; tarsus, ⅞; bill, 1 (nearly).

This interesting species is confined to the interior of New South Wales, being principally found among low scrubby trees and bushes on the banks, or in the neighbourhood, of the Lachlan, Darling, and Namoi rivers, but is not by any means plentiful. The nest is rather large, round, and cup-shaped, formed outwardly of twigs, and lined with grasses. Eggs, delicate greenish blue, sprinkled with purplish black.

———

PSOPHODES CREPITANS.

(Coach Whip Bird.)

———

HEAD, face, ear coverts, throat and chest, black; a large patch of white on the side of the neck; back, wings, and upper tail coverts, olive brown; tail feathers, blackish olive, the three lateral pairs tipped with white; under surface, olive brown; some feathers in the centre of the abdomen, tipped with white; bill, black; feet, reddish brown; irides, hazel.

Length, 10 inches; wing, 3⅞; tail, 5⅞; tarsus, 1¼.

The true habitat of this bird is New South Wales and the southern parts of Queensland. The female is smaller, and wants the patch on the neck. It is one of the first to attract the attention of the stranger when arriving at those parts of Australia of which it is a denizen. Its singular note is like the sound caused by quickly drawing a whip lash through the air, and ending with the sharp crack of the same implement. This note is repeated at short intervals, making the scrubs echo again. Though the bird may be close at hand, it is not easily seen, from the dark color of its plumage, and the ease with which it can hide itself in the dense portions of the scrub. By remaining quiet, the observer may sometimes have an opportunity of watching its movements, which are elegant in the extreme. The crest is moveable, and the tail capable of great expansion; and the contest of two males, as they chase one another through the entangled vines of the scrubs, is a sight worth beholding. It much frequents the ground, where, for the most part, it obtains its food, and where it scratches among the dead leaves and decaying vegetation for the insects so plentifully found in those situations. The nest is rather loosely constructed, being formed of coarse grasses and creeping plants, without any lining, and generally placed in a thick bush near the ground. The eggs are two in number, greenish white, spotted with black and light grey, but most at the large end, the darker spots sometimes resembling Hebrew letters, commas, dashes, &c. Size, 1¼ inch by ⅞.

———

PSOPHODES NIGROGULARIS.

(Black-throated Psophodes.)

———

UPPER surface, olive; under surface, ashy, passing into brown on the flanks, and white on the centre of the abdomen; primaries, brown; tail, light olive brown, the four lateral feathers crossed near the extremity with black, and tipped with white; throat, deep black, with a stripe of white from the angle of the lower mandible; bill and feet, dark horn color; irides, dark brown.

Length, 6¼ inches; wing, 3¼; tail, 4½; bill, ⅞; tarsus, 1¼.

This species is confined to Western Australia. The Wongan Hills and thickets of Leptospermum growing among the sandhills on the coast, are situations known to be frequented by it. It has a singular harsh and grating note, not easily described, and, when once heard, not readily forgotten; which remark will apply to its eastern representative.

ORTHONYX SPINICAUDUS.

(Spine-tailed Orthonyx.)

MALE—Crown of the head and behind the neck, brown; back, brown, with a black patch on each feather; lower part of back and upper tail coverts, rufous; shoulders, and greater and lesser wing coverts, black, much tipped with grey; primaries, secondaries, and tertiaries, blackish brown at the base, the remaining portion, reddish brown; tail, dark brown—the quills naked at the tips; face, dark grey; throat and under surface, white; flanks, grey; bill and feet, black; irides, dark brown.

FEMALE—Is very similar to the Male, but rather redder in plumage, and may at once be distinguished by the throat, which is rich rust red. The young has the under surface obscurely barred with greyish brown, and the feathers of the head are a curious mixture of brown, grey, and rust red.

Length, 8¼ inches; wing, 3½; tail, 3½; bill, ½; tarsus, 1.

The scrubs and bushes which border the coasts of Queensland and New South Wales are the resort of this curious bird; in those situated on the Clarence, Richmond, and Tweed Rivers it is perhaps the most abundant. It is always to be seen upon the ground, its powerful claws being eminently serviceable in procuring its insect food, for which it scratches as a common hen. It is shy, and must be sought for always in the most inaccessible portions of the scrub. The nest, which is a large structure, is built upon the ground, in some situation suited for its protection, such as under the roots of a tree or shelving rock; it is formed of moss, and is domed in shape, with a small entrance near the bottom. The eggs are large for the size of the bird, and are of a whitish tint.

MALURUS

M. SPLENDENS
Banded Wren

M. ELEGANS.
Graceful Wren

M. LAMBERTI.
Lamberts Wren

M. CYANEUS
Blue Wren

M. LONGICAUDUS.
Long tailed Wren

M. MELANOTUS.
Black Backed Wren

MALURUS CYANEUS.

(Blue Wren—Superb Warbler.)

MALE—Crown, sides of the head, and a broad crescent on the upper part of the back, beautiful shining light blue; back of the neck, streak before and behind the eye, throat and chest, back and rump, deep black; abdomen, whitish; wings, pale brown; tail, blackish tipped with white; bill, black; feet, brown.

FEMALE—Brown above; greyish white beneath.

Length, 4¾ inches; wing, 1¾; tail, 2¼; bill, ½; tarsus, ¾.

This species is plentiful in New South Wales, but is rarely met with so far north as Moreton Bay. During the winter months the adult male loses its bright coloring, and the plumage of the sexes is very similar, the only marked distinction being the color of the bill—the male retaining its black bill at all seasons, whereas the female and young males have the mandibles brown. It is very active, generally being met with in grassy situations, among the stems of which it threads its way with great dexterity, carrying its tail in an erect position. The song is something like that of the European wren. Its food consists of insects, especially caterpillars. The nest is a dome-shaped structure of grass, lined with hair or feathers, and has a small hole for entrance at the side. It incubates from September to December, and rears two or three broods. The eggs are four in number, delicate flesh-white, sprinkled with blotches and spots of reddish brown, forming a zone at the broad end : size, 8 lines by 5½ lines.

MALURUS LONGICAUDUS.

(Long-tailed Wren.)

No separate description is necessary for this species, which differs from the former in the greater length of its tail, and in having the blue coloring a little darker. Its habits, food, and nidification are similar to those of the Malurus Cyaneus.

Length, 5 inches; wing, 2; tail, 2¾; bill, ½; tarsus, 1.

Habitat—Tasmania.

MALURUS MELANOTUS.

(Black-backed Wren.)

MALE—Crown, chin, throat, abdomen, upper part of the back, upper and under tail coverts, beautiful metallic blue; ear coverts, verditer blue; lores, band across the breast and lower part of head, velvety black; external margins of all the wing feathers, green; tail, bluish green slightly tipped with white; bill, black; irides and legs, blackish brown.

FEMALE—Has the lores and circle round the eye reddish brown; upper surface, brown; under surface, brownish white; wings, brown; tail, green tipped with white; bill, reddish brown; feet, brown.

Length, 4¾ inches; wing, 2; tail, 2¾; bill, ½; tarsus, ¾.

This species may be regarded as intermediate between the above and the following. It is mostly to be seen on the ground in the neighborhood of scrubs, and runs with astonishing swiftness. Habitat—Belts of the Murray, South Australia.

MALURUS SPLENDENS.

(Banded Wren.)

MALE—Crown, back, and rump, azure blue; throat and under surface, the same, but with a cast of purple; cheeks and ear coverts, brilliant metallic blue; a band behind the head and ear coverts, and a narrow band across the chest, velvet black; external margins of the wing feathers, green; inner webs and tips of primaries, brown; tail, bluish green, slightly tipped with white; bill, black; feet, brown.

Length, 5 inches; wings, 2; tail, 2¼; bill, ¼; tarsus, ¾.

This species is one of the most beautiful of the genus to which it belongs. It is peculiar to Western Australia, where it frequents scrubby situations throughout the colony, associating in companies of five or six. It incubates in September and the three following months. Its nest and eggs are similar to those of Malurus Cyaneus, as are also its food and general habits.

MALURUS LAMBERTI.

(Lambert's Wren.)

MALE—Crown, ear coverts, sides of the neck, and centre of the back, rich verditer blue; throat, breast, crescent across the upper part of the back, and rump, black; scapularies, brilliant chestnut; wings, brown; abdomen, whitish; tail, dark brown, tinged with green and tipped with white; bill, black; feet, fleshy brown.

FEMALE—Brownish grey above; buffish beneath.

Length, 5¼ inches; wing, 1¾; tail, 2¾; bill, ½; tarsus, ¾.

This species has an extensive range, being found in Queensland and New South Wales. It is sometimes seen in gardens in the neighborhood of Sydney, and also on the low scrubs of the sand-hills; but in Queensland it frequents high ferns and reedy situations, and in manners and habits assimilates to its congeners. The nest is also similar, but the eggs are, perhaps, more largely blotched. The Queensland specimens appear to be brighter in color than those of New South Wales.

MALURUS ELEGANS.

(Graceful Wren.)

MALE—Forehead, ear coverts, sides of the face, and occiput, rich verditer blue; centre of the back, light verditer blue; scapularies, chestnut; throat, chest, back of the neck, and rump, deep velvety black; wings, brown; abdomen and under tail coverts, buffy white; tail, dull bluish green, crossed by numerous indistinct bars, and slightly tipped with white; bill, black; irides and feet, blackish brown.

FEMALE—Upper surface and wings, brown; under surface, buffy white; tail, not tipped with white; bill and feet, brown.

This species is very nearly allied to Malurus Lamberti, but is a little larger than that species, and the feathers of the tail are more spatulate. The blue coloring of the back is also lighter. It is found in Western Australia, frequenting swampy situations. The nest is similar in form to that of Malurus Cyaneus, but more slightly put together, the materials used being thin shreds of melaleuca bark, with a lining of feathers—the same being generally suspended from a branch of the same tree. Eggs, four in number, similar in color and markings, but rather larger than those of Malurus Cyaneus. Food—Insects and caterpillars.

ACANTHIZA

A.INORNATA
Plain coloured Acanthiza

A.LINEATA
Striated Acanth

A.PYRRHOPYGIA
Red rumped Acanth

A.CHRYSORRHŒA
Yellow rumped Acanth

A.REGULOIDES
Buff rumped Acanth

A.DIEMENENSIS
Tasmanian Acanth

ACANTHIZA CHRYSORRHŒA.

(Yellow-rumped Acanthiza.)

FOREHEAD, black—each feather tipped with white; line over the eye, cheeks, and throat, greyish white; upper surface and wings, olive brown; rump and upper tail coverts, light yellow; tail, blackish brown, margined and tipped with grey; irides, light grey; bill and feet, blackish brown.

Length, 4 inches; wing, 2¼; tail, 1¾; bill, ⅜; tarsus, ⅝.

This species has a larger range than any other of its congeners, being found at all seasons in New South Wales, Victoria, South Australia, Western Australia, and Tasmania. It has a sweet song, not unlike that of the English gold-finch. It associates in small flocks, and is tame and familiar. The nest is dome-shaped, and has a small hole for entrance; at the top of the dome is a depression like a second nest, which is probably used by the male while the female is incubating. The nest is placed in a low bush, no matter of what kind. Eggs, four or five; flesh color, or the same speckled with reddish yellow: size, 9 by 6 lines. The bronze cuckoo (Chrysococcyx Basalis) frequently deposits its egg in the nest of this species, the young of which are turned out by the more strong limbed intruder, which is fed and cared for by the foster parents with the greatest assiduity. The number of broods reared by a A. Chrysorrhœa is not less than three in the year.

ACANTHIZA REGULOIDES.

(Buff-rumped Acanthiza.)

UPPER surface, delicate olive brown—the feathers of the forehead, tipped with lighter; wings, brown, margined with lighter; throat, white; upper tail coverts, chest, and abdomen, buffish yellow; tail, blackish brown, margined and tipped with brownish buff; bill, brown; feet, olive brown; irides, straw color.

Length, 3¾ inches; wing, 2; tail, 1¾; bill, ¾; tarsus, ⅝.

From Queensland to South Australia this pretty species is to be found. Like the former species, it is gregarious and tame in disposition; it also builds a dome-shaped nest, which is formed of grasses, spiders' webs, etc., and lined with feathers, the same being generally fixed to a hanging piece of bark of the Eucalyptus or Melaleuca. The eggs are four in number. Its food consists of insects, which are procured, not only on the trees, but on the ground.

ACANTHIZA DIEMENENSIS.

(Tasmanian Acanthiza.)

FOREHEAD, rufous—each feather tipped with blackish brown; upper surface, wings, and tail, dull olive brown; upper tail coverts, tinged with rufous; tail, crossed by a band of deep brown; throat and chest, whitish, irregularly streaked with dark brown; the remainder of the under surface, buff, deepening into rufous on the under tail coverts; bill, brown; irides, red; feet, brown.

Length, 4 inches; wing, 2¼; tail, 2; bill, ¾; tarsus, ⅝.

This species is confined to Tasmania, over which island it is to be found pretty plentifully dispersed, frequenting low and scrubby vegetation, and also gardens. Its globular nest is placed in a low bush, and has a small entrance near the top. It is formed of grasses, root fibres, and strips of bark, and well lined with feathers. Eggs, four or five, pearly bluish white, sprinkled and spotted with reddish brown: size, 8½ by 6 lines.

ACANTHIZA INORNATA.

(Plain Colored Acanthiza.)

Upper surface, tail, and wings, olive brown; primaries, dark brown; a broad band of brownish black near the tips of the tail feathers, followed by a spot of whitish; under surface, buffy white; irides, greenish white; bill and feet, black.

Length, 3½ inches: wing, 1¾; tail, 1½; bill, ¼; tarsus, ¾.

This species, which is, perhaps, the most plainly adorned of all the family, is found in South and Western Australia. It is often to be observed upon various trees, such as the Eucalypti and Casuarinæ, and also on shrubs and bushes; the islands along the coast are also frequented by it. Its food consists solely of insects. The nest is formed of grasses, with a lining of feathers, and generally placed in a grass tree or low bush. Eggs, five: size, 7½ by 5¼ lines; color, white, tinged with greenish grey.

ACANTHIZA LINEATA.

(Striated Acanthiza.)

Crown, olive brown, streaked with white; back and wings, olive green; tail, olive green, crossed by a blackish band near the tip, the extreme tip being olive grey; throat, whitish, spotted with dark brown; chest and under surface, dull yellow, slightly ferruginous on the under tail coverts; irides, brown; bill and feet, black.

Length, 3½ inches; wing, 2; tail, 1¾; bill, ¼; tarsus, ¾.

This species is found from Queensland to South Australia. Its favorite habitat is wild and rugged country, especially near mountain streams. Its food consists of those minute insects which are to be found on the smaller branches of the twigs and leaves, and which are overlooked by birds of larger size. The nest is dome-shaped, having a small hole near the top. The same is sometimes suspended from a drooping bough, or in the midst of a bundle of creepers, or a low bush. The bronze cuckoo (Chrysococcyx Lucidus) is parasitical upon this species, and it is remarked that such nests as have been visited by it bear marks of the forcible entrance of the intruder, as the hole is much larger than usual.

ACANTHIZA PYRRHOPYGIA.

(Red-rumped Acanthiza.)

Upper surface and wings, olive brown; the feathers of the forehead margined with whitish buff; wings, brown, margined with lighter brown; throat, white, mottled with black; upper tail coverts, rufous; tail, olive, crossed with a broad obscure band of black, and tipped with whitish; abdomen, whitish; flanks, pale buff; bill and feet, blackish brown; irides, hazel. The sexes are alike.

Length, 4 inches; wing, 2; tail, 1¾; bill, ¼; tarsus, ¾.

South Australia seems to be the peculiar habitat of this lively little bird. The great Murray Scrub is its favorite resort, among the smaller trees and shrubs of which locality (so favorable for the collector of ornithological specimens) it is ever on the move, in pursuit of its minute and often beautiful insect prey.

ANTHUS AUSTRALIS.

(Australian Pipit.)

Upper surface, dark brown, each feather margined with rufous, especially on the shoulders and wing coverts; stripe over the eye, light buff; throat, white; breast, light buff, streaked with brownish black; abdomen and under tail coverts, white; tail, brownish black, except the two outer pairs of feathers, which are white, bordered with black on their inner webs; bill and feet, fleshy brown; irides, dark brown.

This common and familiar bird is distributed all over the continent of Australia, and is also found in Tasmania, and is, I believe, the only representative of the genus Anthus at present known in Australia. Its habits much resemble the common meadow pipit of Britain. It is essentially a ground bird, and runs with considerable swiftness. When disturbed, it takes a short flight and descends suddenly. Its food consists of insects, worms, and seeds. It breeds from September to January. The nest is rather deep, and formed of dried grasses placed in a hole in the ground, frequently in a most exposed situation, but sometimes sheltered by a tuft of grass. The eggs, three or four in number, are whitish grey, spotted and freckled with dark grey: size, 11 lines by 7½ lines.

CINCLORHAMPHUS CRURALIS.

(Brown Cinclorhamphus.)

Crown and all the upper surface, sandy brown, with a broad central mark of deeper brown on each feather; tail greyish brown—the lateral feathers margined with buffish white; lores, brownish black; throat, deep brown, or white, or an admixture of both, forming bars; chest and flanks, greyish brown; centre of abdomen, deep brown; under tail coverts, dirty white, with a broad lancet-shaped streak of blackish brown down the centre of each feather; irides, hazel; feet, light brown. The sexes differ much in size, the female being scarcely half the size of her mate: she is similarly colored, but lighter.

Length, 9½ inches; wing, 4½; tail, 4½; tarsus, 1¾; bill, 1.

This, which is the largest of the genus, is found in various parts of New South Wales, Victoria, and South Australia. It frequents flat grassy country, and is very similar in its habits to the European skylark, often mounting into the air and uttering its animated and pleasing song. Its nest is constructed of grass, in a small hole in the ground. Eggs, four in number, buffy white, minutely freckled with reddish brown, more especially at the broad end.

CINCLORHAMPHUS CANTILLANS.

(Black-breasted Cinclorhamphus.)

Crown, upper surface, and tail, dull brown, each feather edged with greyish buff; edge of the wing, whitish; coverts, brown, margined with rufous buff; tertiaries, margined with whitish buff; a triangular spot in front of the eye, brownish black; throat, chest, and abdomen, dark brown; thighs, greyish buff in front; under tail coverts, greyish white, with a broad central mark of brown; bill and feet, fleshy brown.

Length, 9 inches; wing, 4; tail, 4½; bill, ¾; tarsus, 1¼.

This species is found in Queensland and the northern portions of the continent. The one inhabiting Western Australia is also referred to this species by Mr. Gould, who remarks that it is "smaller in size, and never so black in the breast." It will very probably be found that several other species exist which have been confounded together, and which will eventually have to be separated, the variation in the plumage of these birds making it a matter of much difficulty to decide as to the different species. The C. Cantillans much resembles in its habits the European Bunting, rising like that bird from a bush, with a fine full note, and descending with tremulous wing to another. The nest and eggs are similar to those of the former species.

CINCLORHAMPHUS RUFESCENS.

(Rufous Tinted Cinclorhamphus.)

Crown and upper surface, dull brown, each feather margined with brownish grey; upper tail coverts, light rufous brown; tail, brown; wings, brown, the feathers more or less edged with greyish buff; an obscure streak over the eye, greyish buff; throat, dull white; chest and abdomen, light brownish grey, the upper portion of the former spotted or streaked with brown; bill, fleshy brown; feet, ashy grey; irides, hazel.

Length, 7½ inches; wing, 3½; tail, 3½; bill, ¾; tarsus, 1.

The whole of the colonies of Australia are frequented by this bird, with the exception of Tasmania. Like its congeners, the male is by far the largest. It lives on the ground, and frequently makes a perpendicular ascent into the air, singing most sweetly like a common skylark. It builds in similar situations to the former, but, in addition to the coarse grass which constitutes the exterior, the nest is lined with fine grasses or hairs. Eggs, four in number, purplish white, freckled and marked with small blotches of chestnut brown: size, 10 lines by 7 lines.

SPHENŒACUS GRAMINEUS
Little Grass Bird

S. GALACTOTES

ACHOCEPHALUS AUSTRALIS
Reed Warbler

MYRAFRA HORSFIELDII
Horsfield's Bush Lark

SPHENŒACUS GALACTOTES.

(Tawny Grass Bird.)

FOREHEAD and crown, rufous—the remainder of the upper surface pale brown; neck and flanks, the same color, blending into buff on the under tail coverts; all the central portion of the under surface, whitish; all the feathers of the upper surface marked with blackish brown in the centre, showing very conspicuously on the uppermost tertiaries; tail, light brown, faintly barred with darker—shafts, black; irides, light brown; upper mandible, olive brown, the cutting edges of which are yellowish white; lower mandible, bluish white; legs and feet, reddish flesh color.

Length, 6¼ inches; wing, 2½; tail, 3½; bill, ⅜; tarsus, ⅞.

This species is found throughout the whole of Queensland and Northern Australia, being very rare in the northern parts of New South Wales. It frequents grassy situations in the neighborhood of swamps, among the grasses and reeds of which it threads its way with great dexterity. It is seldom seen, as the means of concealment are so easily available. When disturbed, its flight is of short duration, the small wings not sufficing for a long excursion. Its food consists of insects.

SPHENŒACUS GRAMINEUS.

(Little Grass Bird.)

STRIPE over the eye, white; crown and all the upper surface, light brown; tail, rufous brown; secondaries and tertiaries, dark brown, margined with buff; the centre of all the feathers of the back and wing coverts, blackish brown; under surface, grey, passing into black on the flanks and vent; each feather on the breast with a small line of brown down the centre; bill and feet, fleshy brown.

Length, 5¼ inches; wing, 2½; tail, 2⅞; bill, ⅜; tarsus, ⅞.

The whole of the southern colonies, including Tasmania, are inhabited by this species, it being as frequent in Western Australia as in New South Wales—specimens from both places exhibiting no difference. The sexes are alike in size and color. Like the former species, this is a very shy and retiring bird, being seldom seen except by the more observing collector. It delights in swampy localities, where, among the rank and luxuriant vegetation, it seeks its insect food. Season of incubation, August and September. It builds its nest among the reeds, the same being constructed of the soft flowering portion, or the skin of the stalk of the reeds, and sometimes grasses, but always lined with feathers. Eggs, four; fleshy white, freckled and streaked with purplish red and blotched with reddish grey.

ACROCEPHALUS AUSTRALIS.

(Reed Warbler.)

ALL the upper surface, olive brown; wings and tail, brown; quills, deep brown, margined with olive buff; all the under surface, deep buff, except the throat, which is white; bill, horn color above—whitish beneath; irides, brown. The sexes are alike.

Length, 6 inches; wing, 3; tail, 3; bill, ⅜; tarsus, 1.

This beautiful warbler is very common in South-eastern Australia. Wherever there are reeds on the banks of rivers and creeks its voice may be heard, but, as Captain Sturt remarks, "that is silent when these are wanting." On the banks of the Murray and Darling it sings during the greater part of the night. It suspends its nest from two or three reeds, about two feet from the surface of the water, the same being composed of the soft skins of reeds and dried rushes. Eggs, four; greyish white, marked and blotched with brown and grey; size, 10 by 7 lines.

[OVER.

ACROCEPHALUS LONGIROSTRIS.

(Long-billed Reed Warbler.)

FAINT line over the eye, fawn color; upper surface, reddish brown, becoming more rufous on the upper tail coverts; primaries and tail, deep brown, margined with rufous; chin, whitish; under surface, deep fawn color; irides, yellowish brown.

Length, 6¼ inches; wing, 3; tail, 3; bill, ¾; tarsus, 1.

This species inhabits Western Australia, and is noted for its beautiful song, which is uttered both night and day, and much resembles the European Nightingale. It is a shy bird, and makes its nest of similar materials to the former species. The eggs are four in number, greenish white, blotched all over with large irregular patches of olive: size, ⅝ by ⅜ of an inch.

MIRAFRA HORSFIELDII.

(Horsfield's Bush Lark.)

UPPER surface, ashy brown—the centre of each feather dark brown; wings, brown, margined with rufous; stripe over the eye, buff; chin, white; under surface, pale buff; a series of spots of a dark brown tint form a crescent beneath the throat; bill, fleshy brown, tipped with dark brown; feet, fleshy brown. The sexes are alike, both in plumage and size.

This interesting little bird is found throughout the colonies of New South Wales, Victoria, and Queensland, being very rare in the latter. It frequents every variety of country, but is most abundant to the west of the mountainous portions known as the Main Range. It spends much of its time upon the ground, but is to be seen perched upon trees and shrubs, and, like the Skylark of Europe, occasionally to mount into the air, singing most melodiously.

ESTRELDA BELLA
Pin-tailed Finch

E. ANNULOSA
Black-rumped Finch

E. BICHENOVII
Bicheno's Finch

E. MOD...
Plain-coloured Finch

E. OCUL...
Red-eared Finch

ESTRELDA BELLA.

(Fire-tailed Finch.)

Forehead, lores, and a line round the eye, black; upper surface, wings, and tail, dark olive brown, crossed by numerous bars of black; rump and base of the tail, bright scarlet; under surface, grey, narrowly and minutely barred with black; centre of abdomen and under tail coverts, black; bill, crimson; irides, nearly black; eyelash, light blue; feet, flesh color.

Length 4½ inches; wing, 2¼; tail, 2; bill, ⅜; tarsus, ⅝.

Tasmania is the principal habitat of this beautiful finch, but it is found, though less abundantly, in all the south-eastern portions of Australia. Like many of its congeners, it is usually to be seen upon the ground in small companies, its food being the seeds of grasses. It forms a dome-shaped nest of a large size, having a hole near the top for entrance. The same is constructed of grasses and fine twigs, and is placed in a low bush, frequently in a very exposed position. The eggs are five or six in number, fleshy white. Size, 8½ by 6½ lines. Several broods are reared throughout the breeding season, which extends from September to January.

ESTRELDA OCULEA.

(Red-eared Finch.)

Color and markings of the upper surface and tail, as in E. Bella; a small patch of scarlet behind the eye; throat and breast, light brown, finely banded with black; abdomen, black, with a large spot of white at the tip of each feather; irides and bill, red; the base of the upper mandible, light grey; eyelash, greenish blue; legs, yellowish grey.

Length, 4¾ inches; wing, 2¼; tail, 2; bill, ⅜; tarsus, ⅝.

This species is found throughout Western Australia, to which portion of the continent it seems to be confined. It frequents grassy situations in the neighborhood of swamps and rivers, and is more solitary in its habits than most of the others.

ESTRELDA ANNULOSA.

(Black-rumped Finch.)

Face, ear coverts, and throat, white, surrounded by a jet black band; chest, greyish white, immediately below which is a band of black; abdomen, white; crown, back of the neck, and back, greyish brown, marked with numerous fine bars of greyish white; rump and upper and under tail coverts, black; wings, blackish brown; the wing coverts and secondaries, spotted thickly with greyish white; bill and feet, bluish lead color.

Length, 4 inches; wing, 2; tail, 2¼; bill, ⅜; tarsus, ½.

This rare species is confined to the northern portions of Australia which lie to the west of the Gulf of Carpentaria. It frequents grassy situations on the banks of rivers, feeding in small flocks from six to ten in number.

ESTRELDA BICHENOVII.

(Bicheno's Finch.)

The description of E. Annulosa will apply for the most part to the present species, but it may be distinguished from the former by the white patch on the rump, and by its having the transverse markings on the back more clearly defined. In size it is also similar.

This species is found in the interior of the northern portions of New South Wales and the southern portions of Queensland, specimens having been (though rarely) obtained near Brisbane. It is always to be found feeding upon the ground, usually in small flocks, and when disturbed, flies off among the bushes. Its food consists of the seeds of grasses and plants of various kinds.

[OVER.

ESTRELDA MODESTA.

(Plain-colored Finch.)

FOREHEAD, purple; lores and spot on the chin, black; crown, back of the neck, back, and wings, brown; wing coverts and tertiaries, tipped with white; rump and upper tail coverts, barred with white and brown; tail, black—the two outer feathers tipped with white; under surface, white, barred with brown; middle of the abdomen, white; legs, light flesh color; irides, bright hazel.

Length, 4½ inches; wing, 2¼; tail, 2; bill, ⅓; tarsus, ½.

This species frequents the same portions of the country as the former, and is met with occasionally on the banks of the Brisbane River. It would not seem to extend its range as far as Port Curtis, for among the various species of finch received from thence, I have not seen a specimen of the present one. In its habits it is similar to the others, always to be seen on the ground, grass seed forming its principal food, and, like them, constructing a dome-shaped nest of grasses with the entrance near the top. The eggs are six in number, pinky white: size, ½ by ⅜ of an inch.

ESTRELDA RUFICAUDA.

(Red-tailed Finch.)

MALE—Forehead, face, and bill, bright scarlet; a few white dots on the cheeks; upper surface and wings, brownish olive; upper tail coverts and tail, brownish crimson, each feather of the former having a spot of pinky white near the tip; throat and under surface, greyish buff, spotted with large oval whitish spots; under tail coverts, buff; foot, yellowish buff; irides, lemon yellow.

The *Female* has a general resemblance to the male, but is rather smaller, and not so bright in color.

Length, 4 inches; wing, 2; tail, 1¾; bill, 5-16; tarsus, ¾.

This very handsome species is found in the interior of the northern portion of New South Wales, and also in Queensland. In the neighborhood of Rockhampton, in the district of Port Curtis, it appears in considerable numbers, and, being capable of enduring captivity well, has been in much request for the cage, living very readily on canary-seed. It is generally seen in small flocks, feeding on grass seeds.

ESTRELDA TEMPORALIS.

(Red Eyebrowed Finch.)

CROWN, grey; upper surface and wings, dark olive, inclining to grey; eyebrow and upper tail coverts, brilliant scarlet; tail, dark grey; throat, chest, flanks, and under tail coverts, light grey; abdomen, buff; bill, scarlet, with a small black patch above and below; foot, flesh-color; irides, brownish red.

Length, 4½ inches; wing, 2; tail, 1½; bill, 5-16; tarsus, ¾.

This species is plentiful from South Australia to Queensland, frequenting grassy situations, its food consisting of seeds. Though easily reconciled to the cage, it seldom lives long in captivity, being of a delicate nature. It assembles in flocks of considerable numbers, except in the breeding season, when it associates in pairs, building the nest in a low bush or tuft of rank grass. The structure is rather large, being formed of grasses externally, and lined with vegetable down in the interior. Eggs, five or six, fleshy white.

ESTRELDA PHÆTON.

(Crimson Finch.)

CROWN, bluish black; side of the neck, dark grey; line over the eye, ear coverts, upper tail coverts, and most of the under surface, bright crimson; (the abdomen in the female has a tinge of brown); a few small white spots on the flanks; centre of abdomen and under tail coverts, black; tail, red; bill, rich crimson, shading into whitish at the base; legs and foot, ochre yellow, tinged with red in front; irides, reddish brown.

Length, 5¼ inches; wing, 1½; tail, 2¾; bill, ½; tarsus, ¾.

This elegant species is a native of Queensland and Northern Australia, from the Port Curtis district to Port Essington. Like the former, it frequents situations where grasses abound, its food principally consisting of the seeds of that family of plants. A good many have been received alive from Rockhampton, and seem to endure captivity very well.

AMADINA CASTANOTIS.

(Chestnut-eared Finch.)

MALE—Crown of the head and back, brownish grey; wings, brown; rump, white; upper tail coverts, black, spotted with large white spots; tail, brown; ear coverts and flanks, chestnut, the latter spotted with small white spots; a white patch in front of the eye is bounded before and behind by a narrow black line; throat and chest, grey, finely banded with black; a patch of black in the centre of the chest; abdomen white; bill, scarlet; foot, yellowish flesh-color.

The *Female* differs from the male in wanting the chestnut ear coverts and flanks, the bands and black mark on the chest, &c., but bears sufficient similarity to be easily recognizable.

Length, 4 inches; wing, 2; tail, 1¾ inch; bill, 5-16; tarsus, ¾.

This well-marked species is found in South and West Australia, probably over the whole of the interior, as well as the north-west coasts—a species which seems identical being found in the Malayan Islands. Captain Sturt refers to this bird as the sure indication of water being near. It assembles in large flocks, feeding on the seeds of plants, particularly those of the grasses. It builds in the neighborhood of lagoons and creeks, several nests being often constructed in the same bush. The period of incubation is December. The raptorial birds make great havoc among this species, and frequently carry off a pair at one swoop.

AMADINA LATHAMI.

(Spotted-sided Finch.)

CROWN of the head, ear coverts, and neck, grey; back and wings, brown; upper tail coverts, bright scarlet; tail, band across the chest, and a patch in front of the eye, black; flanks, black, spotted with large oval white spots; throat and under surface, white; bill, purplish red; irides, crimson; foot, lead-color.

Length, 4 inches; wing, 2; tail, 1½; bill, ½; tarsus, ½.

This conspicuous species is very common in various parts of New South Wales, and occasionally in the southern portions of Queensland. Its favourite resort is grassy situations on the banks of creeks, or anywhere where grass-seed is plentiful. As a cage pet it is a great favourite, and is trapped in large numbers by the bird catchers.

PITTA MACKLOTII
Blue-banded Pitta

PITTA MACKLOTII.

(Blue-banded Pitta.)

FOREHEAD, cheeks, and chin, vinous brown; crown of the head, dark brown, with a few slight streaks of greyish blue; occiput and back of the neck, orange chestnut; throat, brownish black, followed by a broad band of verditer blue across the chest, this is succeeded by a narrow band of black; abdomen and under tail coverts, scarlet; upper part of the back and wings, deep olive green; upper tail coverts, upper surface of tail feathers, greater wing coverts, and outer edges of secondaries, greyish blue; spurious wing, primaries, and under surface of tail, black; a spot of white near the base of the third primary is continued across the fourth and fifth, forming a band; under surface of wings, greyish brown; flanks, brown.

Length, 7 inches; wing, 4½; tail, 1¾; bill, 1½; tarsus, 1¾.

This species of Pitta is now introduced for the first time as a member of the Australian fauna. Like many other birds of beautiful plumage, it is a periodical visitant at Cape York. No information accompanied the specimen, which was kindly forwarded to me by G. Krefft, Esq., of the Sydney Museum, for the purpose of being figured. That gentleman informs me that the species has been known to science for many years, having originally been obtained by MM. Müller and Macklöt, naturalists to a French expedition, when on the coast of New Guinea, and that the same is figured in the *Planches Colorès* of Temminck.

OREOCINCLA LUNULATA.

(Mountain Thrush.)

CROWN of the head and all the upper surface, olive brown—each feather tipped with a crescent of black; wings and tail, olive brown—the outermost feather of the tail, tipped with white; throat, white, spotted with dark brown; chest, washed with buffish brown; abdomen and under tail coverts, white—the chest and sides of the abdomen, ornamented with large black lunate marks at the tip of each feather; bill, brownish horn color; feet, yellowish white; irides, dark brown.

Length, 10 inches; wing, 5; tail, 3½; bill, 1½; tarsus, 1¼.

The eastern coast, from Queensland on the north to Tasmania on the south, seems to be the habitat of the present species. It has also been found in Victoria and South Australia, but by no means plentifully. The singular fact that the southern specimens are far larger and more robust than the northern, is very manifest on comparison. Like Pitta Strepitans, the northern specimens are fully a third less than the southern. As its name indicates, it prefers mountainous districts, and elevated forest country, where it may be observed hopping on the ground in search of its food which consists of snails, insects, and perhaps berries. It is generally found in pairs. The breeding season is August and the two following months. The nest is formed of green moss and lined with fibrous roots, and is of large size, being 7 inches in breadth, the diameter of the opening being 3¼ inches, and the depth 2 inches, or a little more. The eggs, two (?) in number, are buff color, freckled all over with reddish brown; size, 1¼ inch by ¾. The sexes are alike, and the young assume the plumage of the adult at an early age.

CINCLOSOMA CINNAMONEUS.

(Cinnamon-colored Ground Thrush.)

MALE—All the upper surface, two middle tail feathers, sides of the breast, and flanks, cinnamon brown; ear coverts, brown, edged below with darker; a narrow stripe of buffy white over the eye; lores, black; throat and chest, white, both having a large triangular patch of black in the middle; wing coverts, spurious wing, and lateral tail feathers, black, largely tipped with white; centre of abdomen, white; under tail coverts, black on the outer and white on the inner webs; irides, brown; feet, blue; bill, black.

The FEMALE has the markings on the throat, breast, and wings, grey instead of black.

Length, 8 inches; wing, 3½; tail, 3½; bill, ¾; tarsus, 1¼.

This pretty species is found throughout the far interior, frequenting the country to the westward of the Darling; making its appearance in the winter months. Of the four species yet known this is the smallest. Our first knowledge of it was obtained by Captain Sturt, who, during his memorable detention at the Depôt, shot one specimen. Since that time Mr. White and others have also met with examples, from one of which, in Mr. Waller's collection, the accompanying figure was drawn.

PTILONORHYNCHUS RAWNSLEYI

PTILONORHYNCHUS RAWNSLEYI.

(Rawnsley's Satin Bird.)

HEAD, throat, neck, chest, abdomen, back, upper and under tail coverts, rich glossy bluish black; wing coverts and spurious wing, jet black, edged with the former color; primaries, black, with the exception of a small portion of the outer webs, and a large portion of the inner webs near the base, which are of a bright yellow color; the secondaries are brilliant orange for the greater part of their length, their basal portions being edged with black, and have a large rounded or oval patch of black near their tips; a narrow stripe of deep orange runs in a wavy form through the centre of the outer webs of the tertiaries, the inner webs being wholly black; the two middle feathers of tail, jet black, the remainder, the same, slightly tipped with golden brown; bill, the same, but lighter at the tip; irides, greenish blue.

Length, 11¼ inches; wing, 6; tail, 4; tarsus, 1¼; bill, 1¼.

This splendid new species must be regarded as a most interesting addition to the avifauna of Queensland. The strong resemblance in its coloring to the common Satin Bird, and also the Regent Bird, might lead to the suspicion of its being a hybrid, but the important testimony of A. C. Gregory, Esq., the explorer, and now Surveyor-General of Queensland, will have much weight in assisting the naturalist to a right conclusion. The specimen from which my figure is taken was submitted to the inspection of that gentleman, who immediately recognised it as a species seen by him on his route from the Gulf of Carpentaria to Moreton Bay, about the month of October, 1856. The locality was the Suttor River, a branch of the Burdekin. Mr. Gregory always took considerable trouble to distinguish the different notes of birds and cries of bush animals, knowing that the natives frequently use them for their own purposes as decoy notes or signals of communication; and his attention was drawn to the present species from its peculiar note, which was a prolonged " o-hoo " several times very distinctly repeated, the same being in the minor key, giving it a very plaintive character. Mr. Gregory states that he had an excellent opportunity of observing its plumage, and cannot possibly be mistaken; and that, on mentioning the circumstance to Mr. Elsey, the surgeon and naturalist attached to his party, it became a matter of discussion between them as to whether it ought to be placed in the genus Ptilonorhynchus or Sericulus. The country in which it was seen was an open box flat, with brigalow scrubs in the neighborhood. The present specimen was obtained by H. C. Rawnsley, Esq., in the scrub behind his house, at Witton, on the River Brisbane, a few miles from the city, on the 14th July, 1867. As a naturalist possessing a large acquaintance with Australian ornithology, I have much pleasure in dedicating this bird to him.

CHLAMYDERA MACULATA.

(Spotted Bower Bird.)

CROWN of the head, ear coverts, and throat, rich brown, each feather surrounded by a narrow line of black; feathers on the crown, small and tipped with silvery grey; a beautiful band of elongated feathers of a light rose pink crosses the back of the neck; all the upper surface, wings, and tail, deep brown; each feather of the back, rump, scapularies, wing coverts, and secondaries, tipped with a large round buff spot; primaries, slightly tipped with white; all the tail feathers, terminated with buffy white; under surface, greyish white; feathers of the flanks, marked with faint zigzag lines of light brown.

The female, with the exception of the tippet, is similar to the male, but is supposed to have, when arrived at maturity, a rudimentary fringe.

Length, 11¼ inches; wing, 6; tail, 4½; bill, 1¼; tarsus, 1⅜.

This prettily ornamented bird is found in South Australia, Victoria, New South Wales, and Queensland. It inhabits the brushes bordering plains, and also the sides of low hills covered with low scrub. In those situations the singular bower which it builds may occasionally be found. The structure is an archway of fine grass, with the heads nearly adjoining; this constitutes the lining and is outwardly strengthened with twigs, the whole being kept securely in their places with small stones or pebbles so disposed as to form a paving to the interior and some distance around, small paths leading to the bower being left bare. The front and back of the bower are similarly arranged. A heap of various materials is piled together opposite each entrance, consisting of shells, small pebbles, bones of small animals, bits of broken crockery, &c. The bower is repaired from year to year, and is resorted to as a playground by numerous individuals who delight in disporting themselves, engaging in various curious and frantic evolutions, and in chasing one another through the avenue. The nest of this species was once found by Mr. Coxen at Jondaryan; it was cup shaped, constructed of dried sticks, and lined with fine grass and feathers. To that gentleman's great regret, he was not able to describe the eggs, as the nest only contained young birds. The food of the Spotted Bower Bird consists of berries, seeds, and insects. It has a harsh grating note, which is frequently the means of attracting the notice of the collector.

CHLAMYDERA CERVINIVENTRIS.

(Fawn-breasted Bower Bird.)

CROWN of the head, back of the neck, and upper part of the back, brown, with a streak of buff down the centre of each feather; scapularies and wing coverts, brown, streaked and tipped with buffy white; the tail coverts are greyish and similarly tipped; primaries, secondaries, and tertiaries, dull brown, the two latter, slightly tipped with dull white and edged with brownish buff; tail, brown; the feathers of the throat are narrow in form and of a rusty buff margined with brown; the rest of the under surface, light fawn color; bill, black; foot, greenish black; irides, hazel.

Length, 11½ inches; wing, 5½; tail, 5; bill, 1¼; tarsus, 1¼.

This new and interesting species was first discovered at Cape York by Mr. Macgillivray, naturalist on board H.M.S. *Rattlesnake*. Of all the examples which have since been obtained, none have had the lovely fringe behind the neck which adorns some of the other species, hence it may be presumed that it is destitute of that ornament. The bower, which was also found by Mr. M., differs somewhat from that constructed by the other species, the walls being thick, nearly upright, and the passage between very narrow. It is formed of fine twigs placed upon a thick platform of thicker twigs, and is about four feet long, nearly two feet in width, eighteen inches in height, and is decorated here and there with snail shells and berries. Its presence is usually announced by a loud churr-r-r as it starts forth alarmed at the approach of the intruder. The bower (which Mr. M. sent home to the British Museum) was situated in a patch of low scrub about half-a-mile from the beach. Specimens have also been obtained by Mr. J. Jardine, late Government Resident at Cape York, who has likewise secured one of the bowers, but not having had an opportunity of seeing it, I can add nothing to what has been stated by Mr. Macgillivray.

SERICULUS CHRYSOCEPHALUS

SERICULUS CHRYSOCEPHALUS.

(Regent Bird.)

MALE.—Head and back of the neck, rich yellow, widened into a collar adjoining the back; the forehead finely tinged with orange; secondaries, deep yellow, narrowly edged along the inner webs with black; primaries, more or less black on the tips and edges of the outer webs, the remaining portion of them (except the first feather, which is entirely black) being bright yellow; lores, a stripe over the eye, throat, cheeks, and the remainder of the plumage, deep black; bill, orange; irides, lemon color; feet, black.

FEMALE.—Head and cheeks, brown; a large patch of blackish brown on the crown; back, wings, and tail, olive brown; breast, light greyish brown, with lunate markings of olive brown; irides, hazel; bill and feet, black.

Length, 11¼ inches; wing, 5¼; tail, 4½; bill, 1⅓; tarsus, 1¼.

Among the many beautiful forms belonging to the avifauna of Australia, the Regent Bird takes the first rank. The richness and beauty of its coloring has always rendered it an object of attraction, and to be desired as an ornament for the glass case. It is found in all the eastern portions of Australia, from the Hunter River on the south to the district of Port Curtis at the north, being most plentiful in the scrubs of south Queensland and the northern portions of New South Wales, frequenting the fig and other trees for the purpose of feeding, which it does in company with many other birds of similar habits. I have seen it in company with Graucalus Swainsonii, and, though rarely, with Pitta Strepitans; and Mr. Gould states he has also seen it feeding on the same tree as the Satin Bird, Cat Bird, and the green Oriole. Though shy, it is not difficult to procure; all that is necessary is to remain quiet with gun in hand under the tree to which it resorts. The females are much less shy, as if conscious that their plain livery was a security. The young males, also, being similar in appearance, are by no means hard to be obtained; it seldom occurs, however, that it is found in the intermediate state of plumage. It is only very recently known that this beautiful bird builds a bower, very similar in character to that of the Satin Bird, but much smaller in size and not arched. The representation in the plate will give a better idea of its form than any description. It is open at both ends and built on a strong platform of sticks, and, in the specimen from which the drawing was taken, further strengthened by being attached to two growing saplings.

This interesting discovery was made about the middle of 1863, by Mr. Waller, of Brisbane, when shooting in the scrub at Eagle Farm, on the River Brisbane. His attention was called to it by seeing what to him was a circumstance of most unusual occurrence: a male Regent Bird descending to the ground, jumping about, and acting altogether in a very strange and singular manner. He shot the bird, but only succeeded in wounding it, and on going to the spot where he expected to find it dead, he came upon the bower, which was in a thick and entangled portion of the scrub. He at once saw the nature of the structure, and that it could not be that of any bower bird known before, and justly concluded that it must have been formed by the Regent Bird which he had just shot. Immediately afterwards the female came and alighted close to the bower. The ground around the bower was clean as if swept, and close to the structure were scattered a few specimens of a common species of helix. More fully to satisfy himself that his suspicions were correct, Mr. Waller visited the spot the next day, and several days following, and was fully satisfied that his conjectures were well founded, as he saw the female again in the immediate vicinity, of the bower, and uttering her call as if in search of her lost mate. Impressed with the importance of his discovery, Mr. Waller determined to have the fact confirmed by Mr. Charles Coxen, an ornithologist of acknowledged experience and known to science. That gentleman accompanied him to the spot, and was fully satisfied as to the correctness of the opinion entertained by Mr. Waller of its being none other than the bower of the Regent Bird. With some considerable trouble it was removed, and is now in Mr. Coxen's possession, having been kindly presented to him by Mr. Waller. The Sericulus is stated by the late Mr. Strange to build its nest during the month of November, the same being rudely constructed of sticks, but he did not succeed in obtaining the eggs.

ORIOLUS FLAVOCINCTUS
Crescent-marked Oriole

O. VIRIDIS
Green Oriole

ORIOLUS VIRIDIS.

(Green Oriole.)

HEAD and all the upper surface, yellowish olive; primaries, blackish brown, narrowly margined on the external webs with light grey; secondaries, tertiaries, and spurious wing, margined and tipped with whitish grey; under surface, white, washed with olive yellow on the sides of the chest, and marked with a tear-shaped spot of black down the centre of each feather; tail, grey—all but the two central feathers largely tipped with white on the inner webs, and the inner webs softening from deep black next the shaft into grey at the margins; bill, light reddish brown; irides, reddish orange; feet, grey.

Length, 10½ inches; wing, 6½; tail, 4½; bill, 1½; tarsus, ⅞.

This species is confined to the colonies of New South Wales and Queensland, being tolerably plentiful in some localities. Though known to feed upon insects, it is to be regarded as a genuine fruit eater. It is particularly partial to the wild fig, and, in situations where that tree abounds, may often be seen feeding in company with other birds of similar habits; it will also, at times, show its appreciation of the cultivated fruits introduced by the settler, and visits the gardens to satisfy its appetite, whether natural or acquired. It has a variety of pleasing notes, and often imitates those of other birds. It forms its nest of shreds of stringy bark or tea-tree bark, lining the same with filaments from the oak (casuarina), or grass and hair. The nest is generally placed in the fork of a horizontal bough, without much regard to concealment. Eggs, from two to four; color, creamy white, spotted and blotched with umber brown, sepia brown, and light grey, most thickly disposed on the larger end: size, 1½ inch by ⅞. The breeding season is from September to January.

ORIOLUS AFFINIS.

(Allied Oriole.)

THIS species belongs to the northern portions of Australia. It needs no separate description, being so similar to the former. The points in which it differs are the following: The body is smaller, the wing shorter, the bill larger, and the white tips of the tail feathers of smaller extent. It has a fine voice, very varied and pleasing. The nest was found by Gilbert, in the month of December, and was attached to the drooping branch of a tea-tree, at the distance of about five feet from the ground; it was large and deep, formed of narrow strips of tea-tree bark, mingled with a few twigs, and lined with fine wiry twigs. Eggs, bluish white, sparsely spotted with dark brown and bluish grey: size, 1½ inch by ⅞.

ORIOLUS FLAVOCINCTUS.

(Crescent-marked Oriole.)

HEAD and all the upper surface, yellowish olive; a stripe of black runs through the feathers of the crown, and a wedge-shaped mark of black down the centre of the feathers of the back and scapularies; under surface, lighter and brighter than the upper; under tail coverts, yellow; wings, black—all the feathers margined with greenish yellow, and tipped with pale yellow; two central feathers of tail, dull blackish olive, the rest much darker, and broadly tipped with yellow; bill, dark flesh color, tipped with greenish; feet, greenish lead color; irides, red.

Length, 11½ inches; wing, 5½; tail, 4½; bill, 1½; tarsus, ⅞.

The female is rather smaller than the male: her wings are marked with lighter yellow, and she has the under surface streaked with black.

This handsome species is a constant resident at Cape York. It has also been found on the opposite or western side of the Gulf of Carpentaria, where it was originally discovered by Captain King, during his survey of that portion of the coast; Gilbert also procured it in the neighborhood of Port Essington. Information respecting its habits and nidification are at present wanting, but will probably be soon supplied by the Messrs. Cockerill and Thorpe, at present (1868) engaged in the study and collection of the birds of the northern portion of the Cape York peninsula.

SPHECOTHERES AUSTRALIS
Australian Sphecotheres

Female of S.Australis

SPHECOTHERES FLAVIVENTRIS
Yellow bellied Sphecotheres

SPHECOTHERES AUSTRALIS.

(Australian Sphecotheres.)

—◆—

MALE—Crown of the head, nape of the neck, and ear coverts, jet black; back of the neck, dark grey; back and upper tail coverts, bright yellowish olive; throat and upper part of the chest, grey, softening into yellowish olive on the flanks and abdomen; shoulders, coverts, and tertiaries, yellowish olive; the inner webs of the latter, blackish grey, softening into whitish grey at the outer edges of the underlying feathers; primaries and spurious wing, black, edged with grey; the four central tail feathers, black, slightly tipped with brownish black; the remaining feathers of the tail are more or less white, the outermost of all being entirely white on the outer webs; ventral feathers and under tail coverts, white; bare skin round the eye, and a narrow line to the nostrils bright red; irides, brownish red; feet, brownish yellow; bill, black.

FEMALE—Head, whitish brown, each feather with a strong brown line down the centre; neck and upper part of the back, dull olive brown; wings, dull olive brown, each feather margined with whitish buff; primaries, brownish black, margined with whitish buff; throat, chest, and abdomen, dull white, each feather having a broad longitudinal streak of brown; rump and tail, dull olive, the three outer pairs of feathers being tipped with dull white, and margined with a fine line of the same on the inner web.

Length, 11¼ inches; wing, 6; tail, 4¼; bill, 1¼; tarsus, 1.

This bird inhabits the dense scrubs of Queensland. Its food consists of wild figs and other fruits. It occasionally visits gardens, and is excessively fond of mulberries. It is to be seen associated with various other frugivorous birds, such as the Regent-bird, Satin-bird, &c.

———

SPHECOTHERES FLAVIVENTRIS.

(Yellow-bellied Sphecotheres.)

—◆—

MALE—Crown of the head, cheeks, and central tail feathers, black; outer tail feathers white, the inner webs being black at their bases; back of wings, olive green; primaries, blackish, margined externally with grey; inner webs of tertiaries, blackish; throat, chest, and abdomen, bright yellow; under tail coverts, white; naked skin around the eye, bright red; bill, dark horn color; feet, yellowish brown; irides, reddish brown.

FEMALE—Head and back, brown; upper tail coverts and tail, olive green; the three outermost pairs of tail feathers broadly margined with white; throat, brown—each feather edged with buffy white; breast, abdomen, and under tail coverts, white, each feather having a large oblong dash of brown in the centre; feet, greyish green.

Length, 10¼ inches; wing, 5¼; tail, 4¼; bill, 1¼; tarsus, 1¼.

This species frequents forest land in the peninsula of Cape York, where it associates in small flocks of seven or eight in number. Its food consists of berries and fruits of various kinds.

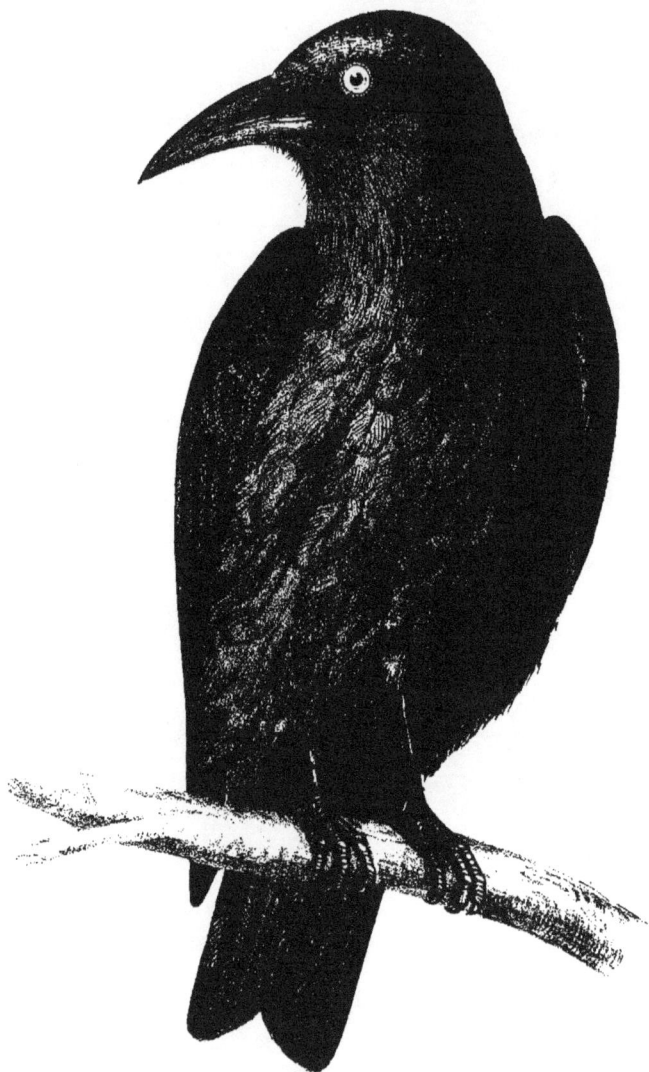

CORVUS CORONOIDES
White eyed Crow

CORVUS CORONOIDES.

(*White-eyed Crow.*)

THE whole plumage, rich glossy black; bill and feet, black; irides, white in the adult, brown in the young.

Length, 21½ inches; wing, 14½; tail, 8½; bill, 2; tarsus, 2¼.

This bird, although differing from the Carrion Crow of England, is more nearly allied to the true Corvus than to any other member of its family. It has been found in every explored portion of Australia, and has probably a greater range of habitat than any other member of the Australian group; and although there is a slight diversity in size between those found in different portions of the continent, there is little doubt of their identity, all having the white eye in an adult stage and possessing habits exactly alike. It is generally seen in pairs, but when opportunities occur for plentiful feeding on offal at stations, slaughter-yards, and at lambing time, it congregates in considerable numbers. Its food in general consists of carrion of all kinds, insects, berries, and other vegetable products; it also at times causes much injury to the farmer by the destruction of seed crops, and many cases are known where whole rows of vines have been stripped of their ripe fruit, but a little attention will soon disperse them. Occasionally a flock of some forty or fifty may be met with in the bush, some on the ground and others on the trees, where they keep up a constant cawing, and in such cases are not easily dispersed, for if disturbed they speedily gather together and commence their noise again. The object of such meeting is not known; but their actions and noise would almost lead to the supposition that they at times, like animals of a higher order, hold high parliament over the past and future. They are almost constant attendants on the camps of the aborigines; indeed, this is generally understood by bushmen, and numerous instances are known of such camps having been discovered and surprised through the instrumentality of these birds. Their cry or caw consists of the first three notes of a common chord, descending from the fifth to the third and first, this last being prolonged to a melancholy groan.

It is but rarely that the nest has been discovered, from the fact of its being placed near the top of the largest and highest trees in such localities as are least disturbed. So little was known of its nidification some few years ago that an impression (of course erroneous) was very common, amongst the working classes of New South Wales, of fabulous rewards having been offered without success, for the nest and eggs of this bird. The nest is of large size and formed of sticks. The eggs—three or four in number—are long in shape; color, pale green, blotched and spotted with umber brown; size, 1⅞ inches by 1¼.

PTILOTIS
Honey Eaters

P. ORNATUS
Graceful H.E.

P. AURICOMIS
Yellow tufted H.E.

P. PLUMULUS
Plumed H.E.

P. FASCIOGULARIS
Fasciated H.E.

P. FUSCUS
Fuscous H.E.

PTILOTIS PLUMULUS.
(Plumed Honey-eater.)

Crown and all the upper surface, olive yellow, inclining to grey on the back; lores, black; ear coverts, throat, and under surface, yellowish grey, faintly streaked with darker. Behind the ear are two tufts—the upper one narrow and black, the lower one broad and of a beautiful yellow. Irides, dark reddish brown; feet, green.

Length, 4½ inches; wing, 3½; tail, 2½; bill, ½; tarsus, ⅔.

This species inhabits the interior of Western Australia. Its movements are quick and darting when occupied among the trees, but its flight is easy and graceful. Its note is a long whistle or shake, like a pea-whistle, and it has also other notes of a more quiet and subdued character. It breeds from October to January, the nest being suspended from a horizontal branch near the ground, the materials used in its construction being dried grasses, and the cotton-like buds of flowers, which constitute the lining. Eggs, two, 10 by 7 lines, pale salmon color, freckled with a deeper tint, which forms a zone at the broad end.

PTILOTIS ORNATUS.
(Graceful Honey-eater.)

Crown, outer edges of wings, and tail, rich olive; back and rump, brown; throat and cheeks, olive brown; chest and under surface, greyish white, each feather broadly marked with dark brown down the centre; under tail coverts, buffy white, striped with brown; a bright yellow tuft on the side of the neck, and an obscure mark of bright olive under the eye; primaries and tail, brown, the latter tipped with white; bill, blackish; legs, light brown; irides, dark brown.

Length, 6½ inches; wing, 2½; tail, 3½; bill, ½; tarsus, ½.

The female is a little smaller.

An inhabitant of Western and Southern Australia. It feeds upon the honey of the flowers of the Eucalyptus and other trees, and builds its nest in a rather exposed situation, on a horizontal branch, the same being small and cup-shaped, constructed with grasses, wool, spiders' webs, and other materials. Eggs, two or three, deep salmon color, minutely freckled with brown at the larger end: size, 9 by 7 lines.

PTILOTIS FASCIOGULARIS.
(Fasciated Honey-eater.)

Crown and all the upper surface, wings, and tail, olive brown; lores, black; ear coverts, yellow, followed by a patch of silvery white on the side of the neck; throat, light yellow, striped with greyish brown; chest, greyish brown, melting away into greyish white on the abdomen, each feather of which is obscurely striped with brown; bill, black; irides, hazel; feet, lead color.

Length, 7 inches; wing, 3½; tail, 3½; bill, ½; tarsus, ½.

This species has only been found in the colony of Queensland, where it must be considered of rare occurrence, being only found in mangrove swamps and the islands near the coast. Its note is a peculiar harsh whistle.

PTILOTIS FUSCUS.
(Fuscous Honey-eater.)

Upper surface, greyish brown, tinged with olive; a ring of black surrounds the eye; ear coverts, blackish brown, followed by a small patch of yellow; throat and under surface, light greyish brown; bill, dull yellow at the base, and black at the tip; feet, fleshy brown; irides, yellow.

Length, 5½ inches; wing, 2½; tail, 2; bill, ½; tarsus, ⅔.

This plainly-colored species is found in Queensland and New South Wales, frequenting the various flowering trees to feed upon the honey, and small insects which are attracted to the blossoms.

PTILOTIS AURICOMIS.
(Yellow-tufted Honey-eater.)

Crown of the head and throat, bright yellow, the former with a tinge of olive; lores, under and above the eye, and ear coverts, black; behind the latter is a long tuft of orange yellow; upper surface, wings, and tail, brownish olive; chest and under surface, olive yellow; bill and feet, black.

Length, 7 inches; wing, 3½; tail, 3½; bill, ½; tarsus, ⅔.

This may be regarded as a plentiful species, inhabiting forest lands and open country adjoining scrubs in New South Wales and Queensland, where it may be seen actively engaged in searching the stems and leaves of trees for insects, which form no inconsiderable portion of its food, though, like the other members of the family, it feeds largely on the nectar of flowers.

P. FLAVIGULA

P. FILIGERA

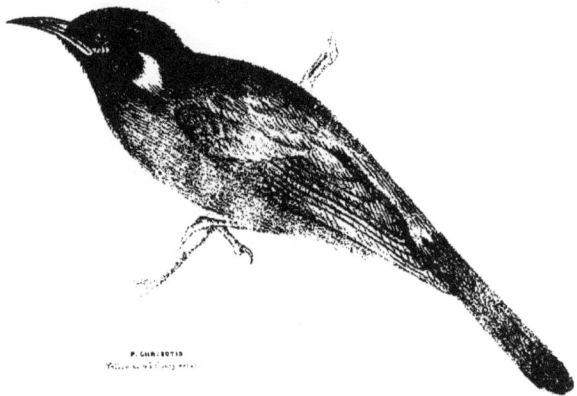

P. CHRYSOTIS

PTILOTIS FLAVIGULA.

(Yellow-throated Honey Eater.)

CROWN of the head and cheeks, blackish grey; back, wing, and tail, yellowish olive; inner webs of primaries and tertiaries, blackish brown—outer edges of the former, bright yellowish olive; throat, bright yellow; ear coverts, blackish grey, tipped with yellow; chest, grey, tinged with olive; centre of abdomen, buff, blending into greyish buff on the flanks; under tail coverts and under surface of tail, olive buff, the former fringed with dull buff; irides, light brown; bill, black; feet, brownish lead color. The female is similar in appearance, but smaller in size.

Length, 8 inches; wing, 4½; tail, 4½; bill, 1; tarsus, 1.

This very well defined species is limited to Tasmania and the southern portions of the continent of Australia. It is abundant in the ravines and gullies about Hobart Town, where its full and melodious note may often be heard. It feeds upon small insects, especially bees, and also upon the pollen of plants. September is the month of incubation. The nest is large and very compactly made; the outer part being formed of stringy bark and grass, and the inner part lined with kangaroo or opossum fur. The eggs, two or three in number, are light fleshy buff, spotted with chestnut and grey: size, 11 by 8 lines.

PTILOTIS FILIGERA.

(Streaked Honey Eater.)

FOREHEAD and lores brown; crown and nape, dark grey, rather indistinctly striped with white; ear coverts, silvery grey, bounded by a tuft of silvery white above, and golden yellow beneath; back and shoulders, olive brown; greater coverts, secondaries and tertiaries, brown, the former largely tipped with buff, and the two latter edged with reddish buff; primaries, blackish brown; throat, light grey; chest and abdomen, brownish buff, obscurely spotted with white; bill, black; feet, dark grey.

Length, 7½ inches; wing, 4½; tail, 3½; bill, 1; tarsus, 1.

This very distinct species is a denizen of the Cape York peninsula. Nothing has as yet been recorded concerning it.

PTILOTIS CHRYSOTIS.

(Yellow-eared Honey Eater.)

CROWN of the head and lores, dark blackish olive; a whitish yellow streak is immediately underneath the eye; face, dark grey, followed by a patch of primrose yellow; all the upper surface and wings, dull olive; under surface, olive grey, darkest on the chest; margin of shoulder underneath, buff; outer webs of primaries, olive green; inner webs, blackish brown, edged with buff; tail, blackish olive, edged with dull olive; under tail coverts buffy white with a broad patch of olive grey in the centre; skin around the gape, white; bill, black; feet, brownish grey; irides, nearly black.

Length, 7½ inches; wing, 3½; tail, 3½; bill, ¾; tarsus, ⅞.

This plainly colored species is apparently confined to the eastern portions of Australia; its range, probably, not extending westward beyond the colony of Victoria. It is very abundant in New South Wales and the southern parts of Queensland. In disposition it is by no means shy, and besides frequenting the brushes, scrubs, or open forest, it is in the habit of visiting gardens to feed upon the insects, pollen, and fruits. It has a loud whistle which may be heard at a considerable distance, and which it utters without ceasing during the spring and summer. The nest is a cup-shaped structure suspended by the rim, and is formed of sticks and lined with fine twigs. The eggs are two or three in number, pearly white, and spotted with purplish brown, the spots forming a zone at the large end: size, 11½ by 8 lines.

PLECTORHYNCHA LANCEOLATA
Lanceolate honey eater
XYNTHOMYZA PHRYGIA
Warty faced honey eater

PLECTORHYNCHA LANCEOLATA.

Lanceolate Honey-eater.

CROWN, ear coverts, and back of the neck, whitish, with a longitudinal mark of black down the centre of each feather; throat and under surface, greyish white, the tip of each lanceolate feather being pure white; back, wings, and tail, light brown; bill, bluish horn color; feet, light blue; irides, brown. The sexes are alike.

Length, 9 inches; wing, 4½; tail, 4½; bill, 1; tarsus, 1.

This species inhabits the western waters, plains, and myall forests of the south-eastern portion of Australia, and is generally to be seen in pairs among the Acaciæ and Eucalypti, feeding on the pollen of these trees, and the insects frequenting the blossoms. The note of this bird is a loud whistle, which is sometimes uttered on the wing. It suspends its purse-shaped nest at the extremity of a branch, the same being built of grass, wool, and a substance resembling cotton. The eggs are two in number, flesh-white, sprinkled with reddish buff, 1 inch long by 8 lines broad.

XANTHOMYZA PHRYGIA.

Warty-faced Honey-eater.

HEAD, neck, upper part of the back, throat, and chest, black; scapularies, black, with broad yellow margins; wings, black, the primaries and secondaries margined with yellow; spurious wing, yellow; the two central tail feathers, black; the remainder, black, more or less tipped with yellow—the latter color predominating in proportion to the distance from the centre; under surface, black, with a well-defined arrow-head-shaped mark near the end of each feather; irides, reddish brown; bill, black; feet, blackish brown; warts of the face, dirty yellowish white. The sexes are alike, but the male is much larger than the female. The young have no warts on the face, that part being partially clothed with feathers.

Length, 8½ inches; wing, 4½; tail, 4; bill, ⅞; tarsus, ⅞.

This very handsome honey-eater is found in Queensland, New South Wales, Victoria, and South Australia, its habitat in the first two colonies being confined to the eastern watershed of the Great Range which divides the eastern and western waters. It often assembles in flocks of more than fifty, and, when actively employed on a particular tree, presents a very beautiful sight, the grace and elegance of its movements and attitudes never failing to excite the admiration of the beholder. But when it takes flight with full expanded wing, the contrast of colors is most pleasing and beautiful. The Banksiæ and numerous species of Eucalypti are the trees most frequented, on account of the honey which they so abundantly furnish; but its food is not entirely confined to the nectar of flowers, being occasionally diversified by an admixture of small insects. It is a courageous bird, and will not allow other species upon the same tree, and generally succeeds in mobbing off any intruder. It utters a loud and peculiar whistle, and has a song which may be considered harmonious. The cup-shaped nest, which is formed of grass and wool, is placed in the drooping branch of a gum tree. The eggs are two in number, deep buff, marked with spots and blotches of chestnut and purple grey, especially at the broad end: length, 11 lines; breadth, 8½ lines.

COMPANION

TO

GOULD'S HANDBOOK;

OR,

SYNOPSIS

OF THE

BIRDS OF AUSTRALIA.

CONTAINING

NEARLY ONE - THIRD OF THE WHOLE, OR ABOUT 220 EXAMPLES,

FOR THE MOST PART

From the Original Drawings.

BY

SILVESTER DIGGLES.

VOL. II.

BRISBANE:

PRINTED BY THORNE & GREENWELL, EDWARD STREET.

MDCCCLXXVII.

INDEX TO VOL. II.

PREFACE TO VOLUME II.

A S the letter-press occupying the usual place generally filled by a preface, in Volume I., is devoted to explanatory matter, and details the causes why this work as proposed in the original prospectus (a copy of which is there given) was not completed, it will not be unfitting for me to make a few remarks on certain peculiar characteristics which are attached to the avi-fauna of our great Southern continent. I shall not go very fully into this subject, as still so much remains to be learned about the feathered tribes of Australia, to supply which will occupy many years to come of diligent observation and research. New comers remark the paucity of song birds, and are prone to contrast our country with Britain in this respect. But it is an error to suppose that we are altogether without; and, though it might be considered presumptuous to compare our songsters to the nightingale, blackbird, or thrush (and we are ready to admit that they cannot vie with them), those we have are sufficiently characteristic and beautiful to demand notice for their remarkable novelty; and the wild calls of many can only obscurely be described in human language, and are generally referred to as "once heard, never to be forgotten," so highly discriminative is their character. Witness those of the Lyre Birds (perfect mocking-birds), and the extraordinary ones of the Coach Whip and Cat Birds. Though most of our birds are confessedly plain in their plumage, yet we have many examples even of whole families which are of the most gorgeous kind—notably the three members of the Pittas,* of which the one most recently discovered is to be found with several other interesting novelties in the present volumes. The generality of the Australian Robins (unfortunately not figured here) are much more brilliantly colored than the British species, and have a sweet and plaintive song. The Wrens, or Superb Warblers, are more than a dozen in number, and the brilliant plumage is confined to the male during the breeding season. Upwards of twenty species of Finches are found, but none can approach in brilliancy of song to the Canary or Bullfinch, yet can easily be distinguished from one another by their notes, which consist of little more than a mere chirp. A short allusion to the bower builders will not be out of place. The one built by the Regent Bird is figured from the original structure, and may easily be mistaken for a nest, but is merely used as a playground. Elaborate descriptions of some are to be found in the hand-book. The Honey Eaters are a numerous family, and are pretty well represented in this work. The singular forms of the Wattle and Fryar Birds belong to the larger members, while others partake somewhat of the character of the Sun Birds or Nectarineas. It is a singular fact, and one which has never been properly accounted for, that not a single species of Woodpecker is to be found in this country. But we have two families of birds which are numerous and, I think, peculiarly Australian *(Climacteris* and *Sittella)*, which are commonly seen in all attitudes fearlessly travelling spirally up and down the bark of various trees in search of their insect food. There are three species of Rifle Birds of magnificent plumage, which are placed by Mr. Gould close to the latter mentioned, and whose mode of existence is very similar. The reckless manner in which they appear to treat their plumage (using themselves as a wedge to prize off large flakes of bark while searching for insects) is wonderful to behold. The Cuckoos demand a passing notice. From the gigantic *Scythrops* to the minute Bronze Cuckoos, all have the parasitical habits of the British species; and it is very amusing to witness the process of feeding—the foster parents, in some instances, attending to the wants of a young bird double their own size. The smaller species deposit their eggs in the nests of *Maluri, Acanthizæ*, and other small birds who lay eggs of similar appearance to their own.

---

* The location of this family is yet undecided.

Having thus far noted the birds principally in Vol. I., I shall now make a rapid review of the contents of Vol. II. It will be perceived that the families are larger and less numerous than in the former volume. The large families of the Cockatoos and Parrots are the distinguishing feature of the avi-fauna of Australia, and are more than sixty in number of species. Many of these will be found in the present work. The great families are principally those of *Cacatua*, or White Cockatoos ; *Calyptorhynchus*, or Black ditto ; the Parrakeets, and the Lorrikeets, many being exclusively arboreal, and others frequenting the ground. In color they can be compared to the *Psittacidæ* of any country. A great many feed upon the honey which they lick out of the blossoms of flowering trees with their hairy tongues, and are named *Trichoglossi* from possessing that wonderful appendage. Others, as the *Platycerci*, &c., feed upon seeds and grain ; and the larger White Cockatoos are very destructive to the farmer whose crops are visited by large flocks to feed. Others, as the Black Cockatoos, are not confined to vegetable diet alone, but excavate holes in the Eucalypti and other trees to obtain the caterpillars or grubs which feed in the interior of the branches. The Australian pigeons are about twenty-four in number ; and many of them are of great beauty, both of form and plumage. The celebrated Wonga Wonga and the Bronze Wing will readily occur to all ; and the little Top-knot Pigeons are models of loveliness and innocence. The gallinaceous birds do not exist with us, but may be considered as represented by the mound-building birds, *Tallegalla*, *Leipoa*, and *Megapodius*. No true Partridge exists ; and the Quails are represented by fourteen species of various genera. The Cassowary and Emu come next, and, in course of time, like the *Dinornis* of New Zealand, doubtless will become extinct. The former will be found in its appropriate place in this work. The latter, I regret to say, is not figured. The wading birds, Ducks, &c., are also duly recorded. The sea birds alone are poorly illustrated.

ANTHOCHÆRA MELLIVORA.

(Brush Wattle Bird.)

ALL the upper surface, dark brown, each feather marked with a fine line of white down the centre; primaries, chestnut brown on the inner webs for three parts of their length from the base; outer webs and remainder of the inner webs, brown, tipped with white; secondaries, wings, and tail coverts, greyish brown, tipped with white; tail, brown, tinged with olive, and all the feathers tipped with white; feathers of the throat and chest, blackish brown at the base, and white at the tip; feathers of the under surface, brown, with a broad conspicuous mark of white down the centre; bill, black; irides, grey; feet, vinous brown.

Length, 11½ inches; wing, 5½; tail, 5½; bill, 1½; tarsus, 1½

This very common species is found in all the south-eastern portions of Australia, and also in Tasmania. Its northern range would appear to be about 27° latitude. Further to the south it is much more numerous, inhabiting all the country round the coast from Queensland to South Australia, preferring those situations where the leptospermums and banksias abound, from the flowers of which it principally extracts its food, consisting of pollen, honey, and the small insects found upon them. It is much more sparingly dispersed over the interior, but its range to the westward is as yet undetermined. It is a courageous bird, attacking with the utmost pertinacity all feathered intruders upon the tree where it is feeding. Its voice is harsh and peculiar, the native name Goo-gwar-ruck being applied in imitation of the sound, which somewhat resembles the act of vomiting. The breeding season is from September to December. The nest is small, generally placed in the fork of a tree at no great distance from the ground, and formed of fine twigs lined with fibrous roots. Eggs, two or three, salmon color, much blotched at the large end, and sparingly over the rest of the surface with chestnut brown; size, 13 by 9 lines.

ANTHOCHÆRA CARUNCULATA.

(Wattled Honey Eater.)

CROWN of the head, a line running from the base of the bill beneath the eye, and the ear coverts, blackish brown; space under the eye, silvery white, bounded behind by an oblong naked flesh-colored spot, below which is a short pendulous wattle of a pinky blood red color; back of the neck and all the upper surface, greyish brown, each feather striped with white down the centre; upper tail coverts, greyish brown, broadly margined with grey; primaries and secondaries, deep blackish brown, the former slightly and the latter broadly edged with grey; all the primaries tipped with white; two middle tail feathers, greyish brown, the remainder, deep blackish brown, the whole largely tipped with white; throat, breast, and flanks, grey, the centre of each feather being lighter; middle of the abdomen, yellow; irides, bright reddish hazel; legs, brownish flesh color.

Length, 14½ inches; wing, 6½; tail, 7; bill, 1½; tarsus, 1½.

This species, like the former, ranges from the southern parts of Queensland round the coast and south coasts, but is also found in Western Australia, though not in Tasmania. Like the former it collects its food from the flowers of trees, principally those of the angophora and eucalypti. Its note is also harsh and disagreeable, and its disposition equally pugnacious. A single specimen shot this year (1866) by Mr. Waller, is the only one he has ever seen in the neighborhood of Brisbane, but serves to prove that it ranges further to the north than was formerly supposed. It breeds in September and October. The nest is usually placed on the horizontal branch of an apple tree (angophora), being round, rather large, formed of small sticks, and lined with fine grass. Eggs (two or three), 1 inch 3 lines long, by 10½ lines broad; color, reddish buff, marked with chestnut, brown, and blackish grey, principally at the larger end.

TROPIDORHYNCHUS CORNICULATUS.

(*Friar Bird or Leatherhead.*)

Head, naked, and greyish black in color; a stripe of brown feathers from the base of the bill to the eye; a patch of whitish lanceolate feathers with silver gloss on the chin; the chest similarly clothed; back, wings, and tail, greyish brown, the latter, tipped with white; upper part of abdomen, brownish grey, fading into the greyish white of the remainder of the under surface; bill, black; irides, red; feet, lead color.

Length, 13 inches; wing, 9; tail, 5½; bill, 1¾; tarsus, 1¼.

This is a bird which generally excites the attention of a stranger, by its noisy and curious note, so well known to the Colonists of Victoria, New South Wales, and Queensland. Hence has originated the variety of popular names by which it is known in various parts of the country. These need not be enumerated, those above mentioned being sufficiently characteristic. Its flight is undulating. It associates in small numbers, which, when alarmed, take flight in succession to some other part of the forest. It is an active bird, climbing most dexterously among the branches in every conceivable position and attitude, especially when in pursuit of food, which consists of pollen, insects, and wild fruits; it is also very destructive in gardens and vineyards. From the great power and sharpness of its claws, it is capable of inflicting severe injury, as many a sportsman has found to his cost on picking up a wounded specimen.

It breeds in November, at which time it manifests the greatest courage, attacking and driving away all other birds, however large and powerful. The nest is placed generally on the horizontal branch of a tree, without much attempt at concealment, and is outwardly constructed of strips of stringy bark and wool, succeeded by a layer of small twigs, and lined with grasses and root fibres. Eggs, three or four, pale salmon color, spotted minutely with a darker tint: size, 1 inch 5 lines by 11 lines.

TROPIDORHYNCHUS ARGENTICEPS.

(*Silvery-crowned Friar Bird.*)

Crown of the head, silvery grey; the remainder of the head, naked and of a blackish brown; throat and all the under surface, white; back, wings, and tail, brown; bill and feet, blackish brown.

Length, 10½ inches; wing, 5½; tail, 4½; bill, 1¾; tarsus, 1¼.

The only portion of Australia from which this species has been obtained is the north coast, from the westward of the Gulf of Carpentaria. Gilbert found it in great abundance in the neighborhood of Port Essington, and says: "It is most pugnacious, a complete mocking-bird, and utters so many cries and notes as fairly to distract the listener." It is found inhabiting almost every possible variety of situation, feeding on the blossoms of the different Eucalypti, Grevilleæ, and the Melaluew; and even when thus employed, it is seen constantly chasing other birds from branch to branch.

ACANTHORHYNCHUS TENUIROSTRIS
Slender billed Spine bill

A. SUPERCILIOSUS
White eye browed Spine bill

MELICOPHILA PICATA
Pied Honey eater

ACANTHORHYNCHUS TENUIROSTRIS

(Slender-billed Spine Bill.)

CROWN of the head, lores, ear coverts, band on the sides of the chest, primaries, and six middle tail feathers, black; the rest of the tail feathers, black, largely tipped with white; back of the neck, rufous chestnut, becoming brown on the upper part of the back; secondaries, greater coverts, rump, and upper tail coverts, grey; throat, white, with a large patch of light rufous in the centre, which deepens into black at the lower edge; cheeks and chest, white; the rest of the under surface, rufous or fawn color; irides, scarlet; bill, black; feet, greenish black.

Length, 5¾ inches; wing, 2½; tail, 2¼; bill, 1; tarsus, ⅔.

This is a common and widely distributed species, and is found in Tasmania, South Australia, the isles of Bass' Straits, the whole of New South Wales, and in Queensland. It is remarkable for the length and slenderness of its bill, which, from its form, has given the bird the name of the "cobbler's awl" in some localities. It frequents the various flowering trees and shrubs, and, like other honey eaters, extracts the luxurious nectar from the deepest recesses of the tubular flowers. The heath-like family Epacris is much favored by its visits, and furnish this and other birds of similar habits abundance both of honey and insects. It is a frequent visitor in the gardens around Brisbane, whither it is attracted by the numerous mellifluous flowers, and, by its graceful movements, excites much attention. The nest is a pretty cup-shaped structure of moss and grasses, lined with feathers; it is usually found in a low shrub a few feet from the ground. Eggs, two, buffy white, much pointed, some having a zone of reddish brown and grey spots at the large end. Size, 9 by 6 lines.

ACANTHORHYNCHUS SUPERCILIOSUS.

(White-eye-browed Spine Bill.)

CROWN, back, wings, and six middle tail feathers, greyish brown; the rest of the tail feathers, black, tipped with white; stripe over the eye, and from the base of the bill half way across the neck, white, divided in the centre by a broad mark of blackish brown; throat, chestnut, followed by a band of white, which is succeeded by another of black; back of the neck, buffish chestnut; abdomen and under tail coverts, light greyish buff; bill, black; irides, reddish brown; feet, dark brown.

Length, 5¼ inches; wing, 2½; tail, 2¼; bill, 1¼; tarsus, ⅔.

This species is an inhabitant of Western Australia, in every portion of which colony it is to be obtained. It is somewhat plentiful, and, like its congener in the eastern colonies, frequents the flowering plants for food. The honeysuckle trees, or banksias, are specially frequented by them, and furnish insects and honey in abundance. It is active in its motions, but its flight is zigzag and uneven. Its note is pleasing, and uttered as it flies. It builds among the large leaved banksias, the nest being formed of grasses, narrow strings of bark, and tendrils, mixed with zamia wool, and lined with feathers. Eggs, two, buff or bluish white, speckled all over with reddish brown, frequently forming a zone at the larger end. Size, 9 by 6½ lines.

MELICOPHILA PICATA.

(Pied Honey-eater.)

THE whole plumage of the male, black, except the upper portion of the wings, the edges of the secondaries, the rump, under surface of the body, and the lateral tail feathers (excepting the tips), pure white; bill, bluish horn color; irides, reddish brown; feet, greenish grey. The female has the wings and tail brown, general plumage light brown, and the under surface buffy white.

Length, 6¼ inches; wing, 3¼; tail, 3; bill, ¾; tarsus, ⅔.

This shy and suspicious bird is found in South Australia and Western Australia. Its strongly contrasted plumage makes it a very conspicuous object; and its slow and plaintive note is repeated several times in succession as it perches on its favorite spot, the upper part of a solitary bush, or the dead branch of a tree.

MYZOMELA PECTORALIS
Banded Honey eater

M. ERYTHROCEPHALA
Red-headed H' eater

M. SANGUINOLENTA
Sanguineous H' eater

M. NIGRA
Black H' eater

M. OBSCURA
Obscure H' eater

MYZOMELA ERYTHROCEPHALA.

(Red-headed Honey Eater.)

MALE: Head, throat, and rump, scarlet; back, wings, and tail, and band across the chest, black; the remainder of the under surface, brown.
Female: Uniform brown above; lighter brown beneath.

Length, 4¼ inches; wing, 2¼; tail, 1¾; bill, ⅝: tarsus, ⅝.

This rare and very distinct species was procured by Gilbert at Port Essington, where it was found to frequent the extensive beds of mangroves bordering the sea,; and to collect its food from the flowers, flitting from one branch to another, and uttering its rather sharp and harsh chirrup.

MYZOMELA SANGUINOLENTA.

(Sanguineous Honey Eater.)

MALE: Head, neck, breast, back, and upper tail coverts, rich scarlet—the two latter much intermingled with black; lores, wings, and tail, black; wing coverts, margined with white, and primaries with light grey; flanks, grey; abdomen, under surface of wing, and under tail coverts, white—the latter marked with light grey down the centre of each feather; bill, black; feet, brown; irides, dark brown. Female: Brown above; light grey beneath.

Length, 4¼ inches; wing, 2½; tail, 1¾; bill, ½; tarsus, ½.

This handsome little honey-eater is common in, and is, I believe, confined to, the eastern portions of New South Wales and Queensland, and frequents the various flowering trees in pursuit of its food, which consists of pollen and insects. Its note is sweet and loud, and frequently uttered as it darts from branch to branch. The nest is a small cup-shaped structure of strings of bark, lined with a cottony substance. It was found near Liverpool in 1857, by Mr. Waller, and contained two young birds.

MYZOMELA PECTORALIS.

(Banded Honey Eater.)

FOREHEAD, crown of the head, upper surface, wings, tail, and a band across the chest, black; throat, upper tail coverts, and abdomen, white.

Length, 4¼ inches; wing, 2½; tail, 1¾; bill, ½; tarsus, ⅝.

This species is pretty plentiful at Cape York, from whence several specimens, collected in 1868, were brought by Messrs. Cockerill and Thorpe. All the specimens obtained by them were mottled with brown on the back. In its habits it resembles its congeners in feeding on honey and insects.

MYZOMELA NIGRA.

(Black Honey Eater.)

MALE: Head, all the upper surface, wings, and a stripe down the centre of the abdomen, black; the remainder of the plumage, pure white; bill and feet, black. Female: Head, all the upper surface, wings, and tail, brown; under surface, brownish white; bill, brown; feet, brownish black; irides, dark brown.

Length, 4¼ inches; wing, 2½; tail, 1¾; bill, ½; tarsus, ½.

This species is found over a large extent of country, but, I believe, has never been seen on any of the waters of the eastern coast. It is not uncommon in the myall country of New South Wales and Western Australia; and it is also occasionally found in the south-western portion of Queensland, actively employed among the blossoms of the myall, varying its nectarine food by the addition of such small insects as are attracted by the highly scented blossoms.

[OVER.

MYZOMELA OBSCURA.

(Obscure Honey Eater.)

———◆———

MALE: All the upper surface, dark brown; wings and tail, blackish brown; under surface, lighter brown. Female: Upper surface, wings, and tail, greyish brown; throat and chest, grey; abdomen and under tail coverts, white; bill, black; feet, dark grey; irides, red.

Length, 5½ inches; wing, 3; tail, 2½; bill, ⅜; tarsus, ⅜.

This species is of larger size than the four former species, and is found from the south of Queensland as far northward and westward as the Coburg Peninsula, where it is stated by Gilbert to be rare. It is often met with in the neighborhood of Brisbane.

ENTOMYZA CYANOTIS
Blue faced Entomyza

E. ALBIPENNIS
White winged Honey-eater

ENTOMYZA CYANOTIS.

(Blue-faced Honey Eater.)

ADULT.—Naked skin around the eye, deep blue, greenish above the eye; crown of the head, stripe underneath the naked part, and space behind the neck, black, with a lunate mark of white at the occiput; a slaty black patch, commencing in a thin line at the throat and becoming broader on the chest; a white stripe, from the base of the lower mandible, divides the black of the head and throat; breast and under surface, white; upper surface, wings, and tail, bright olive green; inner webs of all but the two central feathers of the tail and inner webs of the primaries, brown; tail feathers, tipped with white; base of the bill, bluish grey—tip, black; irides, very light yellow; eyelash, black; foot, lead color.

The YOUNG differs from the adult in having the irides of a dark olive tint, and the base of the under mandible greenish yellow; the bare space around the eye is light greenish yellow.

Length, 13 inches; wing, 5¾; tail, 4½; bill, 1¼; tarsus, 1¼.

This singular but very pretty species of Honey Eater is found throughout the colony of New South Wales and the southern portions of Queensland, being found pretty generally dispersed throughout the year. It differs in size; Queensland specimens being smaller than those from New South Wales. It frequents the flowering gums in search of its food, which consists of honey and insects. It is met with in small companies; and when other birds of similar habits visit its resort it evinces a very pugnacious disposition, and ceases not to annoy and persecute them until they take their departure. On the approach of man near its building place it shows great boldness and courage, swooping down on the intruder and striking at him in passing by. Its actions are graceful and easy as it hangs and clings among the branches and twigs; and the brilliancy of its countenance renders it a very conspicuous object. The eggs are stated by Mr. Gould to be deposited in the deserted nest of the Pomatorhinus Temporalis, in a neat round depression at the top of the dome; they are generally two in number, of a rich salmon color, spotted with rust brown: size, 1⅛ inch by 10½ lines.

ENTOMYZA ALBIPENNIS.

(White-pinioned Honey Eater.)

CROWN and back of the neck, black; lower part of face, chin, and centre of the chest, slaty black; a white crescent at the occiput; a streak of white from the base of the lower mandible joins the white of the under surface; back, wings, and tail, golden olive; primaries, brown; the inner webs, for half their length from the base, pure white; tail, brown, tinged with golden olive—all but the two central feathers, tipped with white; the naked skin round the eye is rich blue in the adult, and saffron yellow in the young; bill, yellow at the base, and black at the tip; feet, green.

Length, 12 inches; wing, 6; tail, 4¾; bill, 1½; tarsus, 1¾.

This species is confined to the northern portions of Australia, and is abundant in the country to the west of the Gulf of Carpentaria. Though bearing a general resemblance to the former species, it is easily distinguished from it by the color of the inner webs of the primaries, and by being rather smaller in size. Its habits are similar to those of E. Cyanotis.

MELITHREPTUS VALIDIROSTRIS.

(Strong-billed Honey-eater.)

CROWN, deep black; a narrow band of white proceeds from behind the eye, and is continued round the occiput; cheeks, chin, ear coverts and band behind the neck, black; upper surface, dull olive, brighter on the rump and outer edges of tail feathers; wings, brown, tinged slightly with olive; throat, white; under surface, brownish grey; bill, black; feet, brown; irides, reddish brown; orbits, greenish white.

Length, 6¾ inches; wing, 3½; tail, 3; bill, ¾; tarsus, ¾.

This is the largest of the genus to which it belongs, and is only found in Tasmania, where it may be observed in every description of country feeding among the flowering Eucalypti, upon insects and honey. It makes a round cup-shaped nest of coarse grass, which is suspended by the rim. The eggs are three in number, dull buff, thickly spotted with purplish brown and bluish grey markings: size, 11 lines by 8 lines.

MELITHREPTUS (NIGRO) GULARIS.

(Black-throated Honey-eater.)

CROWN of the head, ear coverts, and behind the occiput, deep black; throat, white, with a central patch of black; stripe from each eye through the black of the occiput, white; neck, yellowish olive; back, olive; upper tail coverts, bright olive; wings and tail, dark brown; the basal portions of the latter edged with olive; breast, light grey; abdomen, greyish buff; under tail coverts, buffy white; bill, black; irides, hazel; orbits, verdigris green; feet, brownish orange.

Length, 6½ inches; wing, 3½; tail, 2¾; bill, ½; tarsus, ¾.

This species is found in various parts of Queensland, New South Wales, Victoria, and South Australia, frequenting, like the former species, the flowering Eucalypti in search of its food, which consists of insects, pollen, and honey. Its note is often repeated, harsh, and grating, and is uttered by both sexes.

MELITHREPTUS LUNULATUS.

(Lunulated Honey-eater.)

HEAD, chin, cheeks, and ear coverts, black; lunate mark on the occiput; throat and under surface, white; shoulders, dark greyish brown; back and wings, rich yellowish olive; inner webs of quills, brown; outer edges of primaries near the extremities, whitish grey; tail, dull olive—the lateral feathers, brown; feet, olive; orbits, red; irides, dark brown; bill, dark horn color, lighter and yellowish at the base.

Length, 5 inches; wing, 2¾; tail, 2½; bill, ½; tarsus, ¾.

This is a very common species in most parts of New South Wales, Victoria, and South Australia—being a permanent resident in those colonies. In habit it is in every way similar to the former species. It builds a well constructed cup-shaped nest, the materials used being fine strips of bark, mingled with hair or wool, and lined with the fur of the opossum. It is generally suspended by the rim to the extremity of a leafy branch near the top of a high tree. Eggs, two or three, pale buff, distinctly marked with chestnut, brown, and bluish grey: size, 9 lines by 6½ lines.

MELITHREPTUS CHLOROPSIS.

(Swan River Honey-eater.)

THIS is so similar in appearance to M. Lunulatus as to need no separate description—the points of difference being that the orbits are green, and not red, as in the former species; it is also larger in size.

Length, 5¼ inches; wing, 3¼; tail, 2⅝; bill, ¾; tarsus, ¾.

MELITHREPTUS BREVIROSTRIS.

(Brown-headed Honey-eater.)

HEAD and ear coverts, blackish brown; occipital crescent, buff; back, olive, becoming brighter on the upper tail coverts and outer edges of tail feathers; wings and tail, brown; outer edges of quills, dull olive for the greater part of their length, and whitish at their extremities; orbits, bright bluish green; all the under surface, sandy brown.

Length, 4¾ inches; wing, 2¼; tail, 2⅔; bill, ½; tarsus, ⅔.

This plainly colored species is an inhabitant of New South Wales and South Australia.

MELITHREPTUS ALBOGULARIS.

(White-throated Honey-eater.)

HEAD, black, with a distinct crescent of white round the back of the head; chin and all the under surface, pure white; back and wings, rich yellowish olive; tail, brown, margined with bright olive; orbits, dull green; bill, black; foot, greenish grey.

Length, 5 inches; wing, 2¼; tail, 2¼; bill, ⅔; tarsus, ⅔.

This pretty species is found throughout the whole of Queensland, from Brisbane to Cape York, and also on the opposite side of the Gulf of Carpentaria, being very abundant at Port Essington. Like its congeners, it delights to frequent the leafy branches of trees, and may often be seen in small companies of six to ten, feeding upon the pollen, honey, and insects frequenting the flowers. It builds a nest of narrow strips of ten tree bark, and lays two eggs of a light salmon color, marked with blotches and freckles of reddish brown: size, 9 lines by 6 lines.

MELITHREPTUS MELANOCEPHALUS.

(Black-headed Honey-eater.)

HEAD, throat, and a crescent-shaped mark on the side of the chest, black; back and upper tail coverts, yellowish olive; wings and tail, brownish grey; orbits, light green; breast, white; abdomen, greyish white; bill, black; irides, hazel; feet, brown.

Length, 5¼ inches; wing, 3; tail, 2¼; bill, ½; tarsus, ⅔.

This very distinct species is confined to Tasmania, and is in the habit of frequenting the gardens of the colonists in the fruit seasons, although its ordinary food is the same as that of the other members of this peculiarly Australian genus. It is generally seen in small companies of from ten to twenty in number.

1. MYJANTHA GARRULA   2. M. FLAVIGULA   3. M. MELANOPHRYS

MYZANTHA GARRULA.

(Garrulous Honey Eater.)

FOREHEAD, white; crown, ear coverts, and a space fronting the eye, black; back of the neck and back, grey, tipped with whitish; central feathers of tail, greyish brown—the lateral feathers the same, tipped largely with whitish; primaries, dark brown; outer webs of secondaries, yellow, tipped with grey—inner webs, dark brown; chest, light grey, each feather tipped with a darker crescent; abdomen, white; naked skin behind the eye, and feet, yellow; bill, yellowish flesh color; irides, deep brown.

Length, 10 inches; wing, 5½; tail, 5½; bill, 1½; tarsus, 1½.

This is a very common species in Tasmania, New South Wales, and the south of Queensland. It associates in small flocks, and generally attracts the notice of the traveller by its peculiar shrill cry or note of alarm, which frequently is the means of scaring away other birds which the collector may be in search of. Should one be wounded, its companions will linger about the neighborhood for a considerable time. It builds a slightly-made nest in the fork of a young gum, the same being constructed of small twigs, lined with wool, strips of stringy bark, or with grass and feathers. Eggs, two or three—bluish white, marked all over with reddish brown.

MYZANTHA OBSCURA.

(Sombre Honey Eater.)

FOREHEAD, yellowish olive; lores, line beneath the eye, and ear coverts, black; head and all the upper surface, grey, each feather having a streak of brown down the centre; wings and tail, brown—the external webs of the base, yellow; the tail tipped with white; throat and under surface, dull grey, becoming lighter on the lower portion of the abdomen and under tail coverts; the feathers of the breast with a brownish crescent near the tip—the extreme margin, light grey; irides, dark brown; bare skin round the eye, bill, and bare patch on each side of the throat, bright yellow; feet, dull reddish yellow.

Length, 9½ inches; wing, 5½; tail, 4½; bill, 1½; tarsus, 1½.

This species inhabits Western Australia, where it represents the Myzantha Garrula of the eastern portions of the continent. It feeds on insects, seeds, and berries, and builds in a low gum tree, the nest being formed of sticks, lined with grass and feathers. Eggs, orange buff, spotted and blotched with darker. Size, 11½ lines by 9 lines.

MYZANTHA LUTEA.

(Luteous Honey Eater.)

GENERAL plumage, grey above, and white beneath; the rump is also white; primaries and tail feathers, edged with bright yellow; tail, tipped with white; a fine line of bright yellow runs from behind the ear down the sides of the neck; the ear coverts striated with white; a small patch of yellow at the gape; in front and beneath the eye, blackish brown; bill, citron yellow; feet, yellowish brown.

Length, 10½ inches; wing, 5⅝; tail, 5½; bill, 1½; tarsus, 1½.

This very beautiful species is an inhabitant of the north-west coast. Nothing is at present known of its habits, but there is little doubt they are similar to those of the common species, which it may be said to represent in its own domain.

MYZANTHA FLAVIGULA.

(Yellow-throated Honey Eater.)

BILL, forehead, the tips of several feathers down the sides of the neck, and throat, citron yellow; lores and ear coverts, black; back of the neck and back, grey; wing, brown; the outer webs of primaries and secondaries, dull yellow; tail, greyish brown, tipped with white; upper tail coverts, throat, cheeks, and abdomen, white; chest, very light grey, marked with greyish brown crescents; feet, yellow; irides, brown.

Length, 9¾ inches; wing, 5¼; tail, 5; bill, 1; tarsus, 1¼.

This species frequents the interior of New South Wales and South Australia. It is much more shy, and, though possessing a similar voice, is far less noisy and inquisitive than the common **Myzantha Garrula**, but in other particulars it much resembles that species in its habits. It feeds on insects, small fruits, and nectar.

MYZANTHA MELANOPHRYS.

(Bell Bird.)

UPPER surface, yellowish olive; under surface, the same, but paler; forehead and a stripe from the angle of the bill, blackish brown; primaries and secondaries, dark brown, the former margined with grey, and the latter with yellowish olive; skin round the eye, orange; bill and feet, yellow; irides, brown.

Length, 7¼ inches; wing, 3¾; tail, 3¼; bill, ¾; tarsus, ⅞.

New South Wales and south Queensland are the exclusive habitat of the present species. It is gregarious in flocks of from ten to thirty or more, frequenting dense brushes, more especially in swampy situations. Its ordinary note has been compared to the tinkle of a sheep bell; but sometimes it utters a note somewhat similar to that of **Myzantha Garrula**, while sporting amongst the trees. The tinkle of the Bell Bird is a sure indication to the weary traveller of the near presence of water.

NECTARINIA AUSTRALIS.

(Australian Sun Bird.)

MALE—crown, face, shoulders, and upper surface, olive green; throat and chest, dark metallic indigo blue; abdomen, bright yellow; wing feathers and tail, blackish grey, the former edged with olive green, and all but the two central feathers of the latter tipped with white; bill and feet, black. *Female*—upper surface as in the male; throat and all the under surface, bright yellow.

Length, 4 inches; wing, 2¼; tail, 1¼; bill, ⅔; tarsus, ½.

This is the only one of the extensive family to which it belongs at present known in Australia. Many species are found in India, where they are popularly designated "Humming Birds." They are also extensively distributed throughout the Malayan Archipelago, and in their beautiful and resplendent colors almost rival their representatives in the West Indies and South America; their habits, too, are very similar, as they feed chiefly on the nectar of flowers and the minute insects and spiders which are found upon them. The nest of the Australian Sun Bird is an elongated domed structure with an opening close to the top, and is suspended from the twig of a bush or tree. It is composed of shreds of melaleuca bark, leaves, and vegetable fibres, and lined with the silk of the bombax tree, which is common at Cape York. The eggs are much pointed at the narrow end; the color greenish grey, mottled with obscure marks of brown. It is very probable that, when the northern shores of Australia are better known, other species of these beautiful birds may be discovered. It has hitherto been found from Cape York to Port Denison, in the colony of Queensland, and in the isles of Torres' Straits.

PTILORIS PARADISEUS.

(Rifle Bird.)

MALE—Crown of the head and throat, clothed with small scale-like feathers of dark metallic green; the upper surface and chest, deep black with a beautiful purple blush in certain lights, the whole of this part of the plumage being exceedingly soft and velvety; abdomen and flanks, black, each feather broadly margined with bright olive green; primaries, dull black; the two central feathers of the tail rich metallic green, the remainder, deep black; bill and feet, black, with yellow soles; irides, dark brown.

FEMALE—Upper surface greyish brown; wing and tail, ferruginous brown; stripe behind the eye and throat, white; under surface, buffy white, spotted with black lunate marks on the chest, and banded on the abdomen with dark grey. The young male assimilates to the female in plumage.

Length, 11½ inches; wing, 6¾; tail, 4½; tarsus, 1¾; bill, 2¼.

Three species of Rifle Bird are at present known to inhabit Australia; the one represented in the accompanying plate being that with which naturalists were first acquainted. It is limited to a small belt of country bordering the sea from the Hunter River in the south, to Moreton Bay at the north, being seldom found farther inland than twelve or fifteen miles. Its principal place of resort is the cedar and pine scrubs, found on the high ranges bordering creeks and rivers, where it may be seen at sunrise ascending to the tops of the highest pine trees, far out of the reach of gunshot, when its loud harsh call may be heard at a long distance. It ascends in a series of leaps from branch to branch until it gains the summit, where it remains until the heat of the day increases, when it seeks the shade of the lower portions of the scrub. During the middle of the day its call is seldom heard, but towards evening it again utters its shrill note at intervals of about fifteen minutes. The voice of both sexes being similar, the anxious sportsman is often disappointed in his hope of obtaining a fine adult male, such an acquisition alone repaying him for the very severe toil and labor entailed upon all who would see the Rifle Bird in its native haunts. For a single full plumaged male, a dozen or more females or young birds may be obtained. The wings of the Ptiloris are not adapted for long and sustained flight, being short and rounded, and its habits are suited to this conformation, the various thickly crowded trees being visited at short intervals, and afford an inexhaustible supply of insects and berries, on which it feeds. The feet are robust, and well adapted for climbing.

CHRYSOCOCCYX OSCULANS.

(Black-Eared Cuckoo.)

HEAD, all the upper surface, and wings, glossy brown, with a tinge of olive, becoming darker on the shoulders and primaries, and fading into white on the upper tail coverts; tail, dark brown tipped with white—the most external pair of feathers with five bars of white on the inner web; ear coverts, black encircled with white; under surface of throat, breast, and abdomen, pale cinnamon brown, fading into white on the under tail coverts; bill, very dark brown; irides, deep brown; feet, greenish grey.

Length, 7¾; wing, 4¾; tail, 4; tarsus, ⅞; bill, ⅞.

This bird has been obtained in situations very widely apart—the Namoi River in New South Wales, South Australia, and Western Australia. It is a scarce species, and little is known respecting it.

CHRYSOCOCCYX LUCIDUS.

(Bronze Cuckoo.)

HEAD, all the upper surface, and wings, bronzy green; primaries, brown; tail, bronzy green, crossed by a black band near the tip; the two lateral feathers on each side with a series of large oval spots of white across the inner web, with smaller ones on the opposite web; all the under surface, white, crossed by broad well defined bars of deep bronze; irides, brownish yellow; feet, brown.

The Female resembles the Male, but the coloring is not so bright, and the bars on her under surface are less distinct.

Length, 6½ inches; wing, 4; tail, 3; tarsus, ⅝; bill, ⅝.

This handsome species is widely dispersed over the Australian continent. It is quiet and gentle in its habits, the note being only a plaintive whistle. Its food consists of insects, which it seeks with great assiduity among the leaves and stems of the trees. It is parasitical, like most of the Cuckoo tribe, and usually lays its egg in the nest of a wren or other small bird, especially choosing such nests as are domed in shape. The egg is of a clear olive brown—somewhat paler at the smaller end, and about 11-16ths of an inch long by half an inch wide.

CHRYSOCOCCYX BASALIS.

(Narrow-Billed Bronze Cuckoo.)

CROWN of the head and face, dull brown; a line of white above and beneath the eye; upper surface and wings, brown bronzed with green; throat and chest, impure white, indistinctly banded with light brown; flanks banded with broad stripes of dull brown; centre of abdomen, white; under tail coverts, white with a large spot of brown near the tip of each feather; two centre feathers of tail, bronzy greenish brown—all the rest except the outer pair, tipped for about one-third their length with the same color—the remaining portion being of a bright chestnut tint and spotted with white (more or less) on the inner webs; the outer feathers on either side alternately and broadly barred with blackish brown and white.

Length, 5¾; wing, 3¾; tail, 2⅝; tarsus, ½; bill, ¾.

This species is so closely allied to the former as to have been figured by Mr. Gould as that species in his splendid work, but having since had abundant reason to believe it distinct, he has separated it under the above name. It has been occasionally met with in Queensland, several specimens having been procured by Mr. Waller; and Mr. Gould states he has received it both from Moreton Bay and South Australia, and that he has reason to believe it visits Tasmania. In the present species it will be readily remarked that the coloring is altogether lighter, and the bars on the under surface not by any means so strongly defined as in C. Lucidus. Information respecting its habits and economy are much to be desired, very little at present being known respecting it. Mr. Waller says, "I used to shoot this species "in New South Wales, and always considered it distinct from C. Lucidus; its note is also different, enabling me always to distinguish the "one from the other."

CHRYSOCOCCYX MINUTELLUS.

(Little Bronze Cuckoo.)

HEAD, all the upper surface and wings, shining bronzy green; all the under surface, white, barred with bronzy green, the bars being most distinct on the flanks; primaries and secondaries, white on the basal portions of their inner webs; two centre feathers of tail, bronzy green—the next on each side, bronzy green on the outer web, rufous on the inner web, crossed by a broad band of black near the tip, and with an oval spot of white across the tip of the inner web—the two next on each side, bronzy green on their outer webs, their inner webs rufous with large spots of black near the shaft, most conspicuous on the outermost of the two feathers, their inner webs are also crossed near the tip with a very broad band of black, and have an oval spot of white at the tip—the outer feather on each side is barred alternately on the outer web with dull bronzy green and dull white, and on the inner one with broad decided bars of black and white and tipped with white; bill, black; feet, olive.

Length, 5½ inches; wing, 3¼; tail, 2½; bill, ⅝; tarsus, ½.

The above description is by Mr. Gould, and is taken from a single specimen figured in the supplement of his great work. He received it from Port Essington, and remarks, that though so small it has a bill as "stout as some of the larger birds;" in this respect materially differing from C. Basalis, to which species it is in other respects most closely allied.

SCYTHROPS NOVÆ HOLLANDIÆ
Channel Bill Cuckoo

SCYTHROPS NOVÆ HOLLANDIÆ.

(Channel-billed Cuckoo.)

HEAD, neck, and breast, grey; upper surface and wings, dark grey, each feather tipped with blackish brown; primaries, black; tail, grey for more than two-thirds of its length from the base, followed by a broad band of black, and largely tipped with white; under surface and abdomen, whitish grey, crossed by bars of delicate grey; ventral and under tail coverts, whitish, barred with black; under surface of tail, strongly barred with black, which extends nearly across the inner webs only; naked skin round the eyes and nostrils, scarlet; feet, dark lead color; bill, horn color, whitish at the edges.

Length, 24 inches; wing, 13; tail, 11; bill, 2¾; tarsus, 1¾; largest toe and claw, 2¼.

This singular cuckoo is found in Queensland and New South Wales, where it resorts to situations where the wild fig is plentiful, on which fruit it feeds in company with various pigeons and crows, but is as frequently found in forest country, feeding on the various species of Orthoptera that frequent the tops of the Eucalypti and other trees. Its range extends considerably to the westward, not less than 200 miles, and probably much farther. It is known to the colonists of New South Wales as the "Rain Bird," as its presence is supposed to indicate a wet season. It is migratory, appearing in October and departing in June. It is sometimes seen in small companies of five or six, but more frequently in pairs, and endures some persecution from other birds, who seem to be instinctively aware of its peculiar propensities; for, like the family generally, it is parasitical—laying its eggs in the nests of other birds, and principally of birds much smaller in size than itself. It is singular to see so large a bird tended by others sometimes not half as large as itself. Specimens of the Scythrops have been shot, the stomachs of which were filled with small black seeds; and it also feeds largely, as before stated, upon insects, preference being given to grasshoppers and phasmidæ. Mr. Swainson, in his classification of birds, places this species in connexion with the Toucans, to which family (exclusively American) it certainly bears a near relation, only requiring the brilliancy of coloring possessed by those birds to complete the resemblance. Its voice is harsh and disagreeable, but loud and peculiar, and seldom heard but in the morning.

CACATUA LEADBEATERI
Leadbeater's Cockatoo

CACATUA LEADBEATERI.

(Leadbeater's Cockatoo.)

Upper surface of the body, wings, and tail, white; forehead, front and sides of the neck, chest, down to the centre of the abdomen, light rose color; under surface of wing and basal portions of the inner webs of tail feathers, rich salmon color; crest of male, scarlet, tipped with white; crest of female, scarlet, blending into yellow in the centre; bill, horn color; feet, dark brown.

Length, 15 inches; wing, 10½; tail, 6½; tarsus, ⅞.

This elegant bird is found over all the southern portions of the Continent, from the borders of New South Wales to Western Australia, and may be considered as confined to the interior. The river courses bordered by huge Eucalypti are its favorite haunts; and the pine forests near Gawler Town are resorted to for the purpose of breeding. This species is much less noisy than the common white cockatoo, and also much more quiet in its disposition. It thrives well in a cage, and is by far the most ornamental of the genus to which it belongs.

CACATUA SANGUINEA.

(Blood-stained Cockatoo.)

CREST, upper and under surface, wings, and tail, white; the feathers next the bill and underneath the eye, spotted with blood red; bases of the inner webs, of the primaries, secondaries, and tail feathers, sulphur yellow; bill, whitish; feet, mealy brown; irides, dark brown. The sexes are alike.

Length, 14 inches; wing, 10; tail 5½; bill, 1¼; tarsus, ¾.

This species is a denizen of the northern and central portions of the Australian continent. It does not seem to occur on the peninsula of Cape York, but is probably limited in its eastern range to about the 140th meridian of longitude. Sturt met with it in thousands on Evelyn's plains near the Depôt, where it was observed feeding voraciously on the seeds of a species of kidney-bean, and making a deafening noise, its voice being very harsh and disagreeable. At Port Essington and the Alligator River it is of very common occurrence, and is often seen feeding in company with the well known sulphur crested species, C. Galerita. It affects swampy situations, and, though numerous, is wary and not easy of approach.

CACATUA EOS

CACATUA EOS.

(Rose-breasted Cockatoo.)

———◆———

CROWN and occiput, white, tinged with rose color—the basal portions of the latter, bright rose color; cheeks, a collar surrounding the neck, throat, and chest, bright rose color; abdomen, rose color, edged with whitish grey; under surface of shoulder, rose color; wings and upper part of the back and tail, light grey; quills and end of the tail, dark grey; lower part of the back and upper tail coverts, whitish; under tail coverts, light grey; bill, whitish horn color; orbits, brick red; irides, brownish red; foot, dark grey. The sexes are nearly alike in color and size. Specimens vary considerably in the depth and richness of the coloring of the breast.

Length, 14 inches; wing, 9½; tail, 5½; bill, ¾; tarsus, ⅞.

This species of cockatoo is very plentiful throughout the interior and northern portions of Australia, and particularly so in the Maranoa district; all round the Gulf of Carpentaria it is also pretty common. It is very hardy and will live for many years in a cage. Numbers are captured for the English and European markets, as there is but little difficulty in the transport, this bird bearing the voyage better than almost any other. Like the common white cockatoo it associates in large flocks, and, where agricultural operations are conducted, proves an equally troublesome neighbor. A flight of these birds is a beautiful sight, as their movements are simultaneous—one moment displaying the silvery grey back, and then by a sudden change bringing the rich pink of the under surface to view. It possesses great powers of flight. The breeding season commences about October, and the eggs are deposited in the holes or spouts of gum trees, the box being usually preferred for the purpose. The eggs, which are generally three in number, are of a white color: size, 1½ by 1¼ inch.

CALYPTORHYNCHUS LEACHII
Leachs' Cockatoo

CALYPTORHYNCHUS LEACHII.

(Leach's Cockatoo.)

MALE—General plumage, black, with greenish reflections; head, crest, and neck, lighter, partaking of a yellowish brown tint; two central tail feathers and the bases and tips of the lateral feathers, deep black; central portions of the latter, bright scarlet.

FEMALE—Head and crest, blackish brown, each feather tinged with yellow at the tip; cheeks and ear coverts, yellow, tinged with orange, and partly overlapped by other feathers of a blackish brown tint, proceeding from beneath the eye; back and wings, brownish black, glossed with green; chest and abdomen, the same, but duller; the two middle tail feathers, black; the remainder, orange scarlet in the middle, and black at their bases and extremities—the scarlet portion crossed by a series of irregular black bands, which vary somewhat in form in each feather; bill, bluish horn color; eyes, dark brown; foot, mealy grey. The young female has the neck of a uniform greyish brown, slightly spotted with buff.

Length, 20 inches; wing, 14; tail, 10; tarsus, ⅘.

This, which may be regarded as the least of the Australian black cockatoos, is found in Queensland, New South Wales, Victoria, and South Australia. It frequents ridges and forest country, especially where the oak (casuarina) abounds, on the hard nuts of which tree it principally subsists, breaking the same with the greatest ease with its powerful bill. It is generally met with in small companies of from four to six, and is less shy than others of the same genus. On one being wounded, its companions fly around screeching, and fall an easy prey to the sportsman. The note is not very loud, but discordant, and often leads to its discovery. All attempts have hitherto failed to render this bird familiar to confinement, as it speedily languishes and dies.

CALYPTORHYNCHUS FUNEREUS

CALYPTORHYNCUS FUNEREUS.

(Funeral Cockatoo.)

GENERAL plumage, dull black with a greenish tinge; body feathers, edged with brown; ear coverts, dull yellow; tail feathers, blackish, all but the two centre ones, crossed with a broad band of yellow, equal to half their length, much mottled with fine black markings; bill, black in adults, but of a lighter color in the young birds; eyes, dark hazel; feet, dark brown. The sexes are much alike, but the coloring is rather less bright in females.

Length, 30½ inches; wing, 18; tail, 17; bill, 2½; tarsus, 1; longest toe, 2½.

This bird is the largest of the genus, its length of wing and tail being unequalled by any of its family. It is found over the whole of New South Wales, and occasionally in the southern parts of Queensland, although nowhere numerous; its resort being mountain ranges, brushes, forests, and open country, usually in small companies of four or six, except when breeding. Its flight is mostly heavy and laboured, but at times it shows an activity that would not be accredited it from its appearance. Its food consists of the larvæ of insects found under the bark of trees, and the seeds of the Banksia and other trees. Its note is difficult to describe, but very remarkable, and is between a shriek and a whine. It lays two eggs (white) about 1½ inches long by 1½ broad, which are deposited in the hollow branch of a tree.

CALYPTORHYNCHUS XANTHONOTUS.

(Yellow-eared Black Cockatoo.)

CROWN of the head, face, upper surface of throat, and neck, brownish black; ear coverts, pale yellow; breast feathers tipped with olive; back and under portion of body, brownish black; two centre tail feathers, blackish brown—remaining feathers, black at tip and base; centre portions, blotched and mottled with pale yellow, interspersed with brown; irides, black; orbit in adults, pink. Sexes, much alike.

Length, 2½ inches; wing, 14½; tail, 12; tarsus, 1.

This species is principally confined to Tasmania, but occasionally found at Flinders' Island and parts of South Australia. Its habits are very much the same as those of the genus in general, frequenting the thickly wooded districts and mountain ranges. Like them, it delights in proclaiming its whereabouts, on the approach of rain, by its peculiar whining discordant note. Its food consists of seeds, grubs, and a large species of caterpillar found under the bark of the wattle and other trees; the powerful beak cutting and scooping both bark and wood in search of its food. Its nest is formed in a hollow spout of some large tree, and contains two eggs (white) of about 1 inch 8 lines long by 1 inch 4 lines broad. The diet of the young birds consists of seed from leguminous plants; they are very voracious, and consume large quantities of such like food.

MICROGLOSSUS ATERRIMUS.

(Great Palm Cockatoo.)

ADULT— Space fronting the eye and beneath the crest, deep velvety black; the feathers of the crest, greyish black—each feather being narrow and lanceolate in form; all the remaining plumage, black, with green and purple reflexions; cheeks, rose color, narrowly bordered with yellow; irides, dark brown; bill, dark horn color; feet, lead color.

YOUNG—Glossy black, with lemon yellow lunate bands on the breast and abdomen.

Length, 28½ inches; wing, 14; tail, 11; tarsus, 1; largest toe and claw, 2½.

This splendid species, which is by some naturalists termed the Goliath Aratoo, is one of the largest known members of the Parrot tribe in the eastern hemisphere; fully equalling in size many of the splendid Macaws of South America; but the comparative shortness of its tail renders it much less graceful in appearance than the latter family. It is found at Cape York, where it abides throughout the year. Though long known to naturalists as an inhabitant of New Guinea and the neighboring islands, they were not aware of its being a denizen of the woods of Australia until the visit of H.M.S. *Rattlesnake* in that locality, in the year 1849. It is found both in the densest scrubs and the open forest, associating in small flocks of four or five in number. Its harsh scream and loud whistle often betray its presence. The tender shoots at the summits of the palms are uncovered readily from their strong envelopes by its powerful bill, and, with honey-bearing blossoms of various other trees furnish it with abundance of the choicest food. Fragments of gravel have been found in the stomach, which, as in the case of many other birds, materially assists the process of digestion by grinding down the food. The tongue is long and capable of being considerably extended. It breeds in November, the nest being situate in the hollow branch of some huge tree, and formed of strips of bark. The eggs (two in number) are pure white, and very much rounded in form. The young birds are easily tamed, and feed readily on biscuit, rice, etc.,

The figure is a little less than half the natural length. The outline of the upper mandible is of the natural size, and measures round the curve 4½ inches.

POLYTELIS ALEXANDRÆ
Princess of Wales Parrakeet

POLYTELIS ALEXANDRÆ.

(Princess of Wales' Parrakeet.)

FOREHEAD and crown, pale blue; chin, throat, and lower portion of the cheeks, pink, inclining to salmon color; back of the head, nape, sides of the neck, back, and scapularies, greyish olive; lower part of the back and rump, light blue; shoulders and wing coverts, bright pale greenish yellow; outer edges and tips of primaries, narrowly margined with light yellow—the remainder of the outer webs, light greenish blue—inner webs, brown; breast and abdomen, light olive grey; thighs, tinged with rose color; upper tail coverts, olive, tinged with blue; the two middle tail feathers, greyish olive, washed with blue—the next two on each side, the same color on their outer webs and dark brown on the inner; the remaining feathers of the tail, olive black in the middle, margined with bright olive green on the outer webs and bright scarlet on the inner webs, throughout the whole of their length; bill, scarlet; feet, brown.

Length, 10 inches; wing, 7; tail, 10; bill, ½; tarsus, ⅞.

This remarkable and very interesting species was obtained by F. G. Waterhouse, Esq., the Curator of the Institute Museum, Adelaide, while engaged in the exploratory expedition conducted by Stuart in Northern Australia, latitude 16° 54' S.; the locality being known as Purdie's Ponds. The disposition of its colors is unique, and altogether different from the other two known species, which form a trio equally remarkable for elegance of form and beauty of coloring.

1 *PLATYCERCUS FLAVIVENTRIS*
   Yellow bellied Parrakeet

2 *PLATYCERCUS BARNARDI*
   Barnard's Parrakeet

PLATYCERCUS FLAVIVENTRIS.

(Yellow-bellied Parrakeet.)

———

FOREHEAD, scarlet; crown of the head and back of the neck, pale yellow, each feather slightly margined with brown; space under the eye, dull scarlet; cheeks, blue; back and shoulders, dark olive black, each feather edged with green; shoulders and middle portions of the wing, blue; the primaries, blue at the base of their external edges; the remainder, blackish brown; rump and two middle tail feathers, green; the remaining tail feathers, dark blue at the base, and lighter towards their tips; under surface, yellow; bill, flesh-color; feet, greyish brown. The female is smaller and less brilliant than the male.

Length, 13 inches; wing, 7½; tail, 8; tarsus, 1.

This species is limited to Tasmania and the islands of Bass's Straits. . It is gregarious in every description of locality, but principally seen on the ground, over which it runs with great agility. It feeds principally upon grass seeds, but insects and the flowers of gum trees serve to give some variety to its diet. In the neighborhood of farms and homesteads it is frequently so tame as to dispute the food dealt out to the poultry. It is hardy, and thrives very well in a cage

It breeds from September to January, and lays its eggs in the hole of a gum tree; they are six or eight in number, and pure white.

———

PLATYCERCUS BARNARDI.

(Barnard's Parrakeet.)

———

FOREHEAD, crimson; crown, cheeks, chest, abdomen, central portion of the wing, and rump, verditer green; occiput, brown, beneath which is a collar of light yellow; back, dark grey; centre of the abdomen, orange; shoulder and upper coverts, deep blue; primaries and spurious wing, black; the basal portions of the former, deep blue; the two central tail feathers, dark green, passing into deep blue at the tip; the lateral feathers, dark blue at the base, gradually fading into bluish white at the tips; bill, bluish horn color; feet, brown. The sexes are almost alike, the male being the brightest.

Length, 13 inches; wing, 6¼; tail, 7½; tarsus, ⅝.

This elegant species may be regarded as one of the finest of the Platycerci. Like its congeners, it is equally at home among the trees and on the ground, and it procures its food in both situations. Its stronghold is the Murray, Darling, and Namoi rivers, in which localities it may be met with in companies of five or ten. When alarmed and caused to take flight simultaneously, the sight is beautiful, as in the full blaze of the sunshine its gorgeous coloring shows to the best advantage.

PLATYCERCUS PALLICEPS.

(Pale-headed Parrakeet.)

Crown of the head, very pale yellow; feathers of the nape, back, and scapularies, black, broadly margined with gamboge yellow; cheeks, whitish; rump and upper tail coverts, yellowish white, with a tinge of blue; shoulders, rich deep blue; middle of the wing, light blue; primaries, deep blue at the base, paler towards the tip; inner webs, brown at the base; chest and abdomen, light greenish blue; under tail coverts, scarlet; two middle tail feathers, olive green at the base, merging into light blue towards the tip; the outer webs of the remaining feathers, deep blue at the base, becoming lighter towards the tip; the inner webs, dark brown; all the feathers tipped with white; bill, horn color; feet, dark brown; irides, dark brown.

Length, 12½ inches; wing, 6½; tail, 6¾; tarsus, ⅞.

This species is widely spread over the colony of Queensland, being most plentifully found in the southern and western portions, occupying the place of P. Eximius of New South Wales, to which beautiful species it is nearly allied. It is commonly known as the Moreton Bay Rosehill (corrupted into Rosella). Its plumage, especially before assuming the adult state, is exceedingly variable, so much so that any one unaware of the fact would readily suppose several species to exist on inspecting the more extreme instances of variation, the same being principally on the face and under surface. Sometimes the former is pure white, at other times much suffused with, or altogether, light blue. The figure in Mr. Gould's supplement, which he names P. Cyanogenys, taken from a single specimen shot by Mr. Macgillivray at Cape York, is probably only a variety of P. Palliceps more richly colored than usual. It is often obtained alive in the neighborhood of Brisbane and Darling Downs, and bears confinement well, being a favorite and very ornamental bird for the aviary. Like others of the family, it is in the habit of trespassing upon the crops of the farmer; maize being a description of food to which it is particularly partial, and on which it thrives best in the cage. It lays two white eggs, which like those of the family in general are deposited in the hole of a tree (principally apple tree) in the flats.

PLATYCERCUS FLAVEOLUS.

(Yellow-rumped Parrakeet.)

Forehead, crimson; cheeks, light blue; crown, back of the neck, back, rump, upper tail coverts, and all the under surface, pale yellow, the feathers of the back being black in the centre and pale yellow on their outer edges; middle of wing, pale blue; spurious wing and outer webs of the basal part of the primaries deep violet blue, the remainder, dark brown; two central feathers of tail, tinted with green at the base, passing into very pale blue at the tips; the internal feathers have their basal parts deep blue, passing into very pale blue at the tips, the inner webs, brown for a greater or less portion of their length, the extreme tips of all being white; bill, light horn color; feet, dark brown.

Length, 13½ inches; wing, 7; tail, 7½; tarsus, ⅞.

This well marked and not very variable species is found in considerable numbers on the Lachlan and Darling rivers.

PSEPHOTUS PULCHERRIMUS.

(Beautiful Parrakeet.)

FOREHEAD, deep scarlet, followed by a large blackish-brown patch, which covers the crown and nape; feathers round the eye, dull yellow; sides of the neck, light shining bluish green; chest, bright yellowish green; back, greyish brown; upper tail coverts, light blue, but with a greenish cast next the tail, where they are tipped with black; a bright scarlet patch runs from the shoulder longitudinally more than one-third across the wing; edge of the wing, black; primaries, bluish black; external webs towards the extremities, light grey; secondaries and tertiaries, blackish brown, more or less tinged with light buffish brown, especially on the edges of the outer webs; upper part of abdomen and the flanks, verditer blue; centre of abdomen and under tail coverts, scarlet, each feather delicately margined with white; the two central feathers of the tail, dark blackish olive, the basal portion being much lighter; the remaining feathers of the tail are green at their bases, light blue in the middle, and very largely tipped with white, particularly on the inner webs. The female is not so brightly colored as the male. Bill, horn color.

Length, 11 inches; wing, 5; tail, 7; bill, $\frac{1}{2}$; tarsus, $\frac{1}{2}$.

This species is found most plentifully in the district of Darling Downs, but has been obtained in other parts of Queensland, specimens having been shot occasionally near both Ipswich and Brisbane. It feeds upon grass seeds, and also those of small papilionaceous plants. It prefers open forest country, where it associates in pairs. The eggs (five in number) are deposited on the bare ground in a deserted anthill, the entrance being a small hole in the side. The young are covered with a thick white down, and much resemble those of hawks.

PSEPHOTUS MULTICOLOR.

(Many-coloured Parrakeet.)

FOREHEAD, gamboge yellow; crown of the head, cheeks, throat, and chest, lightish shining bluish green; a patch of reddish brown on the occiput; back, dull green; tip and under surface of shoulder, brilliant blue; on the middle of the shoulder is a deep yellow patch; outer webs of primaries, deep blue at the base, and grey towards the tips; secondaries and greater coverts also are edged with lighter blue; the remainder of the wing is green; abdomen, orange scarlet; vent, lemon yellow; upper tail coverts, green, with a band of scarlet in the middle; tail, green at the base, the two middle feathers graduating into dark blue, and tipped with black; the remaining feathers pale blue, tipped moreor less with white.

Length, 11$\frac{1}{2}$ inches; wing, 5$\frac{1}{2}$; tail, 7; tarsus, $\frac{1}{2}$; bill, $\frac{1}{2}$.

This bird is found on Liverpool Plains and the surrounding country, as well as in the Murray and Darling River districts. It is similar in its habits and nidification to the preceding.

1. EUPHEMA CHRYSOSTOMA 2. E. SPLENDIDA 3. Female
Blue banded Grass Parrakeet. Splendid Grass Parrakeet.

EUPHEMA CHRYSOSTOMA.

(Blue-banded Grass Parrakeet.)

FOREHEAD, crossed by a band of deep blue, edged above by a line of pale blue; lores and stripe behind the eye, deep yellow; shoulders and wing coverts, bright blue; primaries, black, edged with bluish green; abdomen and under tail coverts, yellow; the four central feathers of tail, greenish blue—the remainder, blue on the outer edges at the base, and largely tipped with yellow; the remainder of the plumage, olive green; irides, bill, and feet, brown. The sexes are similar.

Length, 9 inches: wing, 4; tail, 5; tarsus, ½.

This species is an inhabitant of the southern portions of Australia only—Victoria, the isles of Bass' Straits, and Tasmania, being merely a summer visitant of the latter colony. It is constantly to be seen on the ground, its food consisting of the seeds of various grasses, through which it threads its way with great dexterity. When disturbed, it flies off to the nearest tree, and when the danger is over returns to the ground. It breeds in October and November. The eggs are, as usual with the parrot tribe in general, deposited in the hole of a tree; they are white, and from five to seven in number.

EUPHEMA SPLENDIDA.

(Splendid Grass Parrakeet.)

MALE.—Head, deep ultramarine blue, tinged at the throat with purple; behind the neck, back, upper tail coverts, sides of the chest, and flanks, rich olive green; upper portion of wing, beautiful light blue, deepest on the shoulder; secondaries, greyish green on the outer webs, dark brown on the inner webs; outer webs of spurious wings and primaries, dark indigo blue, shading into brown at their tips; inner webs, brown; centre of chest, fine scarlet; the remainder of the under surface, deep yellow; the four central feathers of tail, bluish green—the outer margin of the inner webs black; the remainder of the tail feathers are more or less largely tipped with yellow, the basal portions being green shading into black; bill, dark horn color; feet, brownish grey.

FEMALE.—Forehead, obscurely banded with blue; feathers of cheeks, green, tipped with blue; shoulders and upper portions of wings, light blue; edges of primaries and spurious wings, greenish blue; chest, and upper surface, green; abdomen, bright yellow; under tail coverts, greenish yellow; tail, similar to that of the male, but darker in color.

Length, 8 inches; wing, 4½; tail, 4½; tarsus, ½.

Of all the Parrakeets belonging to the genus Euphema this must be regarded as the most beautiful. The richness and splendour of its coloring, no doubt, suggested the appropriate name given to it by Mr. Gould. It is a rare species, and exclusively confined to the interior, where its range must be wide, as it has been obtained in Western Australia and also on the Darling River, and in the Murray Scrub. The beautiful but common species, E. Pulchella, is the most nearly related to the present, but may at once be distinguished by the absence of the glowing scarlet breast, and the possession of a bright patch of chestnut near the shoulder.

EUPHEMA AURANTIA.

(Orange-Bellied Grass Parrakeet.)

MALE—Forehead, banded with blue, margined before and behind with greenish; crown and upper surface, grass green; shoulders, part of the secondaries, and outer edges of the primaries, deep blue; cheeks and breast, yellowish green, becoming still more yellow on the abdomen and under tail coverts; centre of abdomen, bright orange; the two central tail feathers green—the others are green on the outer webs and tipped with yellow, the inner webs being brown; irides and bill, dark brown; feet, brown.

The Female differs from the Male in being much less brightly colored, but still retains sufficient resemblance to be very easily recognised.

Length, 8¼ inches; wing, 4½; tail, 4½; tarsus, ½.

This species is found in Victoria, South Australia, the islands of Bass' Straits, and (though rarely) in New South Wales, and also, during the summer season, in Tasmania, the small islands to the south are its principal habitat; it is almost the only land bird found in these solitary spots. In common with the other members of the family, this species is usually observed feeding upon the ground in grassy situations; its food consisting principally of the seeds of such as are found in damp swampy localities.

EUPHEMA ELEGANS.

(Elegant Grass Parrakeet.)

FOREHEAD, deep blue, bordered above with metallic light blue, which is continued over the eye; lores, bright yellow; upper surface, rich olive green; shoulders, blue; primaries and secondaries, black; throat and chest, greenish yellow, graduating into bright yellow on the abdomen and under tail coverts; centre of abdomen, pale orange; two middle tail feathers, greenish blue, the rest being blue at the base and broadly tipped with yellow; bill and feet, blackish brown; irides, dark brown. The Female and young have no bar across the forehead.

Length, 9 inches; wing, 4½; tail, 5½; tarsus, ½.

This Parrakeet has only occasionally occurred in New South Wales. It becomes more numerous in Victoria and South Australia, and is also met with in great numbers in Western Australia, where it appears to be confined to certain localities. Like the former species it resorts to situations where its favorite food (grass seed) is abundant, remaining in the same neighborhood the greater portion of the year. In dry seasons it may be observed near the water holes in great numbers morning and evening. Its flight is rapid and often at a great height in the air. The breeding season is in September and October. Eggs, from four to seven in number, white, 11 lines long by 8½ broad; they are merely deposited in the hole or "spout" of a gum tree.

MELOPSITTACUS UNDULATUS.

(Warbling Grass Parrakeet.)

CROWN of the head and throat, light yellow; ear coverts and back of the neck, yellowish green, striped on and near the head finely, and lower down the back more boldly, with black, assuming the form of crescents on the tertiaries, shoulders and wing coverts, which are all edged with yellow; lower portion of back, bright green, as is also the under surface of the chest and abdomen; several spots of bright blue and black ornament the throat, looking very conspicuous on the yellow ground; two central tail feathers blue, the remainder being bright yellow, except the bases and tips, which are green; irides, straw color; nostrils of male, light blue—of female, fleshy brown; legs, pale bluish lead color. The young has the whole of the head barred and is destitute of the spots on the throat; the irides also are grey.

Length, 7½ inches; wing, 3½; tail, 4.

This very pretty and interesting Parrakeet is a denizen of the interior of Australia, ranging over the vast plains in incredible numbers. It frequents the southern portion of the continent in Spring, when grass seed is abundant, but always in some situation where water is near, as it drinks morning and evening. For some unknown cause it is in the habit of paying occasional visits to districts where its presence has not before been observed, and, departing suddenly, will not be again seen for many years. It bears captivity well, and besides surviving the voyage to England, has been known frequently to rear its young there. Its usual breeding place is the spout of a gum tree, the eggs (four in number) being laid upon the bare vegetable earth which is usually found therein; their length is 9, and breadth 7 lines; color, pure white.

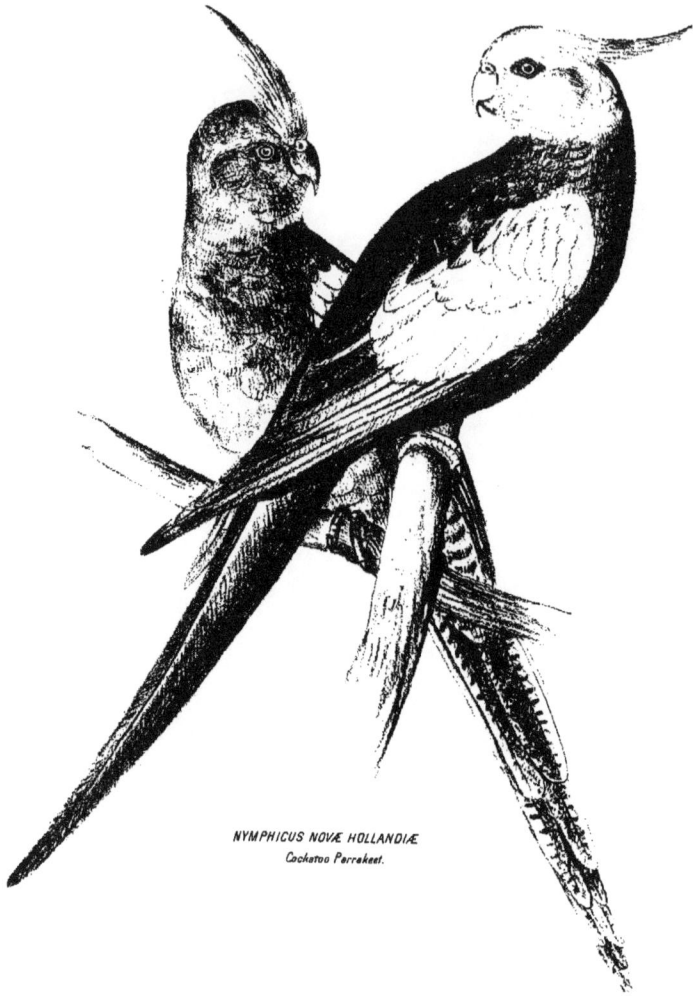

NYMPHICUS NOVÆ HOLLANDIÆ
Cockatoo Parrakeet.

NYMPHICUS NOVÆ HOLLANDIÆ.

(Cockatoo Parrakeet.)

MALE—Head and throat, yellow; a patch of reddish orange on the ear coverts; crest, yellow at the base, grey at the tip; back of the neck, two central tail feathers, and the external margins of the primaries, grey; back, shoulders, all the under surface, and outer tail feathers, greyish brown. A white mark extends from the shoulders lengthwise down the centre of the wing. Irides, dark brown; bill, bluish lead color; legs and feet, bluish grey.

FEMALE—Face and crest, dull olive yellow; throat, greyish brown; back, lighter than in the male; lower part of the abdomen and upper tail coverts, yellow; the four middle tail feathers, grey; the remainder, yellow—all being crossed with brownish bars except the external webs of the outermost, which are pure yellow.

Length, 13½ inches; wing, 6½; tail, 8; tarsus, ½.

This species is found all over the interior, from New South Wales and Queensland to Western Australia, but rarely approaching the coast nearer than 100 miles. Its most northern limit is somewhere about latitude 24°. It is migratory, and makes its appearance at both extremities of its range in September, at which time the work of incubation occupies a great share of its attention. It breeds in the holes of trees in the neighborhood of water. The eggs, five or six in number, are white, 1 inch long by ⅔ broad. It returns northward about February or March.

This bird is often caged, and is capable of uttering short sentences. It endures captivity well, and feeds upon canary seed, bread, &c., and has been known to breed in confinement, and rear its young. Its natural food consists of the seeds of grasses. It assembles in immense flocks in various localities at the time of migration, and, being very powerful on the wing, may be seen at long distances from water.

●

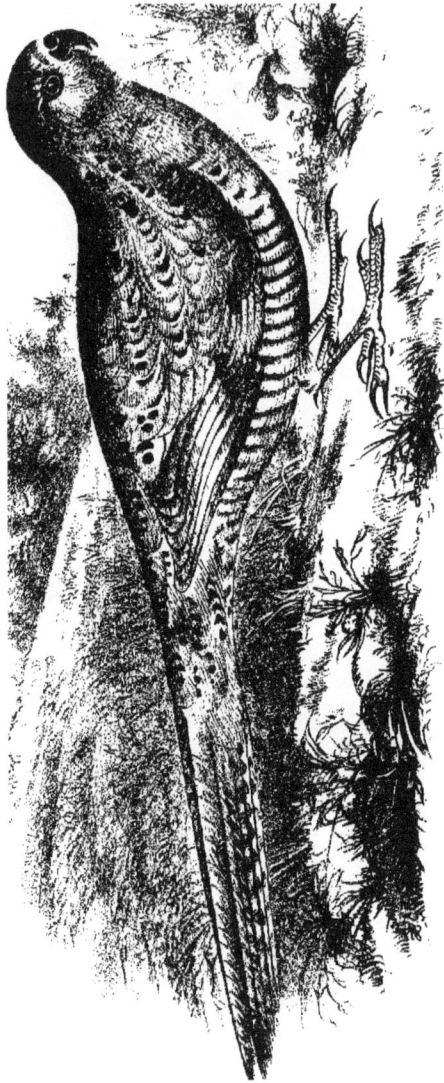

PEZOPORUS FORMOSUS.

(Ground Parrakeet.)

FOREHEAD, scarlet; head and nape, grass green, each feather broadly streaked with black; back, scapularies, shoulders, and upper tail coverts, grass green, broadly and irregularly barred with black, and narrowly with yellow, on the central portion of each feather; spurious wing, black, edged with green on the outer webs; secondaries, dull green, edged and tipped with yellowish grey; primaries, brownish black, tipped with whitish grey, and margined on their external webs with bright green—all but the three outermost have a triangular mark of bright yellow in the centre; throat and chest, light yellowish green, the latter streaked with black; abdomen and under tail coverts, greenish yellow, numerously marked with blackish bands; the four central feathers of tail, green, crossed by numerous narrow bars of yellow; the remainder of the tail feathers, yellow, crossed with bars of bright green; irides, black, surrounded by a grey ring; feet, flesh color, tinged with blue claws, black; bill, greyish horn color.

Length, 11½ inches; wing, 5; tail, 7; tarsus, 1½.

This species is essentially terrestrial in its habits, never being seen anywhere but upon the ground. I have not heard of its occurrence in Queensland or any portion of the northern territory. In New South Wales and the southern colonies it occurs more or less plentifully, as well as in Western Australia; being also common in Tasmania and the Isles of Bass' Straits, in such situations as are suited to its requirements, being those portions of the country which abound with rank grassy herbage. From the similarity of its coloring to the objects by which it is surrounded, it is seldom seen until flushed, when, after a short flight, it alights and endeavors to elude observation by hiding among the tufts of rushes or thick swampy vegetation. Its flesh is of excellent flavor, being much like that of the Partridge, and as it emits a powerful scent is easily followed by the pointer. It makes no nest, but lays its white eggs upon the bare ground, the number being either five or six.

GEOPSITTACUS OCCIDENTALIS.

(Western Ground Parrakeet.)

FOR a knowledge of this species we are indebted entirely to Mr. Gould, who describes it from a specimen received from Perth in Western Australia and which has been in his possession for many years. In its general coloration it resembles Pezoporus, but differs from that bird in several important particulars. In contour Pezoporus is graceful and well proportioned; the present species is short and dumpy, the wings being large and long and the tail short; the head is also disproportionately large, the tarsi and toes short and diminutive, and the claws very small.

Length, 10 inches; wing, 5½; tail, 5; bill, ½; tarsus, ½.

LATHAMUS DISCOLOR
Swift Lorikeet.

CYCLOPSITTA COXENI
Coxen's Lorrakeet.

LATHAMUS DISCOLOR.

(Swift Larikeet.)

FOREHEAD, scarlet; cheeks, yellow and scarlet; crown, ear coverts, and the upper surface, bright green; under surface, yellowish green; secondaries, bluish green; and primaries, blackish blue—both margined with yellow; lateral feathers of tail, blue at the tip, passing into brownish red at the bases—the central feathers tipped with black; shoulders, under wing coverts, and under tail coverts, scarlet; bill, horn color; feet, fleshy brown; irides, yellowish hazel.

Length, 9 inches; wing, 4¾; tail, 4¾.

This species is found in New South Wales and Tasmania, which latter colony it visits in the summer time, and is then found plentifully distributed over the island; as cold weather approaches it migrates northward. It is essentially a honey eater; and while engaged in feeding it is very unwary, and will permit a very near approach. In beauty and disposition of coloring this Lorikeet is scarcely to be excelled; and in its native state, silently and dexterously clambering among the branches and foliage of the various flowering Eucalypti, is always and must ever be admired, as it assumes a thousand different graceful attitudes. It is not, however, to be seen readily without optical assistance, on account of the similarity of its coloration to that of the foliage of the tree; but the aid of the opera glass will reveal an interesting sight; in fact no sportsman or collector should go unprovided with this important and useful instrument. It breeds in the holes of high and inaccessible trees. The eggs are said to be two in number, and white. This species is essentially arboreal in its habits, never being seen on the ground.

CYCLOPSITTA COXENI.

(Coxen's Parrakeet.)

FOREHEAD and lores, scarlet, intermingled with bright yellowish green; ear coverts, bright scarlet; cheeks, green, with a few patches of light blue; upper surface, bright yellowish green, inclining to olive on the back; tail, darker; upper part of the wings, grass green; outer edges of the primaries, rich blue, edged with bright verditer; inner webs, blackish brown; outer webs of secondaries, bluish green, edged with grass green; the inner webs of the four uppermost tertiaries, scarlet; flanks, deep yellow; all the under surface, yellowish green; under surface of shoulder, green mottled with blue; upper mandible, dark bluish horn color, with a line of white at the base—tip, black; under mandible, whitish, suffused with bluish horn color at the cutting edge—tip, black; feet, dull light green; irides, yellowish hazel.

Length, 7½ inches; wing, 3¾; tail, 1¾; tarsus, ⅜; bill, ⅜.

The only locality in which this new and interesting species has as yet been found is the mountainous region near Mount Sampson, thirty or forty miles to the north of Brisbane, where, among the dense and almost impenetrable scrubs, enormous fig trees rear their magnificent heads far above all other vegetation. We are indebted to Mr. Waller for the introduction of this species to the notice of science. The first specimens were brought to him by Mr. J. Mackenzie, a timber getter, whose employment lay in that district, and, having a liking for natural history, he brought them to Mr. Waller, who immediately perceived them to belong to a genus and species hitherto unknown to Australia. The large size of the bill and excessive shortness of the tail struck him immediately, and he kindly placed a specimen in my hands for the purpose of being figured in the present work. All that he dissected were found to have the stomach filled with the fruit of the wild fig in an unripe state. To kill this bird is a most difficult task, and a large quantity of ammunition may easily be expended without success, as the immense trees, the tops of which are frequented by it, often attain a height of 200 or even 250 feet; but at this distance so small an object is quite indiscernible, and frequently larger birds, being mistaken for the present one, are shot instead. Pigeons, cat and satin birds, and a host of others, all feed together, and the same discharge sometimes brings down several at once. This is, I believe, the way in which the first specimen of Cyclopsitta Coxeni was obtained, falling a victim to a discharge aimed at a larger bird, and both coming to the ground together. Specimens of this new parrakeet were sent to Mr. Gould by his brother-in-law (Charles Coxen Esq., of Brisbane), and, I am happy to add, have been named after that gentleman—a tribute long due to one who, during the progress of Mr. Gould's great work, has frequently rendered him important information and assistance. Although this is the only species of the genus Cyclopsitta at present known in Australia, there are several found in the Malayan region.

TRICHOGLOSSUS SWAINSONII.

(Swainson's Lorikeet.)

Head, sides of the face, and throat, blue, with a stripe of lighter blue down the centre of each feather; an occipital band of greenish yellow; all the upper surface, rich grass green—in some specimens blotched behind the neck with scarlet; wings, deep grass green; inner webs of primaries, black, crossed by an oblique band of yellow; upper surface of tail, green—the two central feathers tinged with blue towards the tip; under surface of the inner webs of tail feathers, greenish yellow; tips and outer webs, olive grey; chest, under surface of shoulder, and flanks, rich orange scarlet (these portions vary much in the coloring of different specimens, no two being alike—sometimes having a large admixture of lunate patches of rich orange yellow, and towards the lower part of the chest crescentic marks of bluish purple, which is the color of the abdomen); under tail coverts, yellow, tipped with green; bill, scarlet, tipped with yellow; nostrils and space surrounding the eye, brownish black; irides, scarlet, with a yellow ring next the pupil; feet, greyish olive. The sexes are alike.

Expanse, 17 inches; length, 12; wing, 6¼; tail, 6¼; bill, ½; tarsus, ½; mid-toe, 1¼.

This magnificent but very common species is found throughout the whole of the eastern coast of Australia, and occasionally in Tasmania, being especially abundant in the neighborhood of Brisbane. Large flocks may be seen at such times as the different species of Eucalyptus come into blossom. It migrates from one part of the country to another as these trees successively flower, their principal food being honey. A gorgeous and animated scene presents itself to the observer when a large flock is engaged feeding high up among the rich glossy foliage of some giant of the forest, darting about from branch to branch, uttering their shrill screams, and clinging and climbing in every conceivable position, often in company with other parrots similarly engaged. A large number may often be obtained when they are thus occupied. Though several may fall at each discharge of the gun, so absorbing is their employment that a considerable time frequently elapses before they are fairly driven off, when in an instant, with whirlwind rush and deafening screams, the whole flock depart to some more secure locality. The popular name of this bird is the Blue Mountain Parrot, probably so named by the first colonists of Sydney in consequence of its being plentiful on the Blue Mountains near.

Many attempts have been made to cage this handsome bird, but in nearly every case without success. For a short time all seems to go on very well, but when the owner least expects it generally dies suddenly. Exceptions occasionally, though very rarely, occur; special precautions being taken to protect it against cold, and also to furnish it with food as nearly like that to which it is naturally accustomed. Its disposition is mild and affectionate, and it may be taught to use articulate sounds. A fine example was kept near Brisbane for seven years, and was so tame and familiar that it was allowed the full range of the house, its cage door being always open. When flocks of its own species were feeding on the trees close by it would join their company, and, after associating with them for a short time, return. It exhibited great partiality for a cat, on whose back it used to climb and remain seated for hours together. This bird was fed entirely upon bread and sugar. I have been credibly informed of another instance of a specimen being kept for the long space of thirteen years. Its food was dry bread, a diet which I suspect it must have been brought to by degrees. This species breeds in the holes of trees, the mangrove not unfrequently being selected for the purpose. The eggs are five in number, white, very round, and nearly an inch in length.

TRICHOGLOSSUS RUBITORQUIS.

(Red-collared Lorikeet.)

Head and cheeks, resplendent blue, lighter down the middle of each feather; throat, olive green; chest, scarlet; a narrow band of the same color across the occiput, followed by another of bright blue—the basal portions of the feathers of the latter, scarlet; upper surface and wings, rich grass green; basal half of the inner webs of the primaries, yellow; centre of abdomen, deep olive black—the basal portions of each feather, scarlet; lower part of the abdomen, yellow, mottled with green; under tail coverts, green; irides, red, with a narrow ring of yellow next the pupil; bill, scarlet; feet, greenish grey.

Length, 12 inches; wing, 6; tail, 5½; bill, ½; tarsus, ½.

Northern Australia alone seems to be the exclusive habitat of this lovely species. Since the opening of Port Albany, at the northern extremity of the Cape York peninsula, I was in hopes that it would be found to be a denizen of that portion of the continent, but have hitherto seen no specimen from thence, and have reason to believe that it does not extend its range to the eastward of the Gulf of Carpentaria. What its southern range may be still remains to be determined. Gilbert found this species numerous at Port Essington, and says that in habit it assimilates in all respects to its congener, T. Swainsonii. The figure is from an Adam Bay specimen, kindly lent by F. G. Waterhouse, Esq., of the Museum, Adelaide.

TRICHOGLOSSUS CHLOROLEPIDOTUS.

(Scaly-breasted Lorikeet.)

UPPER surface, neck, throat, wings, and tail, shining grass green; under surface, bright yellow, each feather tipped with a broad crescent of green; under tail coverts, green, washed with yellow; under surface of shoulder and base of primaries and secondaries, scarlet; bill, scarlet, inclining to orange at the tip; cere and orbits, olive; irides, pale yellow. The sexes are alike.

Length, 8½ inches; wing, 5½; tail, 4; bill, ⅔; tarsus, ½.

This well marked species inhabits New South Wales and Queensland, and is only found on the lands near the coast. It associates in common with several other species of Trichoglossus, and may be generally found feeding together on the same tree. The blossoms of the various Eucalypti are visited by it for the purpose of feeding on the honey which is so abundantly secreted; and as some one or other species of that genus of trees is always to be found in flower, a supply is always available in one part of the country or another at any time of the year; the seeds of the Casuarina and other trees also furnish it with food of a more solid description. Like its congeners, it lays its white eggs in the spouts or holes of gum trees. Many attempts have been made to preserve it alive as a cage bird, but seldom with success, as, after living a few weeks, it generally dies suddenly. Young birds confined in the vicinity of the breeding place are often visited by the old birds, which are then easily trapped.

TRICHOGLOSSUS CONCINNUS.

(Musky Lorikeet.)

FOREHEAD and ear coverts, rich scarlet; crown of the head, greenish blue; upper part of back, brownish olive; a patch of rich yellow on the side of the body near the shoulder; back, wings, tail, and under surface, rich grass green; inner webs of quills, black; inner webs of lateral tail feathers, scarlet at the base, blending into yellow, and terminating in green; bill, blackish brown, tipped with red; cere and orbits, olive brown; irides, buff, encircled with yellow.

Length, 9 inches; wing, 5; tail, 4; bill, ⅓; tarsus, ½.

This species has an extensive range, being found in south Queensland, New South Wales, South Australia, Victoria, and Tasmania. It has derived its name from the peculiar odour emitted by it. Like the former species, it associates with other Trichoglossi feeding upon the same trees, and is very plentiful, being, in fact, one of the most common of the Psittacidæ in Australia. In its habits and nidification it also resembles the former species, and is very tame and familiar, allowing many successive discharges of the gun before becoming sufficiently alarmed to cause it to take flight. It is a noisy bird, keeping up a perpetual harsh scream while feeding or flying overhead. This bird becomes very tame in confinement; but, like the rest of the honey eating parrots, it requires very careful and judicious treatment in dietary.

PTILONOPUS SUPERBUS.

(*Superb Fruit Pigeon.*)

MALE.—Crown, purplish crimson; cheeks and a collar behind the neck, bright green, beneath which follows a broad band of orange scarlet; throat, white, passing into grey at the sides; chest, pearly grey, the feathers being rather squarely pointed and detached, showing indications of the lilac coloring at their bases; back and wings, rich olive green; tail, bright green, with a whitish spot near the tip; the scapularies and all but the three outermost tertiaries have a blackish purple circular spot; primaries and secondaries, slightly margined and more broadly tipped with light yellow; shoulders, dark purplish black; a band of blackish green on the upper portion of the abdomen, followed by one of pure white; flanks, white, interrupted by patches of green; under tail coverts, white, with a central patch of green on each feather; feet, crimson; claws, whitish, tipped with dark horn color; irides, pale yellow.

The female has less red on the head, and her plumage is less bright than that of the male.

Length, 8¾ inches; wing, 5; tail, 3¾; bill, ¼; tarsus, 1.

This elegant species is found in the peninsula of Cape York; some of the East India Islands and New Guinea are also frequented by it. The various wild fruits found in the dense and tangled scrubs near Port Albany, which are the usual haunts of this richly decorated bird, supply it with abundance of its favorite food. It flies well, but is so shy and wary as to render the procuring of specimens a matter of considerable difficulty. It is said to be excellent eating.

CARPOPHAGA MAGNIFICA.

(Magnificent Fruit Pigeon.)

HEAD, cheeks, and throat, grey; neck, grey, shading into yellowish olive above and down the sides of the neck; back and shoulders, golden olive—the basal portions of the feathers, deep grass green; the central wing coverts, bright grass green, ornamented with large yellow spots; secondaries, bright green with a narrow bordering of brownish yellow; primaries, beautiful deep grass green—the inner webs, blackish; tail, deep grass green, with chestnut shafts; breast and upper portion of the abdomen, deep purplish maroon color, interrupted sometimes in a few places by small patches of green; ventral portion and underneath the shoulder, rich orange; under tail coverts, greenish yellow; under side of tail grey—the shafts, buff; orbits, greyish blue; irides, reddish orange; bill, red at the base, the tip being horn color; feet, greyish green, with dull yellow soles; claws, blackish horn color. The female is similar, but not quite so highly colored.

Length, 18 inches; wing, 8½; tail 6½; bill, 1½; tarsus, 1; middle toe, 1⅞.

This truly magnificent bird is found in the scrubs on the Manning, Mackay, Clarence, and Richmond rivers of New South Wales, and all the eastern rivers of southern Queensland, where it may be said to be pretty abundant. It has been obtained in the Illawarra district, which is probably its southern limit. This species is confined to the country bordering the sea, never being found far inland. Its favorite food is the wild fig; other fruits and berries found in the coast brushes are also greedily devoured. It is gregarious in flocks of ten to twenty or more, and although from its feeding upon the tops of the towering and widely spreading trees which far overtop the general growth of the brushes, it is somewhat difficult to be obtained, it cannot be termed shy. Mr. Coxen informs me that he has known instances in which a sportsman has ascended high into a feeding tree, and, from the advantage of his position, obtained a number of specimens before the birds were sufficiently alarmed (even after successive discharges of the gun) to take their departure. The flight of C. Magnifica is heavy and cumbrous, and its note is a peculiar bubbling, cooing, hoarse sound. The natives on the Manning call it "Dubblo Bubblo Maru," from its note. It builds a nest, rather carelessly constructed, with a few sticks, and placed in the fork of a tree in the midst of the scrub. The eggs are two in number, white, and about 1¼ inch in length. The flesh is dark in color, but very good eating, in the winter time being so fat that it is difficult to get a perfect specimen, as on falling from the tree when shot it generally bursts.

CARPOPHAGA LUCTUOSA

CARPOPHAGA LUCTUOSA.

(Torres' Straits Pigeon.)

UPPER and under surface, creamy white; the middle feathers of the tail are tipped with black to the extent of about one third of their length; the remaining tail feathers terminate in the same color, but less in proportion to their distance from the central feathers—the outermost of all have a very slight tip of black, but the outer edge for the greater part of its length, towards the base, is black; primaries, secondaries, and spurious wing, dark grey; under tail coverts, banded with black near the extremity of each feather; a few feathers about the legs, spotted with black; bill, greenish grey, tipped with yellow; feet, blackish green.

Length, 15 inches; wing, 9½; tail, 5½; tarsus, 1¼; bill, ⅞.

This species is plentiful at Cape York and throughout Northern Australia, during the spring and summer months, and generally makes its appearance about October. It frequents the scrubs to feed upon the berries and wild figs. During the mid-day heat it seeks the thick shade, but may be commonly seen in the morning or evening in flocks, or clustering on the tops of bare trees. The flight of this species is strong and rapid. It commences breeding immediately on its arrival, the nests being often built among the mangroves close to the shore; they are constructed of fine sticks, but in such sparing quantity as barely to prevent the eggs from falling through. The eggs are one or two in number, and white. At certain times the flesh of this species is dry and without flavor, but at others is esteemed very good eating. Leichhardt mentions this bird as being pretty common in the forest country round the Gulf of Carpentaria, being generally seen in pairs, and very shy in disposition. It exists in prodigious numbers on Cairncross Island, on the N.E. coast, where it feeds upon the red plum-like fruit of the Minnusops Kaukii. Its note is a loud and deep coo, like that of other pigeons, but more powerful.

CARPOPHAGA LEUCOMELA.

(White-headed Fruit Pigeon.)

HEAD, neck, and breast, white, tinged with buff, especially on the crown; back, wings, and tail, blackish grey; rump and upper wing coverts, bordered with bronzy purple or green; abdomen, dingy buff, passing into slate color on the flanks; bill, reddish pink, tipped with light yellow; irides, reddish hazel; orbits, pink; feet, buff—the scales rose color, and the claws white. The female is smaller in size than the male, and her markings less defined.

Length, 15½ inches; wing, 9½; tail, 6; tarsus, 1¼; bill, ⅞.

This swift-flying species is found throughout the scrubs of New South Wales and Queensland, such situations abounding with the various wild fruits on which it feeds, and which are more or less plentiful at all times of the year. It builds a slight nest of sticks, and the eggs are one or two in number; color, pure white.

CHALCOPHAPS INDICA NATALIS
Little Green Pigeon

H.G.E. GATES

CHALCOPHAPS CHRYSOCHLORA.

(Little Green Pigeon.)

HEAD, upper part of the back, neck, chest, and abdomen, rich vinous brown; shoulder white, margined above with blackish grey; lower portion of the back, and upper tail coverts, deep grey, crossed with three lighter bands; wing coverts, scapularies, and uppermost tertiaries, shining bronzy green; primaries and spurious wing, brown; tail, blackish brown, except the two outer feathers on each side, which are light grey, broadly banded with black near the tip; ventral portion, brownish grey; under tail coverts, black; feet, purplish red; tip of the bill, orange red—the base, purple; eyelids, lilac red; irides, nearly black. The female is similar to the male, but less brightly colored.

Length, 11 inches; wing, 6; tail, 4; bill, ½; tarsus, 1.

This very beautiful little pigeon is plentiful in the scrubs of Queensland, and the northern portions of New South Wales, becoming less abundant to the south. It is generally seen feeding on the ground. The berries and seeds of various wild trees furnish it with an abundant supply of food; and it is sometimes in the habit of visiting gardens, to feed upon the fruit of the mulberry, of which it seems to be excessively fond. The stomach of a specimen shot near Brisbane, which I examined, was filled with an oval-shaped purple berry, about half an inch in length, which Mr. Hill, the curator of the Brisbane Botanical Gardens, informed me was the fruit of "Psychatria Daphnoides" (order Rubiaceæ). When disturbed, this bird rises rapidly, and flies to a short distance, and then, alighting suddenly, remains so quiet as to be with difficulty discovered. It is rather strange that nothing should be known of the nest or eggs up to the present time; and it would afford me much satisfaction to receive any intelligence concerning them.

CHALCOPHAPS LONGIROSTRIS.

(Long-billed Green Pigeon.)

THIS species is here given on the authority of Mr. Gould. It differs from the former in the plumage, being brighter, and the bill much longer. In other respects, it is altogether similar in size, color, and markings, to the above. Habitat, Port Essington.

PHAPS CHALCOPTERA
Bronze Wing

PHAPS HISTRIONICA
Harlequin Bronze Wing

PHAPS HISTRIONICA.

(Harlequin Bronzewing.)

FOREHEAD, a stripe from behind the eye forming a circle round the ear coverts, and a crescent-shaped mark across the throat, snow white; the rest of the head, throat, and ear coverts, jet black; all the upper surface, wing coverts, flanks, and two central tail feathers, deep cinnamon brown; edge of shoulder, dull white; primaries, brownish grey, outwardly margined with rufous, and tipped with white; secondaries, banded near the tips with crimson bronze; lateral tail feathers, bluish grey, passing into black and tipped with white; breast and centre of abdomen, bluish grey; under tail coverts, buff; nostrils and bill, black; bare skin around the eye, purplish black; irides, dark brown; front of feet and legs, lilac red; hind part, flesh red.

The female is much less brilliant in her appearance than the male.

Length, 10½ inches; wing, 8; tail, 3½; bill, 1; tarsus, 1.

This species is found in vast flocks in various parts of the interior. On the Mokai and Namoy rivers it was first observed by Mr. Gould; Leichhardt met with it on his journey, and followed it up to Port Essington. It sometimes appears in countless numbers in a locality where not one has been seen before, and leaves the same for many years, until a combination of circumstances, as drought or scarcity of food, renders a migration beyond its usual boundary a matter of necessity, when it again makes its appearance. It feeds on the open plains, and comes to water at sunset, drinking but sparingly. It lives, in March and April, for the most part on the seeds of the rice-grass, which is also used by the natives for food, when it is delicious eating, but at other seasons very inferior. It incubates in February, laying its eggs, two in number, under the salt bush and other low shrubs found on the open plains; the color of the eggs is white.

PHAPS CHALCOPTERA.

(Bronzewing Pigeon.)

FOREHEAD, buffy white; stripe below the eyes and throat, white; crown, brown tinged with reddish; cheeks and sides of the neck, bluish grey; breast, reddish grey; abdomen, purplish grey; back, scapularies, rump, and upper tail coverts, greenish brown; wing coverts, bluish grey, the outer webs bronzed with large oval spots of various metallic colors: outer edges of primaries, brown; tail, bluish grey. with a band of black near the tip; bill, black in front and red behind; legs and feet, red; irides, hazel.

Length, 14 inches; wing, 10; tail, 6; bill, 1; tarsus, 1⅔.

This elegant species is found in every part of Australia, and in some of the South Sea Islands. It prefers sandy country, and is generally found feeding on the ground underneath various trees, especially wattles, the seeds of which are shed and fallen to the earth. When disturbed, it rises with a loud burring noise, and pitches again at no great distance. It builds in various situations—in holes of trees or among the branches, and even on the ground—the nest being a loose structure of twigs; the eggs are two in number, and of a white color. In consequence of the excellence of its flesh, great numbers of this bird are shot for the table. It drinks sparingly, and its presence at the close of day is a sure indication of water being in the immediate neighborhood. It is generally seen in pairs, but sometimes in considerable numbers. In the neighborhood of Goulburn, Yass, and the Hunter River, this species is especially abundant after the harvest, in the stubble of corn fields, and affords excellent shooting, equal to partridge shooting in England. Indeed, so plentiful are they at certain seasons, that during Mr. Gould's visit to Yarrundi in January, 1840, from thirty to forty brace were shot in two mornings' shooting by that gentleman, and Messrs. S. and C. Coxen, in the wheat stubble adjacent to the house. Mr. C. Coxen informs me that it was raining the whole of the time, and that it is probable the birds were on a migratory passage, but delayed temporarily by the weather.

GEOPELIA CUNEATA
Diamond Ground Dove

GEOPELIA TRANQUILLA
Peaceful Ground Dove

GEOPELIA TRANQUILLA.

(Tranquil Ground Dove.)

CROWN of the head, face, and, throat, light grey; back of the neck, back, shoulders, and wing coverts, ashy vinous brown, banded with a deep black line at the extremity of each feather; spurious wings and primaries, blackish brown; chest and sides of the neck, light grey, narrowly banded with black; abdomen, of a light vinous tint; the four central feathers of tail, ashy brown—the remainder black, largely tipped with white; irides, nearly white; bill and orbits, greyish blue; legs and feet, pink; the front scales of the tarsi, purple.

Length, 7¼ inches; wing, 4½; tail, 4; bill, ⅔; tarsus, ⅔.

This tame and familiar species is found all through the country bordering the eastern coast of Australia, from New South Wales to Cape York. It is subject to some variation in size, the northern specimens being the smallest. The species described, but not figured, by Mr. Gould, under the name of G. Placida, is now considered by Australian naturalists to be only a small variety of the present one, many other birds varying much more in this particular which have never for a moment been doubted as identical. This little dove is very common in many parts of Queensland, and also in the interior, especially on the Darling, Murray, and other large streams. It is generally to be found in small flocks, feeding upon the seeds of the various species of acacia which have fallen from the trees, and is also not uncommon in the gardens around Brisbane. When disturbed, it rises with a whirr, and alights on a branch of the nearest tree, anxiously watching the cause of alarm, whether man or beast. It will allow of a very near approach, and during the progress of the line of railway from Ipswich to Toowoomba, would frequently attend upon the tents of the workmen to pick up crumbs. It is trapped in considerable numbers, and forms a quiet and interesting source of attraction in the cage, where it is often to be seen in company with finches and parakeets, and generally fares the worst among them, as I have seen many specimens with their heads almost totally denuded of feathers by their bolder and more active, though more diminutive companions. The nest is a small, careless, and loose structure of small twigs, and so fragile that the eggs can be seen through it. The latter are two in number and white. The little architect is not particular as to the kind of tree in which to build—the wattle tree being, perhaps, preferred above others—and at no great height from the ground.

GEOPELIA CUNEATA.

(Graceful Ground Dove)

HEAD, neck, and breast, delicate grey, passing into white on the abdomen; back and four central feathers of tail, drab; wing coverts, grey—each feather of the coverts and scapularies with a spot of white on each web, near the tip; spurious wing and primaries, brown—the latter rufous on the inner webs; the remainder of the tail feathers, greyish black, largely tipped with white; irides, red; orbits, salmon color; bill, olive brown; feet, yellowish flesh color.

Length, 7½ inches; wing, 3⅔; tail, 4½; bill, ½; tarsus, ⅔.

This species is equally tame and familiar as the former, and is almost as frequently seen caged in the colonies of New South Wales and Queensland. Like the former species, it is generally to be seen on the ground, and in its habits is quite similar. Its note is very soft and plaintive. The range of this pretty species is very great, it being a denizen of both east and west, and all over the interior. The nest is described by Mr. Gould as a frail but beautiful structure formed of the stalks of a few flowering grasses, crossed and interwoven. The eggs are two in number, white. Size, ⅘ by ⁷⁄₁₀. A nest in Mr. Waller's collection, from which the female was shot about the latter end of August, 1868, was formed of small twigs, loosely put together, and was about four inches in diameter. It was discovered in a small gum sapling, about four feet from the ground.

MACROPYGIA PHASIANELLA
Pheasant tailed Pigeon

MACROPYGIA PHASIANELLA.

(Large-tailed Pigeon.)

CROWN and occiput, rich deep chestnut brown; back and wings, umber brown; wing coverts, broadly margined with deep reddish chestnut; upper tail coverts, brownish chestnut; tail, brown, except the three outermost feathers on each side, which are buffish chestnut at the tips and bases, and have a broad black band in the middle; primaries and secondaries, blackish brown, very narrowly edged with chestnut; throat, whitish, each feather edged with buffish brown; chest and sides of the neck, reddish buff, mingled or barred with blackish brown; abdomen, bright rufous, slightly or indistinctly barred with blackish brown; under tail coverts and under surface of tail, buffish chestnut, becoming greyish near the tips of the longer feathers—the three outer feathers are barred with grey; flanks, deep rufous; irides, blue, surrounded by a scarlet ring; bill, deep olive brown; feet, light crimson. The sexes are alike.

Length, 17¼ inches; wing, 7¾; tail, 9; bill, 1; tarsus, ¾.

This bird, so different in form from the others of its family inhabiting Australia, is seldom seen beyond the outskirts of the dense scrubs which are so frequent on the banks of the eastern waters. It is to be found from Twofold Bay, on the south, to the Mary River, on the north. Its food consists of berries and seeds, most of which are procured upon the ground after having fallen from the trees. It may be occasionally seen in gardens when the same are situated near to its favorite residence, the scrub, and evinces a liking to fruits of a cultivated description. Its note is not very unlike the Bronze-wing Pigeon, but is more mournful and monotonous. The flesh is dark, but of good flavor.

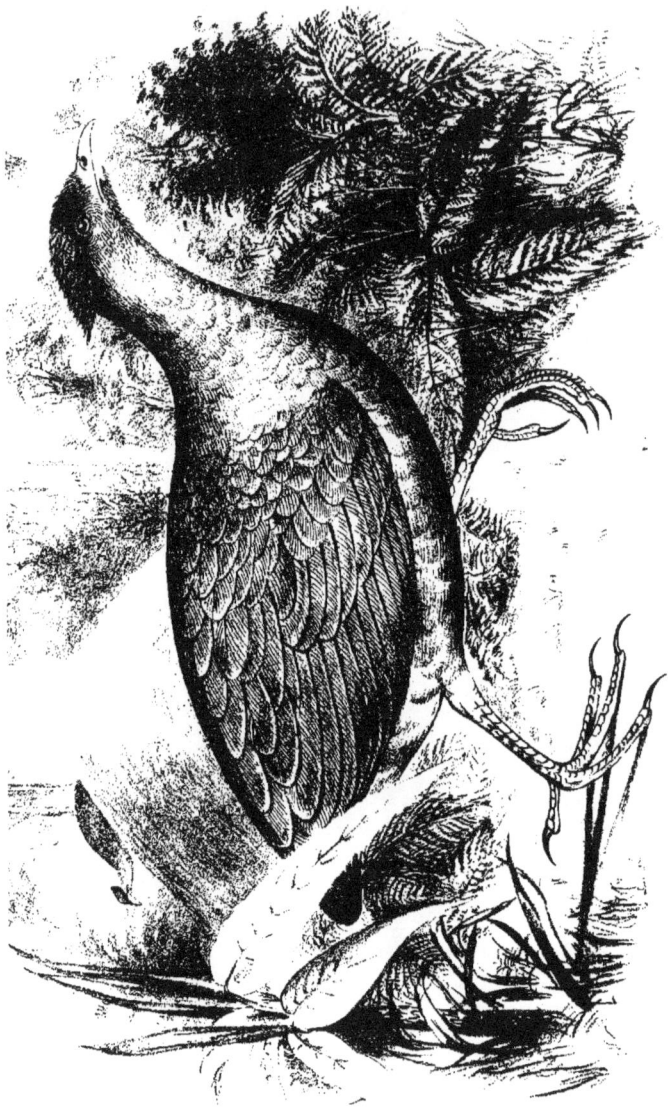

MEGAPODIUS TUMULUS (GOULD).

(Mound-raising Megapode.)

HEAD and crest, dark reddish brown; behind the neck, dark grey; upper surface and wings, deep cinnamon brown; upper and under tail coverts, still darker brown; throat and all the under surface, grey; tail, blackish brown; legs and feet, orange; claws, black; bill, reddish brown, edged with yellow; irides, reddish hazel, or dark brown.

Length, 17 inches; wing, 10; tail, 5; bill, 1½; tarsus, 2½; centre toe and claw, 2¾; hind ditto, 1¼.

This interesting bird is confined to the northern coasts of Australia, being found both at Port Denison, Cape York, and Port Essington, and probably in all the intervening country. It is extremely shy in disposition, and though often heard is seldom seen, as it secretes itself among the dense brushes on the slightest alarm. When fairly disturbed, however, it flies to an adjacent tree, and stretching out its neck, watches and listens intently for the intruder, who must use the greatest caution in making an approach, which the bird will permit to the distance of eighty or one hundred yards, but if any attempt is made to approximate still nearer it takes wing, and then it is of little use to follow. The flight is very heavy and laborious, but it can run with considerable swiftness. The note is described as something like the cluck of the domestic fowl, with a termination similar to the scream of a peacock. The singular habit of mound building invests this, and some allied species, with more than ordinary interest. When first discovered it was thought these structures were tumuli of the aborigines, but further enquiry showed that they were fashioned by a bird. The mounds vary much in size; those recently made are not above four or five yards in circumference, and about five feet in height, but old ones have been met with many times that size, and as high as fifteen feet, with good sized trees growing out of them. The material used in their formation varies with the locality—sand, black soil, shells, &c., with an admixture of vegetable matter, as leaves, grass, small sticks, &c. The feet are very powerful, and well adapted for accomplishing this purpose. The eggs are deposited at a considerable depth in a hole excavated by the old birds, and then covered lightly over and left to themselves, the spontaneous heat of the decaying vegetable matter sufficing to bring them to maturity. The natives probe the mounds with sticks, when, on finding a place easily penetrated, they dig down, and are often rewarded with a considerable number of eggs. Several females lay in the same mound. The eggs are placed on their ends, and in shape are nearly perfectly oval; the shell is white (with a brownish skin outside when fresh). Some are larger than others, the average being three inches five lines long, by two inches three lines broad. When hatched the young are well clothed with feathers, and being uncommonly strong, manage to scratch their way out, when they are taken charge of by the old ones. The food consists of berries, seeds, and insects of all kinds, but especially grasshoppers and beetles.

PEDIONOMUS TORQUATUS *nigricans*
Collared Plain-wanderer

COTURNIX PECTORALIS
Pectoral Quail

PEDIONOMUS TORQUATUS.

(Collared Plain Wanderer.)

MALE.—Crown of the head, back, and upper surface, mottled with black, brown, and fawn color, the latter color occupying the external edges of the feathers, and the black and brown forming alternate circular markings on each feather; throat, neck, chest, and flanks, dull fawn color; the feathers of the neck, chest, and flanks blotched with brown, which, on the latter, assumes the form of bars; tail feathers, almost invisible; centre of abdomen and under tail coverts, buffy white; irides, straw color; feet, greenish yellow.

Length, 4½ inches; wing, 3½; bill, 11-16ths; tarsus, ⅞.

FEMALE.—Crown of the head, reddish brown, speckled with black; sides of the head and neck, light buff, speckled with black; neck, surrounded by a broad band of white, thickly spotted with black; all the upper surface, reddish brown, each feather having several transverse crescentic marks in the centre, and margined with buff; tail, buff, crossed by numerous narrow brown bars; centre of the breast, rufous; the remainder of the under surface, buff; the feathers of the breast marked in a similar manner to those of the upper surface, and the flanks with large irregular spots of black; irides, straw yellow, passing into black at the point; feet, greenish yellow.

Length, 7 inches; wing, 3¾; tail, 1½; bill, ⅞; tarsus, ⅞.

Such is the description and measurement of this singular bird as given by Mr. Gould; The figure, which is that of the female, is also copied from his plate. Up to the present time I have not succeeded in obtaining a specimen, and have every reason to believe that it must now be of rare occurrence, the settlement of the country having driven it farther back into the interior. From the smallness of the wing this bird flies with difficulty. When disturbed it generally hides by crouching among the grass. Its note is a sound not unlike that of the emu, but much fainter, resembling the noise caused by tapping an empty cask. Dogs easily run it down, that being the general mode of its capture. The true habitat of this species is the arid plains of the interior.

COTURNIX PECTORALIS.

(Pectoral Quail.)

MALE.—Lores, ear coverts, and throat, buff; two parallel lines of white over the eye, and a central one of the same color from the forehead to the nape; the remainder of the head and neck, deep brown, each feather of the latter having a central streak of yellowish white, and blotched with black on each side; upper surface, brown, with zig-zag markings of black, each feather with a central mark of yellowish white; wings, brown, marked transversely with zig-zag lines of grey and black; primaries, black; sides of chest, brown; centre of chest, black; abdomen, white, each feather marked with black down the centre; flanks, rich brown; the centre of each feather white, bounded by a fine line of black on each side; bill, blackish brown; irides, hazel; feet, light flesh color.

FEMALE.—Differs from the male in having the throat white, and in not having any black marks on the chest.

Length, 6½ inches; wing, 3¾; bill, ½; tarsus, ⅞.

This species, which much resembles the common European Quail, is found in almost every known portion of Australia, and also in Tasmania. Its food consists of grass seeds, &c., and also insects. In the cultivated parts, after the harvest, the fields are frequented by large numbers of these birds; hence the name of Stubble Quail, by which it is popularly known. It broods from September to December. The eggs are numerous, seldom less than twelve being found in a nest, and the same is generally placed in a thick tuft of grass. The eggs vary much, some being more profusely marked than others. The ground color is straw white, and the markings consist of blotches or spots of brown.

SYNOICUS AUSTRALIS
Swamp-Quail

SYNOICUS CHINENSIS
Least Swamp-Quail

SYNOÏCUS AUSTRALIS.

(Swamp Quail.)

Forehead, lores, throat, and cheeks, brownish buff in summer, but generally very much lighter in the winter season, as is also the rest of the plumage; crown and back of the neck, dark brown, with a broad line of buff down the centre, and a narrow one on each side; upper surface of the back and tail, irregularly banded with grey, black, and light chestnut; wing coverts, reddish, or buffish chestnut, freckled with zigzag marks of light brown; primaries, brown, the outer edges with irregular bands of reddish buff; chest and abdomen, sandy buff, washed with grey, each feather crossed by zigzag or lunated bands of black, which are largest on the abdomen and flanks; all the feathers of the back, and some on the flanks, having a clear, whitish, buff, or greyish line, down the centre; irides, orange; feet, fleshy yellow; bill, bluish black.

Average length, 7 inches; wing, 3¼; tail, variable—1¼ to 2½; bill, ⅜; tarsus, 1.

The sexes are very much alike, but the markings are of a bolder character in the female than the male.

Much confusion exists respecting this species, which is found all over the continent of Australia, and also in Tasmania. The specimens from Cape York and Port Essington are of smaller size, but lighter, and more brightly colored. The Tasmanian specimens are generally the largest, sometimes measuring upwards of 8¼ inches in length; but the color and markings are like those of Queensland, where, also, specimens occasionally occur of equal size. The want of a sufficient number of specimens in all their varieties of plumage, has led Mr. Gould to suppose that we have four species of large swamp quail. But the favorable opportunities I have had of examining numerous Queensland examples shot by Mr. Cockerell, (who, by the aid of his valuable dogs, is able to procure this and other species of quail in great plenty,) enable me to arrive at the conclusion that there is only one. Specimens in Mr. Cockerell's collection of every variety of color, size, and markings justify me in speaking positively concerning the S. Diemenensis and S. Cervinus of Gould; and S. Sordidus, I believe, will be found to be only a plainer variety than usual. No necessity exists for a description of the two former, as they would nearly read like the one above. The last, which I give in the words of Mr. Gould, may assist other observers in arriving at a correct conclusion concerning it. "S. Sordidus: General plumage, dark brown, minutely "freckled with black, each feather of the upper and under surface with a broad stripe of bluish grey down the centre; feathers of the "head and back of the neck with a spot of blackish-brown at the tip; those down the centre of the head, and a few of the back "feathers, with white shafts; chin, buff; flank feathers, with an arrow-head shaped mark near the tip." The measurements are almost "identical with the one above; and the remark by Mr. G., that this "species differs from its congeners in the absence of any variety "in the markings of its plumage," will nearly apply to some specimens of S. Australis which I have seen. In fact, it is difficult to conceive of a bird varying more than this one. A covey of fourteen shot by Mr. Cockerell, varied from light to dark, small to large, bold to more or less inconspicuous markings. The natural habitat of this species is swampy districts, surrounded by thick vegetation, but more especially (in Queensland) near gardens or cultivated spots. When disturbed, it rises with a loud burr, takes a short flight to the distance of about one hundred yards, and endeavors to conceal itself in the nearest cover. If much persecuted, it removes to a greater distance. When a covey rises, the birds scatter in every direction; and if the sportsman remain quiet, he will hear them calling to one another like a monotonous note, consisting of two sounds like a minor third in music, and in a very short time they collect together again. The eggs are usually laid under a tuft of grass in a small depression of the earth, with a few root fibres for a lining; and sometimes are even deposited beneath cabbage plants in gardens. The eggs, from twelve to eighteen in number, are rather variable, some being of a light buff, or olive buff, with scarcely any markings; others are sprinkled with minute spots of brown, or smeared with dirty brownish olive. Size, 1¼ by 1 inch (nearly). The swamp quail is considered a great delicacy for the table, and occupies the same position with us as the partridge does in England.

SYNOÏCUS CHINENSIS.

(Least Swamp Quail.)

Male.--Crown of the head and upper surface, brown, irregularly blotched with black, some of the feathers with a stripe of buff down the centre; wings, brown; face, breast, and flanks, fine blue-grey; throat, black, above which is an oblong mark of white under the eye, and another below the black of the throat, forming a white lunate collar in front; it is bounded below by a line of black; abdomen and under tail coverts, rich chestnut red; irides, hazel; bill, black; feet, light yellow. Female: space surrounding the eye, throat, and abdomen, sandy buff; crown of the head, and all the upper surface, buffish brown, blotched and striped with blackish brown; breast narrowly, and flanks broadly, striped with the same; a blackish streak through the middle of the face; irides, dark brown.

over.]

Length, $4\frac{1}{4}$ inches; wing, $2\frac{1}{4}$; bill, $\frac{1}{4}$ (nearly); tarsus, $\frac{7}{8}$.

Every portion of Australasia, except, perhaps, Tasmania and Western Australia, is frequented by this beautiful species. Its favorite haunts are open, flat, swampy situations, without trees. It is nearly impossible to flush it without the aid of a well trained dog. It rises with a loud burr, but seldom flies far, and on setting, drops like a stone; but is so easily tired, as to allow itself to be taken alive rather than fly, preferring to stick its head in a tuft of grass, and remaining perfectly quiescent in the presence of the pointer, by watching whose nose it may be secured. It is plentiful near Brisbane, as many as fifty pair having been shot by Mr. Cockerell in a hundred acre paddock in a fortnight. The nest has a small run leading to it, and is situated under an overhanging tuft of grass, in a small depression, lined with root fibres, forming a structure sufficiently strong to allow the eggs to be lifted upon it: they are four or five in number, nearly 1 inch long by $\frac{11}{16}$, and rather pointed at the small end; color, creamy whitish grey, finely sprinkled all over with blackish brown: some have also a few dark blotches of brown on the large end. The young are curious little things, and follow the parents like chickens. The forehead, throat, and face, are of a light olive buff; the rest of the plumage, blackish brown, barred above with buffish chestnut, and with a sharp, whitish streak down the centre of each feather.

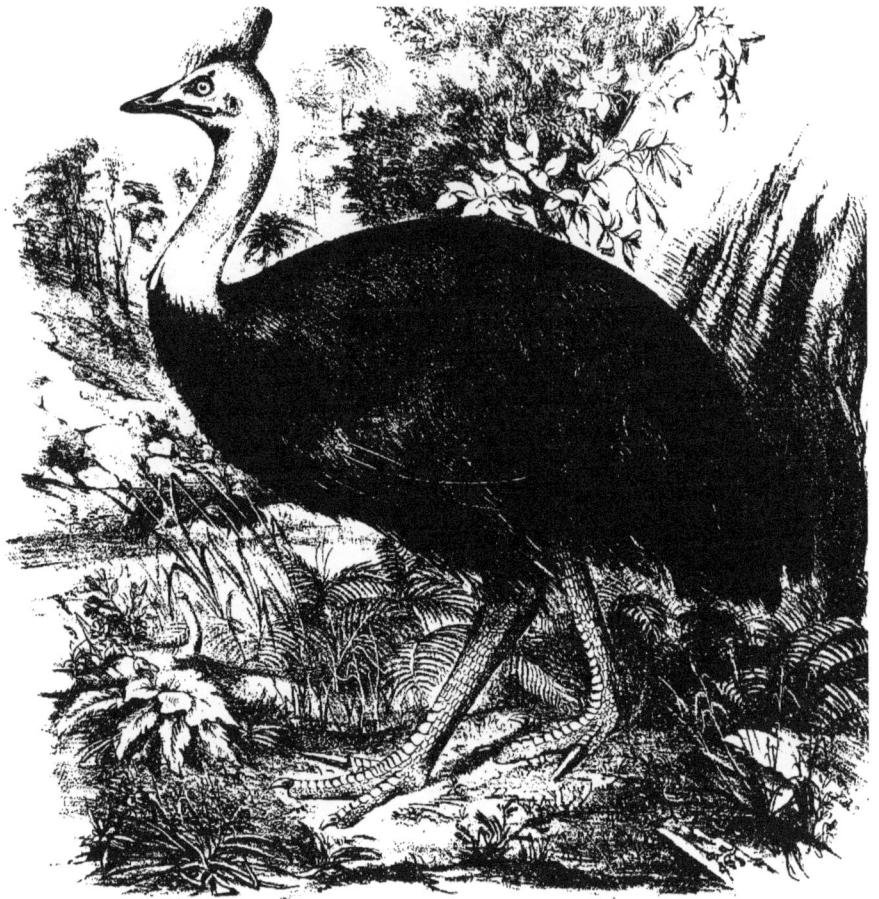

CASUARIUS JOHNSONII (Krefft).

(Johnson's Cassowary.)

MALE.—The general plumage is black (at a distance resembling coarse hair), with the exception of the tail, which is a good deal intermixed with brownish feathers—all the feathers brown at the root; legs, stout; the inner toe very short, with a strong straight nail, which is broad at the base, and ends in a sharp point; wings, rudimentary, and supplied with five or six webless shafts of various lengths; head, surmounted by a horny helmet of a dirty brown color, the height of which is equal to, or greater than, the length of its base; neck, covered with a thin smooth skin, at the lower part of which, on each side, are a few glandular folds; the neck wattles in front are two in number and four or five inches in length; the head and neck are almost entirely bare of feathers; the skin from the bill along the top of the head and extending about five inches behind the neck is of a marine blue tint, below this, and adjoining the plumage, is a patch of cinnabar red; the remainder of the neck is bright ultramarine, except the lower triangular portion adjoining the plumage, where it becomes a deep indigo tint; the neck wattles are bright red; bill, black; irides, rich light brown.

Height, 4 feet 6 inches; length, 4 feet 3 inches; bill, 4 inches; tarsus, 12; mid-toe, 7; outer and inner toes, 5; inner claw, 3; helmet, 5½ to 6½.

The discovery of so large and important a bird as a Cassowary in Australia is an event of much interest. One result of the opening up of the northern portions of Queensland for the purposes of settlement is an increased knowledge of many beautiful birds, and an addition to our fauna of several forms which were supposed to be exclusively confined to New Guinea and the neighboring islands. A report for some years existed relative to a cassowary shot by Kennedy's party during their disastrous expedition skirting the Cape York peninsula; now, even supposing the same to refer to the present bird (of which we are by no means certain) the description attempted does not apply in any one respect.

The Casuarius Galeatus of Coram, &c., is nearly allied to Casuarius Johnsonii, but the following particulars will sufficiently show its distinctness :—

C. GALEATUS.	C. JOHNSONII.
Height of helmet less than the length of the base.	*Height of helmet, greater than the length of the base.*
Skin of neck, thick and furnished with regular tubercular ridges behind; glands on the sides next the plumage much developed.	*Skin of neck, thin and smooth—no ridges behind; glands on the sides of the neck, scarcely developed.*
Inner claw curved and not sharp.	*Inner claw straight and very sharp.*

The above description and characters are furnished by Gerard Krefft, Esq., of the Australian Museum, Sydney, who has kindly furnished me with photographs of both birds, and thus afforded material for careful comparison and the means of supplying a correct figure. The coloration is derived from the original notes of Mr. Johnson, taken at the time the bird was shot by him, in September, 1866, at Gowrie Creek Scrub, Rockingham Bay, and which, together with a sketch by that gentleman, were also forwarded to me by Mr. Krefft. I have much pleasure in adding that G. H. Davidson, Esq., of Rockingham Bay, has also succeeded in shooting a fine specimen of this bird, but, unfortunately, did not succeed in preserving it. On his last visit to Brisbane he brought with him certain portions of it, which I was permitted to inspect. They correspond almost completely, as also do his notes taken at the time, with the able description of Mr. Johnson, the measurements differing very slightly; for instance, the helmet in Mr. Johnson's specimen is 5½ inches in front—the one I saw in Mr. Davidson's possession measured 6½ inches in front. The neck wattles in Mr. Johnson's were 4 inches, and in Mr. Davidson's 5 inches in length, and only the tips of the wattles were orange red and rounded like balls, from which particulars we might be led to infer that the latter specimen, which weighed more than 200lbs., was more aged. The naked quills of the wing which that gentleman showed me were of various lengths, some being broken and all blunt. What the use of these curious appendages is it is difficult to conceive; that no important character can be founded on the number or size of them may be evident from the fact that in the specimen of C. Johnsonii, in the Sydney Museum, the right wing has six, and the left five; and those supposed to be pairs are not of the same length but differ considerably, the disposal of them being somewhat faulike, the shortest on each side and the longest in the middle, varying from ½ an inch to 12 inches in length; the average length of the third, fourth, and fifth, being 11 inches. The skin contains a large quantity of oil, and is difficult of preservation. Little is at present known as to the habits and economy of this bird, which is exceedingly shy and wary. It had been known for some time to exist in the neighborhood, but until Mr. Johnson's visit "had managed to escape every attempt to catch or kill." He says, "The bird seems to confine itself almost entirely to the more open parts of the scrub, and seldom ventures far out into the plains. During "the months of July, August, and September, its food consists of an egg shaped blue skinned berry, the fruit of a large tree; this, together "with herbage, probably forms its diet, at least for that portion of the year." The contents of the stomach of Mr. Davidson's specimen consisted of "a fruit resembling a lemon," which had a "stone inside."

EUDROMIAS AUSTRALIS
Australian Dottrel.

ERYTHROGONYS CINCTUS
Banded Red knee

EUDROMIAS AUSTRALIS.

(Australian Dottrell.)

FOREHEAD and upper surface, light sandy buff, with brown in the centre of each feather; primaries, brownish black, the shafts of the same sandy buff; and all but the first four feathers broadly margined with the same color; throat, buffy white, below which is a crescent-shaped mark of blackish brown; chest, flanks, and under surface of the wings, buff, passing into reddish chestnut on the abdomen; vent and under tail coverts, white; tail, brownish black, the centre feathers margined with buff, the lateral ones with white; bill, dark olive brown; feet, yellowish brown.

Length, 9 inches; wing, 5; tail, 2¾; bill, ¾; tarsus, 1¼.

This bird inhabits the low hills and plains of the interior. It runs very fast, and sometimes makes its appearance on the plains of Adelaide in considerable numbers, having apparently migrated from the north.

ERYTHROGONYS CINCTUS.

(Banded Red-knee.)

HEAD, lores, ear coverts, back of the neck, and chest, black; a small patch under the eye, throat, chest, side of neck, centre of abdomen, and under tail coverts, white, the latter spotted with dark brown; back, centre of wings, and tertiaries, olive, tinged with brown; tips of secondaries and of the outer webs of the six adjoining primaries, white; rump and two middle tail feathers, olive; the remaining feathers, white; flanks, chestnut; thighs and tarsi, purplish red; knee, purplish grey; bill, red at the base, and tipped with black; irides, dark brown. The sexes are alike.

Length, 7 inches; wing, 4¾; tail, 1½; bill, ¾; tarsus, 1¼; middle toe, ¾.

The Banded Red-knee visits the interior of New South Wales, South Australia, and the southern parts of Queensland in the summer season, resorting to swamps and reedy waterholes, where it feeds in company with other birds of similar habits. It is by no means common anywhere. It displays much grace and agility in its movements, and is said by some to be of a tame and familiar disposition. Such, however, is not the experience of collectors in general, who assert that it is with great difficulty they were enabled to obtain specimens. A fine specimen was shot in 1865, at Gammie Swamp, in the neighborhood of Ipswich, by Mr. J. T. Jameson. The nest and eggs are as yet unknown.

4

GLAREOLA ORIENTALIS.

(Oriental Pratincole.)

———

Crown and all the upper surface, brownish olive; primaries and secondaries, black; throat, white, surrounded by a broken ring of black beneath; chest, greyish olive; upper part of the abdomen, buff, fading into the white of the remainder of the under surface; central feathers of tail, black—the remainder white, each feather more or less largely terminated with black; upper tail coverts, white; under surface of wing, rust red; bill, black; feet, blackish brown.

Length, 8¾ inches; wing, 7¼; tail, 3½; bill, 1½; tarsus, 1¼.

This curious bird is not confined to Australia, its wonderful powers of flight enabling it to traverse immense distances, being found in India and the intervening countries. It has occasionally been obtained in the neighborhood of Brisbane, but must be considered of rare occurrence. It is exceedingly difficult to shoot, as its flight is very rapid. Its favorite resort is swampy ground, where it is to be seen in small companies of about twelve. When disturbed it rises to a considerable height, performing immense circles in the air in an ascending spiral direction until it becomes almost invisible, when on a sudden it descends like a flash of lightning, and as it nears the ground it flies for some distance horizontally, and suddenly alights near the spot from whence it arose.

======

GLAREOLA GRALLARIA.

(Australian Pratincole.)

———

Crown of the head and wings, greyish brown, tinged with rufous; lores, deep brown; cheeks, chest, and back, light rufous; abdomen, rich chestnut; throat, upper and under tail coverts, white; the four central tail feathers, white at the base, black in the centre, and tipped with grey; the most exterior tail feathers, pure white—the remainder more or less marked with black at the tips; primaries, black on the outer, and brown on the inner webs; quill of first and longest primary, pure white; under surface of wing, blackish; bill, red at the base and black at the tip; feet, dusky brown; irides, brown.

Length to tip of tail, 8 inches; ditto of wing, 10; expanse, 22; wing, 7½; tail, 2¾; bill, 1; tarsus, 1¼.

This species appears to be confined to the interior. Mr. White, of Reed Beds, near Adelaide, informs me he met with it in moderate abundance at Lake Hope, where he saw it wading in the shallows in small companies, or flying over the surface of the water, as if in search of prey. Sometimes it is to be seen walking about on the sand hills, at some distance from the water. Its flight is most rapid, and it bears up against the wind like a swallow or tern. At times it is seen to rise high in the air and to fly off apparently to some distant quarter, continually uttering its loud whistling note. It is very difficult to shoot. The stomachs of those examined by Mr. White were found to contain the remains of beetles and grasshoppers.

LIMOSA UROPYOIALIS
Barred rumped Godwit

LIMOSA UROPYGIALIS.

(Barred-rumped Godwit.)

ALL the upper surface brownish grey—the centres of the feathers dark, and the edges whitish; primaries, brown; rump, upper tail coverts, and tail conspicuously barred with white and brown; throat and abdomen, white; neck and breast, brownish grey; under wing coverts and flanks, barred with brown and white; tertiaries, edged with white on both webs—the centres, dark brown; bill, yellow, tipped with brown; irides, dark brown; legs, brownish black.

Length, 17 inches; wing, 8¾; tail, 3; bill, 4¼; tarsus, 2½; midtoe, 1¾.

The present species is almost identical with the Limosa Rufa of Europe and Asia, but may be at once discriminated by the conspicuous markings or bars on the rump and upper tail coverts, the "Bar-tailed Godwit" having those portions perfectly white in its winter plumage; in other respects the birds are quite similar, and the singular variations in the length of the bill in different specimens is observable in the present species, some having that organ much longer than others. It is found, in company with other birds of similar habits, on the sea coast or banks of tidal rivers, where at low water it may be observed walking about in considerable companies in search of its food, which consists of various small marine animals, shell fish, etc. Tasmania and various parts of the coast of New South Wales and Queensland are known to be frequented by it; and it is not improbable that it is distributed all round our shores.

SCOLOPAX AUSTRALIS   Australian Snipe
RHYNCHÆA AUSTRALIS   Australian Rhynchæa

SCOLOPAX AUSTRALIS.

(New Holland Snipe.)

LINE down the centre of the head, a broader line over each eye, cheeks, and throat, whitish buff; a broad line of rich brown on each side of the head; neck and chest, whitish buff, mottled with umber brown; back and scapularies, deep blackish brown, each feather broadly margined on the external edge with buff, and more or less regularly striped with rufous; shoulders, greyish brown; coverts, dirty buffy white, barred with dull brown; primaries and spurious wing, brown, the latter slightly tipped with whitish; secondaries and tertiaries, regularly striped with blackish brown on a lighter ground, and more or less tipped with buffy white; rump, rufous buff, closely barred with brown; tail, black at the base, followed by fawn color, and tipped with white; flanks, greyish white, striped with greyish brown; middle of abdomen, white; thighs and under tail coverts, buffy white; bill, greenish yellow at the base, and tipped with brown; irides, very dark brown; feet, olive.

Length, 13½ inches; wing, 6¼; tail, 3; bill, 2¼; tarsus, 1½.

This is larger than the English species (Scolopax Gallinago), but very similar in appearance, and the only one found in Australia, being distributed over the whole of the continent and Tasmania. It frequents marshy and swampy localities, living upon the worms, insects, and molluscs always obtainable in such situations. The long and narrow bill is covered with a soft pulpy membrane, endowed with an exquisite sense of feeling, enabling it to detect its food among the soft mud with unerring certainty. The flesh is delicious, and snipe-shooting in Australia is similar in every respect to the same sport in England. Nothing certain is known concerning its nidification, but it is supposed to breed in Tasmania.

RHYNCHŒA AUSTRALIS.

(Australian Rhynchœa.)

MALE—A stripe from the bill over the centre of the crown to the nape, and another behind the eye, light buff; the rest of the crown, dark brown; throat and cheeks, greyish white, mottled with brown; chest, deep greyish brown, mottled with white; back, brownish olive, finely banded with dark brown; shoulders, buffish grey; wing coverts, scapularies, and tertiaries, the same, but ornamented with large whitish buff spots, each surrounded with a dark brown line; tail, grey, banded with dark brown, and spotted with large oval buff spots; primaries, black, banded with rich buff; a broad band of white across the chest, followed by a blackish patch on the side of the chest—the patch marked with grey and white spots; the remainder of the under surface, pure white; legs and feet, light olive; irides, dark brown; bill, greenish tipped with brown.

The female has the wings more of an olive brown tint, finely barred with deep brown, and destitute of the spots on the scapularies and wing coverts. Her coloring on the neck and chest is more intense, the patch on the side of the chest being nearly black, and without spots. She is also larger than the male.

Length of male, 8½ inches; wing, 4½; tail, 2; bill, 1¼; tarsus, 1¾.

This rare and elegant species, the "painted snipe" of the colonists, is found in New South Wales and Queensland. The Pine Mountain, near Ipswich, and Eagle Farm Flats, near Brisbane, may be mentioned as localities where it has been recently met with. Captain Sturt found it in the interior, and mentions it in his journal, with the remark that it was nowhere common, and delighted to bask in the shade of a tree during the mid-day heat. Its food is similar to that of the common snipe, and its flight, though laborious, is straight and powerful. When disturbed, it seeks to hide itself among the bushes or reeds, and is not easily driven from its lurking place. Although nothing is known of its nidification, it probably breeds in the colony of New South Wales, as Mr. Gould mentions having met with it on the rich alluvial flats of the river Hunter, and, on dissecting a female, an egg was found in the ovarium, of the full size, but destitute of its calcareous covering. He also mentions a peculiarity in the structure of the trachea of the female, which makes four convolutions underneath the skin of the breast before entering the lungs. The use of this curious arrangement is unknown, the supposition being that it assists in the utterance of some peculiar cry; but there is no instance recorded of its doing so, the bird appearing to be perfectly voiceless.

NUMENIUS AUSTRALIS.

(Australian Curlew.)

Crown of the head and back of the neck, blackish brown, each feather margined with buff; back, blackish brown, each feather blotched with reddish buff on the margin; wing coverts, blackish brown, margined with greyish white; tertiaries, brown, irregularly blotched on the margins with lighter brown; rump and under tail coverts, dark brown, barred across the margins with greyish buff; tail, light brown, barred with dark brown; greater coverts, blackish brown, slightly tipped with white; the first five primaries, dark brown, with white stems—the remainder and the secondaries, crossed by irregular interrupted bars of white; sides of the face, throat, and all the under surface, pale buff, with a fine streak of blackish brown down the centre of each feather; bill, flesh color, tinged with olive for half its length from the base—the other portion to the tip, blackish brown; legs, lead color; irides, dark brown.

Length, 29 inches; wing, 12½; tail, 4½; bill, 7; tarsus, 3¼.

This large and conspicuous species so much resembles the common European Curlew that it might be easily supposed to be identical; but the Australian representative possesses a longer bill, and differs in other particulars. It is found in every portion of Australia and Tasmania, especially on the coast, where it frequents rivers and mud flats to feed upon the various crustacea, mollusca, and other living creatures left by the retiring tide. The shallow waters are also frequented by it, and should it step out of its depth it can swim sufficiently well to secure its own safety. Flocks of this bird may be often seen on the banks and mud flats of Moreton Bay, in company with the Mycteria and a great variety of other waders; at such times the sight through a good telescope is one of no ordinary interest.

THRESKIORNIS STRICTIPENNIS.

THRESKIORNIS STRICTIPENNIS.

(White Ibis.)

ADULT.—Head and down to the middle of the neck, quite bare, the skin being of a dull black color—the back of the head and neck have a series of stripes of a maroon tint, the crown being also spotted with the same color; general color of plumage, buffish white; primaries, tipped with greenish black, and several of the uppermost tertiaries for a considerable portion of their length are black—those immediately underneath, gradually becoming white on the inner webs; secondaries have black shafts and an oblong mark of black at the tips; bill and feet, blackish purple; irides, brown. The sexes are alike in appearance, but the male is the largest.

YOUNG.—Head and neck thickly covered with small scaly feathers of various tints, as brownish black, grey, and white, giving that portion of the bird a pied appearance; the remainder of the plumage as in the adult. Frequently the bird when obtained is so much soiled that it appears of a dirty grey tint.

Length, 32 inches; wing, 14½; tail, 6½; bill, 6¾; tarsus, 4.

This large species is a periodical visitant to the settled districts of Australia. There can be no doubt that the remote interior is its proper habitat, as its presence in the southern or eastern colonies is considered a sure indication of drought in that direction. Its visits are made in company with the Straw-necked Ibis, which would seem to indicate that both come from the same quarter. The food of the White Ibis consists of frogs, insects, etc., which it captures by wading among the rushes and acquatic plants which grow so luxuriantly in swampy situations and on river banks.

FALCINELLUS IGNEUS

FALCINELLUS IGNEUS.

(Glossy Ibis.)

HEAD, neck, upper part of the back and shoulder, and all the under surface, rich deep chestnut brown; the feathers of the crown are narrow, pointed, and glossed with purple; lower portion of the back, rump, and tail, shining blackish green, bronzed with green and purple; wings, rich deep reddish brown, glossed with green and purple; primaries, nearly black, with green reflexions; bill, olive black; irides, brown; legs and feet, blackish green. The female is similar to the male, but rather smaller in size. Weight, 16 to 18 ounces.

Expanse of wings, 2 feet 9 inches; length, 21 inches; wing 10½; tail, 4; bill, from 4½ to 6; tarsus, 3½; mid-toe, 2¾.

This beautiful species of Ibis is very widely distributed over the globe. It is recorded as occurring in every portion of Europe, its range extending even to Norway. In Britain it has not unfrequently been observed, and many specimens have been obtained throughout the various counties, though always considered a rare and only occasional visitant. In Africa and Asia it is more commonly distributed, and in America it is said to have been observed in various parts. Audubon says it is very numerous in Mexico; but that eminent ornithologist, the Prince of Canino, asserts the same to be another, though closely allied species. In Australia it is certainly very rare, but is recorded to have been taken in a variety of situations—South Australia, New South Wales, Northern Australia, and Brisbane and Cape York in Queensland. It is interesting to know that, in company with the common Sacred Ibis, this species was also regarded with veneration, by the ancient Egyptians, and that its remains are to be found carefully preserved in the catacombs. It is not to be expected that much should be known respecting so rare a wanderer to our shores, from personal observation in Australia; but it is known to feed upon fish, insects of every kind, snails, frogs, &c., in search of which it frequents swampy situations, and occasionally wades pretty deep, and even swims. The nest is formed of materials collected from the banks of the swamp, and placed upon a more elevated situation among the reeds. Sometimes several nests are to be found in close proximity. The eggs are two or three in number; color, pale green. During incubation the female is supplied with food by the male. This Ibis is usually to be found in small companies, but is very shy and difficult to approach. At the time of migration these birds assemble in immense numbers, the flight being in a series of regular rows forming a closely compacted line. The reduced figure is taken from a fine male shot at Eagle Farm, near Brisbane, by Mr. James Cockerell, in October, 1867.

MYCTERIA AUSTRALIS
Australian Mycteria.

MYCTERIA AUSTRALIS.

(*Australian Mycteria.*)

ADULT—Head and neck, shining metallic green, with the exception of the occiput, which is of a brilliant metallic purple tint; the lower portion of the back, tail, secondaries, and greater coverts, glossy blackish green, with metallic reflections; primaries, upper portion of the back, and also of the wings, the chest and abdomen, pure white; bill, black; irides, hazel; legs and feet, vermillion red.

In the young bird, the legs and feet are black, with a tinge of red.

Height, 52 inches; length, 56; wing, 24; tail, 11; bill, 13; tarsus, 12½; middle toe, 4½.

The genus Mycteria comprises only three known species—one being American, a second Asiatic, and the third Australian. The Mycteria Australis is found in various parts of the continent of Australia, for the most part frequenting the coast. It is shy and wary in the extreme, choosing the most quiet and secluded bays and sandy beaches, where it roams about in search of food, and may be occasionally seen in company with a variety of other birds having similar habits. It also visits some of the rivers of the interior, Leichhardt having met with it on the Burdekin, in lat. 20° 47'. It has a most voracious appetite, and consumes great quantities of fish, eels being especially preferred. To obtain a specimen of this bird is a matter not easily accomplished: a native is generally employed, who, creeping on all-fours, and artfully hiding behind rocks or bushes, is able sometimes to approach near enough to make a successful shot. The Australian Mycteria flies well, and can sustain itself upon the wing for a considerable time. When on the wing the long legs are thrust behind in a horizontal direction, and look like a long red tail. It appears to have no voice. A specimen kept for about seven months by Dr. Bennett, of Sydney, became very tame and familiar, and, in his "Gatherings of a Naturalist in Australia," that gentleman treats very fully and interestingly of its ways and doings while in a state of captivity. Flies and cicadas were choice morsels. When lying down, the legs were doubled up underneath the body, and it somewhat resembled a large goose with a disproportionate size of bill.

·

HERODIAS PLUMIFERUS
Plumed Egret

HERODIAS PLUMIFERUS.

(Plumed Egret.)

THE entire plumage is pure white. From the centre of the back and lower part of the neck depend a series of graceful plumes, long and finely divided. Bill and orbits, bright yellow; legs and feet, black, except the upper part of the thigh, which is yellow; irides, straw yellow.

Length, 22 inches; wing, 11; tail, 4½; bill, 3½; tarsus, 4.

Of the three species of white Egret inhabiting Australia, this takes the intermediate position in size. It is an extremely beautiful and delicate bird. The ornamental plumes are probably assumed only during the breeding season, as at certain times the bird does not possess them. The range of this species is considerable from north to south, and it is also probably found in Java—a species described by Wagler as Herodias Intermedia being apparently identical. Nothing is known of its nidification, which must assimilate to that of its congeners. It is not unfrequently met with on the mud banks at the mouth of the Brisbane river; also among the small islands at the southern part of Moreton Bay, and all such like places on our eastern coast. Of its presence in Western Australia we have as yet no notification. Its food consists of small reptiles, fish, and crustacea.

ARDETTA FLAVICOLLIS.

Yellow-necked Bittern.

Crown of the head, back of the neck, upper surface, and wings, deep brown; spurious wing and primaries, dark grey; sides of the neck, buff; under surface, buff mingled with grey; throat, white. Down the front of the neck, from the bill to the middle of the breast, is a row of dark blackish triangular patches, regularly disposed, and largest on the chest. Irides, straw yellow; orbits, greenish yellow; bill, olive brown above, yellowish grey beneath; tarsi and upper part of toes, olive brown; back of tarsi, fore part of tibia, and knees, citron yellow. The female is not so bright in her markings.

Length, 22½ inches; wing, 8¼; tail, 3½; bill, 3½; tarsus, 2¾.

This species is found in every portion of Australia, and is probably also an inhabitant of Java and India; but the specimens from the latter localities are smaller. It varies somewhat in color, some specimens being more brightly tinted than others. Its place of resort is exclusively the belts of mangrove found on the banks of tidal rivers and swamps, from which situations, although by no means shy, it is not easily driven, as it dexterously evades pursuit among the thick and entangled roots of the trees, running over the mud with considerable speed. The nest is usually built on the horizontal branch of a mangrove tree, and is formed of small sticks. The eggs, two to four in number, are of a greenish white color, and rounded in form: 1½ by 1¼ inch. Season of incubation, November to January.

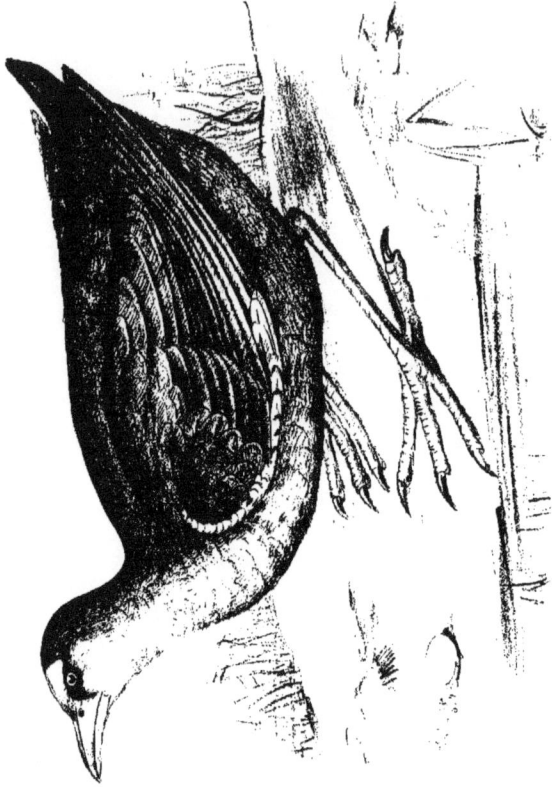

PORPHYRIO BELLUS
Azure breasted Porphyrio

PORPHYRIO BELLUS.

Azure-breasted Porphyrio.

UPPER surface, wings, and tail, blackish brown; cheeks, throat, and under surface, violet blue, which is brightest on the chest, and becomes of a greyer hue on the flanks and abdomen; shoulder and edge of the wing down to the spurious wing, azure blue; primaries, tinged with green on the outer webs; under tail coverts, white; irides, bright red; bill, red; legs and feet, grass green, except the knees, lower portion of tarsus, and inside of the feet, which are dark greenish grey. The male is larger than the female, and somewhat brighter in color.

Length, 18 inches; wing, 10½; tail, 4½; bill, 1¾; tarsus, 3¼.

This species is confined to Western Australia, and inhabits swampy situations, lagoons, and reed beds, feeding upon insects, molluscs, and also some kind of vegetable substance. It is by far the finest of the two species inhabiting Australia, being not only larger but more brilliantly colored than the P. Melanotus of the southern and eastern districts.

CEREOPSIS NOVÆ HOLLANDIÆ.

(Cereopsis Goose.)

———•———

Geneeral plumage, light dingy grey—darker on the upper than the lower surface; a patch of dull white on the crown; primaries, for about one-third of their length from the tips, and secondaries, for about a quarter their length from the tips, black; upper tail coverts and tail, dull black; wing coverts and scapularies, spotted, the former with small and the latter with large, blackish grey spots near the tips; bill, light green, with a narrow black line adjoining the head, the tip is also black; cere, yellow; irides, vermilion or claret color; legs, crimson or reddish orange; toes and webs of the feet, black. The sexes are alike in plumage. The young assume the adult plumage at an early age.

Length, 29 inches; wing, 15; tail, 6¼; bill, 1½; tarsus, 4; mid-toe, 3¼.

This singular bird is about the size and weight of a common goose, and is found widely dispersed over the islands in Bass' Straits and the southern coast of Victoria. When first discovered by our early explorers it was very tame, and frequently killed with sticks and such like weapons; it is now much more wary, and anything but numerous. It has rarely been found in the northern portion of New South Wales. It breeds freely in confinement, and would be a valuable addition to our poultry yards were it not for its pugnacious habits, which make it undesirable. It is strictly, or nearly so, a vegetable feeder, and its flesh is excellent. The gardens of the London Zoological Society have possessed them since their formation, and have been the means of distributing them to many private collectors. Its note is hoarse and disagreeable. The eggs are creamy white, about 3½ inches in length by 2½ broad.

ANSERANAS MELANOLEUCA.

(Pied or Semi-palmated Goose.)

MALE—Head, wings, middle of back, tail, and thighs, bright greenish black; the rest of the plumage white; upper mandible enlarged into a knob where it joins the head; the bill to a little beyond the nostrils, dark dull purplish flesh color—the extremity, blue; legs and feet, orange.

The Female is not so bright in her plumage as the Male, being more of a brownish black tint, with much less bright reflections of green. Her bill is also destitute of the excrescence.

Length, 34 inches; wing, 18; tail, 7½; bill, 3½; tarsus, 3¾; middle toe, 5.

This large and conspicuous species is found all throughout the interior of Australia, becoming more numerous to the north. It pays irregular and by no means frequent visits to the coast, and has been shot in the neighborhood of Brisbane. Its usual and favorite resort is fresh water rivers, and lagoons. Leichhardt found this species in great plenty all round the Gulf of Carpentaria, and being excellent eating, it proved a valuable addition to his scanty supplies of food, when on his arduous journey to Port Essington. A fine specimen will weigh from six to seven pounds. It is only an occasional visitor to some districts, an interval of many years elapsing before it is again seen. The *Darling Downs Gazette* mentions one of these visits in March, 1865, in the following terms: "Wednesday evening, " the 15th instant, Warwick was visited by large flocks of geese, which took to the river and the trees in the neighbourhood of the town. " So stupid were they, or so unaccustomed to the effects of fire arms, that out of a flock of twenty-one which roosted in one locality, twenty " fell before the guns of the sportsmen." The trachea is very long, measuring considerably more than a yard, and makes four convolutions before entering the lungs. The webs of the feet are short—a modification necessary to its habits as a perching bird. The eggs are said to be of a cream color.

BERNICLA JUBATA
Maned Goose

BERNICLA JUBATA.

(Maned Goose.)

MALE.—Head and neck, deep brown; behind the neck, a mane of deep black; the under eyelid, clothed with minute white feathers; upper part of the back, deep grey, with darker lunate markings; lower portion of the back and the tail, deep black; breast, light creamy grey, each feather margined at the eye with intense black, giving that part a spotted appearance; the tip of each feather, whitish, delicately spotted with black, which feature is continued to a considerable extent down the abdomen, the centre part of which is jet black; the flanks are beautifully and regularly barred with minute stripes of black on a light grey ground; under tail coverts, black; shoulder and upper wing coverts, reddish grey, followed by a stripe of white; secondaries, bright metallic green for about one-third their length, and terminating with pure white for the remainder; primaries, deep brown at the tip; inner webs, externally, black; tertiaries, grey—several being margined with black, the lowest pair showing the beautiful metallic green which adorns the secondaries; bill, olive brown; irides and feet, dark brown.

The FEMALE is smaller, and has the head and neck paler than the male, and though possessing the spotting as conspicuously on the breast, has only a small indication of the glossy green speculum; the centre of the abdomen and under tail coverts are white. She differs in other minor particulars, but bears so general a resemblance to the male as not to be mistaken. She is also destitute of the mane.

Length, 19¼ inches; wing, 10¾; tail, 5; bill, 1⅛; tarsus, 1¾.

This beautiful species, the "Wood Duck" of the colonists, is found very largely distributed over the Australian continent. It has been found in every locality except the extreme north, but does not probably visit Tasmania. Its beautiful appearance and the excellency of its flesh (scarcely inferior to that of the black duck), render it an object much coveted by the sportsman, and being by no means shy, there is little difficulty in shooting it when it is to be found. It associates in small companies of from six or eight to thirty or forty; and when feeding among the grass in the neighborhood of lagoons, a flock presents a picturesque appearance, the brilliant plumage of the adult male forming a pleasing contrast to the more unassuming tints of the other sex. It perches commonly on trees, as do also several other species of Australian ducks and geese. It builds in the hollows of trees, sometimes at a considerable distance from water. The young are not unfrequently obtained, and are easily domesticated, feeding and associating readily with common poultry.

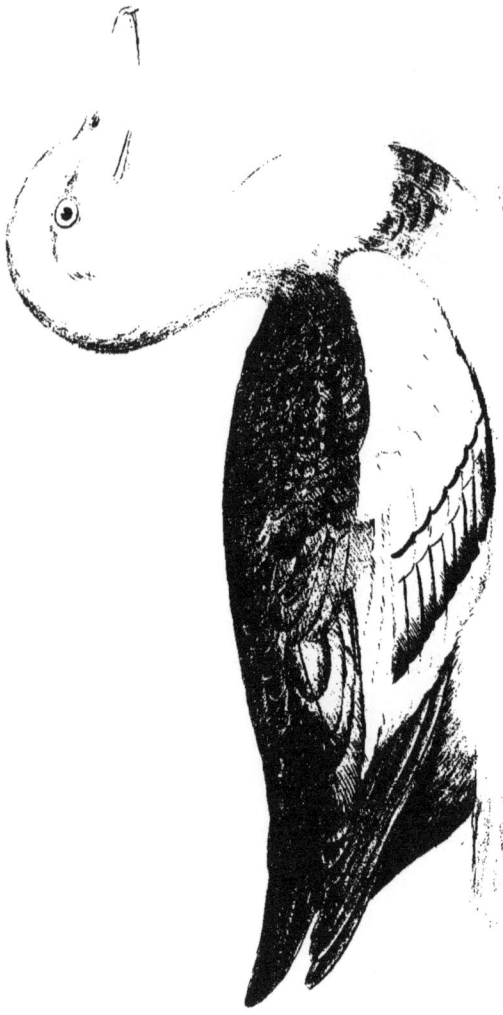

TADORNAH RADJAH
Radjah Shieldrake

TADORNA RADJAH.

(*Radjah Shieldrake.*)

HEAD, neck, upper portion of the wing, breast, and abdomen, pure white; back, scapularies, and a band across the chest, black, marked with fine pencillings of chestnut—the latter color also adorns the outer edges of several of the tertiaries; tail, black; the greater wing coverts are crossed by a broad line of black; secondaries, for about two thirds of their length, shining metallic green, the remaining portion, white; primaries, deep black; under tail coverts speckled with grey; bill, whitish flesh color; foot, salmon color; irides, straw color.

Length, 22 inches; wing, 11; bill, 2¼; tail, 5½; foot 2½.

This handsome and conspicuous species is found in immense flocks about the northern coast, and is by no means of uncommon occurrence in the vicinity of Brisbane, which may be called its southern limit. It is not known to inhabit the interior, but occurs in various islands of the Malayan Archipelago. Its usual habitat is mud flats and mangrove swamps on the banks of tidal rivers, and its food consists for the most part of small shell-fish. The flesh is coarse, and of an unpleasant flavor.

SPATULA RHYNCHOTIS
Australian Shoveller

SPATULA RHYNCHOTIS.

(Australian Shoveller.)

MALE.—Crown to the nape, lores, and stripe behind the neck, dark brown; back and scapularies, brownish black—each feather edged with reddish buff; a stripe of white runs from the front of the eye in a curved direction backwards down the sides of the upper part of the throat; face and sides of the neck, dark grey, suffused with green; at the point where the neck joins the body is an indistinct ring of white, broadest above and mottled with brown; throat, brown, delicately streaked with whitish; shoulders, lesser coverts, and outer edges and tips of some of the tertiaries, greyish blue; greater coverts, black, externally edged and tipped with pure white; edge of wing, white, mottled with greyish brown; under surface of shoulder, pure white; secondaries, brilliant metallic green; primaries, brown; the remainder of the tertiaries, green, black, and white, arranged longitudinally in various proportions of color; chest, buff, lunated with dark brown; abdomen, rich chestnut red, mottled with black, and banded with black on the flanks; lower portion of the back, upper and under tail coverts, blackish brown, glossed with green; tail, brown, very narrowly tipped with whitish; at the base of the tail, on either side, is a patch of white delicately mottled with black; irides, legs, and feet, yellow; bill, purplish black.

FEMALE.—Head and neck, buff, streaked with dark brown; all the upper surface dark brown, each feather margined with whitish brown; wings, similar, but not so brilliant as in the male; under surface, mottled brown and buff.

Length, 20 inches; wing, 9¼; tail, 3⅞; bill, 2⅞; tarsus, 1¼; mid-toe, 2¼.

The above description of the male is the plumage of the pairing season; at other times it is very similar in appearance to the female. It is found in almost every part of Australia, except, perhaps, the extreme north. It is frequently found in company with the common black duck (Anas Superciliosa), and falls a victim to the gun of the sportsman more by accident than design. Its flesh is excellent. The nest and eggs of this bird are still desiderata.

SPATULA CLYPEATA.

(European Shoveller.)

MALE.—Head and upper part of the neck, deep glossy green; lower part of the back, breast, scapularies, and sides of the rump, white; back, blackish brown—each feather margined with grey and tinged with green; lesser wing coverts, and some of the scapularies, greyish blue; tips of the larger coverts, white, forming a bar across the wing; speculum, rich green; tertials, rich purplish black, with a streak of white down the centre; middle tail feathers, brown, edged with white; outer ones, entirely white; upper and under tail coverts, black, tinged with green; under surface, reddish brown; flanks and vent, pale brown, crossed by numerous irregular lines of black; bill, blackish brown; legs, orange red.

FEMALE.—The whole of the upper surface, deep brown, each feather barred and margined with white.

This is the description of the plumage at the termination of the breeding season, which, when over, gives place to the following :—
Male.—Cheeks, sides of the neck, and throat, reddish white, speckled with brown; crown of the head and nape of the neck, black, glossed with green, and each feather with a paler margin; back and scapularies, deep brown, margined with pale, yellowish brown; breast, mingled yellowish brown and white; abdomen, mingled yellow and orange brown.

The above description is by Mr. Gould, whose attention was first directed to this species from a specimen in the possession of, and shot by, the late Mr. Coxen, of Yarrundi. That eminent ornithologist at once perceived the difference between it and the S. Rhynchotis, and, after careful examination, found it to be identical with the European species. An accident occurring by which the specimen was lost, precluded him from making use of it, and he never met with another. It doubtless is a rare and only occasional visitant to this country.

MALACORHYNCHUS MEMBRANACEUS
Membranaceous Duck

MALACHORHYNCHUS MEMBRANACEUS.

(Membranaceous Duck.)

CROWN of the head, occiput, and a rather narrow line behind the neck, greyish brown; a ring of white round the eye, narrow above and broader beneath, the ring being surrounded by a large patch of blackish brown, which is much expanded beneath the eye; throat and front of the face, pure white; a tuft of pink feathers above the ears; hinder part of the face, sides, and front of the neck, light grey, crossed by fine bands of greyish brown; lower portion of neck, upper part of back, chest, and flanks, broadly banded with black and white; centre of abdomen, white; back and wings, brown; central feathers of tail, dark greyish brown; the remainder the same, but slightly tipped with white; upper tail coverts, white, tipped with black; under tail coverts, light buff; secondaries and several of the shorter primaries, tipped with white; irides, hazel; bill, brown; feet, greenish lead color.

Length, 17 inches; wing, 7; tail, 3½; bill, 2¼; tarsus, 1.

This, which may be regarded as one of the prettiest of the duck tribe belonging to Australia, is found in New South Wales, Victoria, Western Australia, Queensland, and occasionally Tasmania. The singular conformation of the bill may be supposed to give it peculiar advantages in procuring its food. The comb underneath the upper mandible is largely developed, and, in addition, it is provided with a piece of loose membrane or skin at each side of the bill, which has the effect of widening that organ to a considerable extent, and being doubtless endowed with great sensibility, probably enables it to discriminate its food more easily than other species not thus furnished. It occurs in small flocks, and, in the act of flying, utters a shrill whistle. When wounded, its habit is to quit the water, and endeavor to hide among the reeds or nearest vegetation. On one being wounded, the rest of the flock show much sympathy, and the greater portion sometimes fall victims to the gun of the sportsman in consequence. The flesh is not much appreciated, because of its fishy flavor. There is no difference in the sexes, except sometimes a little more brightness in the plumage of the male. Nest and eggs unknown.

D. ARCUATA
Whistling Tree Duck

DENDROCYGNA EYTONI
Eyton's Tree Duck

DENDROCYGNA EYTONI.

(Eyton's Tree Duck.)

CROWN of the head and face, greyish brown; a broad central line of deep greyish brown down the back of the neck; a narrow stripe of white next the bill, and the throat white; sides of the neck and the breast, fawn color; back and upper part of the wings, greyish olive—each feather margined with lighter; rump and tail, brownish black, crossed by a band of buff; upper part of the abdomen, light chestnut red, barred with black; elongated lanceolate flank feathers, buff, margined with black; lower portion of the abdomen and the under tail coverts, buffy white; feet, bright rose color; bill, reddish flesh color, with a large blackish mottled patch in the centre; irides, orange.

Length, 20 inches; wing, 8½; tail, 3½; bill, 1½; tarsus, 2⅜.

This species may be regarded as one of the finest of its family in the Australian continent, to the north and north-eastern portions of which it is for the most part confined. The country around the Gulf of Carpentaria is frequented by it in large numbers; being noticed by Leichhardt in abundance at Murphy's Lake, and by Capt. Stokes as very plentiful in the Adelaide River. Like several other Australian ducks, this species is in the habit of perching on trees, whence the name of "wood duck" has been applied to them. When on the wing this bird utters a loud whistle, which can be heard at a great distance. When alighting on a tree it is some time before it gains its equilibrium, tossing to and fro in a very awkward manner. The figures in the plate are much reduced in size. The specimen from which the drawing is taken was shot near Brisbane in 1864, and is now (1869) in Mr. Waller's collection.

DENDROCYGNA ARCUATA.

(Whistling Tree Duck.)

FOREHEAD, crown, a line down the back of the neck, wings, and the tail, brownish black; back and scapularies, dark brownish black—each feather margined with deep buff; breast, deep fawn buff, passing into chestnut on the abdomen—each feather of the chest crossed by a short bar of black; face and sides of the neck, buff; centre of abdomen, buff, mottled with black; under tail coverts, white; wing coverts, chestnut; flank feathers, white, broadly margined with black below; irides, deep brown; bill, black; tarsus, greenish grey.

Length, 18 inches; wing, 8½; tail, 2½; bill, 2½; tarsus, 2.

This species is not uncommon in some parts of Queensland, having a range from south to probably the extreme north, as it is known to inhabit Port Essington, to the west of the Gulf of Carpentaria. It is frequently found in company with other species of duck, and is sometimes shot in mistake for the common black duck (Anas Superciliosa), like which species it is excellent eating. Like D. Eytoni, this bird is a percher, and utters a loud whistle when on the wing, from whence its popular name is derived. It is very rarely to be found so far south as Brisbane; but on each occasion of such visit its stay has been but short, and had the character of a migratory passage. Thus, in 1854, about August, it appeared in the Brisbane River in large numbers, and might have been seen in the middle of the stream, gathered closely in flocks of from fifteen to thirty, floating with the tide. They were approached and shot without much difficulty, and, when disturbed, they made but a short flight and clustered again on the water. Since that date I am only aware of some two or three visits, and in each case the numbers were much diminished.

NYROCA AUSTRALIS.

(White-eyed Duck.)

MALE.—Head and neck, dark chestnut brown; back and tail the same color, each feather margined with buffish chestnut; shoulder margined with white; wing coverts, blackish brown; secondaries, white, largely tipped with blackish brown; primaries, blackish brown, the basal portions and inner webs, white; chest and flanks, ferruginous, each feather margined with a lighter tint; centre of abdomen and under tail coverts, white.

FEMALE.—Head, dull chestnut brown; upper surface, umber brown, each feather margined with buffish brown; under surface, light brown, each feather tipped with buff or white, which two colors are pretty equally mingled on the centre of the abdomen. The remainder of the plumage is similar to, though not so bright as, that of the male; irides, white in the male—brown in the female; bill, black, banded with bluish grey at the tip; feet, blackish brown.

Every portion of Australia is, in all probability, visited by this species, some localities being more frequented than others. It is decidedly uncommon in the northern parts of the continent, as Cape York and Port Essington; but is found frequenting the rivers and lagoons in various parts of New South Wales and Tasmania in considerable numbers. It swims and dives well—the latter qualification eminently serving it, as its food consists of aquatic insects, mollusca, &c., besides vegetable substances, most of which are obtained beneath the surface of the water. It is subject to the attacks of the Falco Melanogenys, or "duck hawk," and forms the favorite food of that bird. It is usually found in company with ducks of other species, associating with them in the utmost amity. This species very much resembles the *Nyroca Anas* of Great Britain, differing chiefly in size.

BIZIURA LOBATA
Musk Duck

BIZIURA LOBATA.

(Musk Duck.)

Crown of the head and back of the neck, brownish black; wings and tail, blackish brown; back, chest, and flanks, the same, numerously and narrowly barred with buffish white; throat, cheeks, and abdomen, dark brown, also barred with buffish white; bill and lobe under the chin, greenish black; irides, dark hazel; legs and feet, dark grey. The female is much smaller in size, and has the markings much less distinct; she is also destitute of the lobe.

Length of male, 26 inches; wing, 9; tail, 5; bill, 2¼; tarsus, 2¼; middle toe, 3¾.

This remarkable species is peculiar to Australia. Its appearance is more singular than beautiful. The curious appendage, or lobe, beneath the chin is flat, and of a leathery consistency. The tail is very stiff and horny; the strong musky odor, emitted during the breeding season, flavors the flesh to such a degree as to render it uneatable, and preserved skins retain the scent for years. The wings are so short as scarcely to be available for flight. Instead of taking wing on being alarmed, it invariably dives, and rises at a considerable distance, with its head only visible. It is very difficult to shoot, as it dives at the flash. With the exception, perhaps, of the extreme north, every portion of Australia and Tasmania is frequented by this curious bird. The rivers both of the coast and the interior, inlets of the sea, solitary lagoons, and even small water holes are situations in which it may be met with, usually in pairs. On the Murray and Lake Victoria it is especially plentiful. Its food consists of aquatic insects and molluscs, the various species of bi-valves being favorite morsels. The fine specimen shot by Mr. Jameson, near Ipswich, from which the figure was taken, had its stomach crammed with a small spiral univalve about half an inch in length. The season of incubation is September and October; the nest being formed among reeds, frequently level with the water, and lined with down plucked from the breast of the bird. The eggs are also covered with the same material, are very thick shelled, and of a pale sea green color: size, 3 inches long by 1 inch broad.

■

XEMA JAMESONI.

(Jameson's Gull.)

HEAD, neck, under surface, and tail, pure white; back and wings, light grey; spurious wing, white; primaries, black, with patches of white; the basal portion of all but the two outer feathers, grey; bill, legs, and eyelids, bright red; irides, white. The sexes are much alike, but the female is the smallest. The young birds are more or less mottled with brown, especially on the back and wings; the tail is also tipped with the same color.

Length, 17½ inches; wing, 13; tail, 5; bill, 1¾; tarsus, 2.

This fine species is found from Queensland round the eastern and southern coasts; has been met with at Cooper's Creek, in the far interior; and is very common about Sydney at times, especially in dull weather, frequenting the paddocks, at no great distance from the city, in great numbers. It is a beautiful and graceful bird, and frequently abundant in certain localities, such as Goose Island, in Bass' Straits. Its flight is easy and buoyant, like that of the gull tribe in general. It breeds on the low islands of Bass' Straits, great numbers incubating in company. The nest is formed of rushes and grasses. The eggs, four or five in number, are variable both in color and shape, no two being alike; they are either greenish or olive brown, more or less streaked and blotched with blackish brown.

PELICANUS CONSPICILLATUS.

(Australian Pelican.)

ADULT.—Head, neck, and all the upper and under surface, white, except a line along the shoulder, lowest row of wing coverts, primaries, secondaries, several of the upper tail coverts, and tail, which are black; bill and pouch, flesh color, the former tipped with light yellow; orbits, light yellow, surrounded by a ring of light blue; irides, dark brown; feet, pale bluish grey.

YOUNG.—Forehead, throat, under side of neck, all the under surface of shoulders, and upper portion of back, pure white; crown, occiput, and back of the neck, light grey; rump, white in the centre, with two rows of dark feathers at the sides; the remainder of the coloring as in the adult, but brown instead of black.

Expanse, 8 feet; length, 5 feet 8 inches; wing, 22 inches; tail 6; bill, 16½; tarsus, 4; mid-toe and claw, 5.

Every portion of Australia and Tasmania is frequented by this species of Pelican. It is most generally found in creeks and inlets of the sea, but is also not infrequently met with in the lakes, lagoons, and rivers of the interior. It sometimes occurs in numerous flocks in situations where food is abundant, as in the larger streams, and resorts to quiet, solitary, land-locked estuaries for the purpose of breeding. The eggs are sometimes deposited in a nest formed of sticks and grassy herbage, placed just above high water mark, or (as in Cook's Island, a rocky islet south of the Tweed) in hollows of the bare rock. They are two in number: color, impure white: size, 3½ inches long by 2½ broad. The food of the Pelican consists of fish of various kinds. It is very voracious. Its flight is well sustained and powerful, considering the weight of so large a bird. The flesh is fleshy, coarse, and scarcely eatable.

PHALACROCORAX SULCIROSTRIS.

(Groove-billed Cormorant.)

THE general plumage, dark shining black, with greenish tint; wing feathers, grey, margined with greenish black; irides, deep grass green; orbits, dark lead color; bill, dark grey, black along the ridge of the upper mandible; feet, dark grey, inclining to black; pouch, dark bluish grey.

Length, 25 inches; wing, 10; tail, 6½; bill, 3; tarsus, 2; longest toe, 3.

This species is rarely found along the coasts, but is common on all the rivers, creeks, and lagoons, of the interior, and is frequently seen sitting on the branches of trees overhanging the water, or on fallen timber protruding above its surface, in small companies of five to ten. Its food consists of frogs, small fish, water lizards, etc. Information concerning its nest and eggs is still a desideratum.

PLOTUS NOVÆ HOLLANDIÆ

PLOTUS NOVÆ HOLLANDIÆ
New Holland Darter

PLOTUS NOVÆ HOLLANDIÆ.

(New Holland Darter.)

MALE.—Throat for two inches, and a broad stripe from the bill down the middle of the neck, glossy white; head, back of the neck, and upper surface, black, glossy, and slightly tinged with green; front of the neck, rusty brown; wing coverts, dull buff margined with black; scapularies, lanceolate, with a central stripe of dull buff, and margined with black; the four internal tertiaries have a broad stripe of dull buff on their outer webs immediately adjoining the quill, the rest and all the primaries, shining greyish black; the largest and lowest of the tertiaries and uppermost tail feathers, corrugated transversely on the outer webs; plumage generally, wiry and stiff.

FEMALE.—Crown of the head, back of neck, and upper part of back, blackish brown, with greyish margin to the feathers of the latter; throat and under surface, buffy white; remaining parts very much like the male, excepting the white marks on the wing coverts, which are larger; bill, blackish green, the basal portion, yellow; feet, pale yellow; irides, yellow.

Length, 37 inches; wing, 14½; tail, 10; bill, 3½.

This, which is the only species inhabiting the Australian continent, is found in New South Wales, Victoria, and Queensland, frequenting tidal and fresh water rivers running into the sea. It has also been met with on the Victoria River on the northern coast. It is of very common occurrence on the Brisbane River, where it may generally be seen perched upon a bough by the water side, intently watching for its fishy prey. On being disturbed it assumes various curious attitudes, its long snake-like neck being moved about in every direction; when fairly driven off it takes a short flight at a small distance above the surface of the water, and alights again without delay. Sometimes it will dive and swim about, its head and neck only being visible, at which time it is very difficult to shoot. The late Mr. Elsey, surgeon to Gregory's expedition into the interior, says, "During February and March it was incubating. It chooses large trees that hang over the water, above or through the mangroves, and in them a number of them build a colony of large coarse flattish nests of dead sticks and twigs, which seem, from the quantity of dirt about them, and their stained appearance, to be used year after year. Each season they place in the centre a few fresh green leaves, and on these lay three or four white eggs with a very opaque but brittle shell, the lining membrane of which is of a blue grey color; they are rather smaller than hens' eggs. We have enjoyed many meals off these eggs; sometimes getting from forty to fifty in a single tree. Both birds sit." Its time of incubation in the neighbourhood of Brisbane is about December and January. The edges of the upper mandible are furnished with small sharp serrations, enabling it to retain its slippery prey with great ease. Complaints have lately been made that the Salmon, introduced at so great an expense in Victoria, have suffered considerably from the depredations of this bird, specimens having been killed with the crop literally stuffed with the young fry.

PODICEPS AUSTRALIS
Australian Tippet Grebe

PODICEPS AUSTRALIS.

(Australian Tippet Grebe.)

FOREHEAD and crown, dark greyish brown; the crest, which stands out behind, is divided into two parts, and of a darker color; lores, throat, and cheeks, white, blending into ferruginous downwards and behind, and forming a ruff nearly round the neck, which, with the crest, is erectable at pleasure; the tippet is edged with dark brown; neck, glossy white in front and sides, brown behind; all the under surface, glossy white; back, brownish grey, sometimes tinged with ferruginous, and showing greenish reflexions on the darker parts; wing coverts, light brown, washed with grey; greater coverts and primaries, blackish brown; secondaries, white, forming a band across the wing; tail (very short), dark brownish black; irides, light scarlet; bill, crimson, blackish on the culmen; legs and feet, blackish olive—the scales in front tinged with buff.

Length, 23 inches; wing, 8; bill, 2¼; tarsus, 2½.

The sexes are much alike, the female being the smallest.

This species has been found for the most part in the south-eastern and southern colonies of Australia, and more recently in Queensland. The fine specimen from which my figure is taken was shot near Brisbane; and there can be little doubt that, as our knowledge is extended, this bird will be found in every portion of Australia, as it is more than probable that, like many other birds hitherto supposed to be exclusively Australian, it will be ascertained to have a much greater range of habitat, and in the present instance to be only a mere variety of the Podiceps Cristatus found in so many parts of the world. In its habits and economy it assimilates in all respects. The situations frequented by this species are lagoons, rivers, creeks, and arms of the sea, especially where rushes, reeds, and other water plants are plentiful. The Tippet Grebe can fly very well, and for a considerable distance, and its swimming and diving powers are amazing. It frequently only raises its head above the surface of the water to take breath, hence the difficulty of shooting it. The legs being situated so far behind, preclude its walking with ease, and its attitude is in consequence nearly upright. Its food consists of almost every animated thing obtainable in the water: fish, frogs, small crustacea, insects, etc., and vegetable matter, has been found in the stomach. The nest will prove the same as that of P. Cristatus, which is described as being made very carelessly—a mere mass of reeds, flags, or other vegetable substances, partly under and partly above the water, the upper surface hollowed to contain the eggs, which are from three to five in number, and of a greenish white. During the absence of the birds they are carefully concealed by vegetable debris, such as fragments of rushes, etc.

OEDICNEMUS GRALLARIUS.

(Southern Stone Plover.)

CROWN of the head, back of the neck, and back, grey, striped with brownish black; loros, chin, and space surrounding the eye, white; ear coverts, a broad stripe down the side of the neck, and a narrow streak in front and beneath the eye, dark brown; upper wing coverts and tertiaries, brown, broadly striped with black down the centre—the latter margined with white; lower coverts, white, tipped with brown, and also striped with black; primaries, brownish black, irregularly banded with white towards their extremities; tail, brown, crossed by bands of white and brown, and tipped largely with black; breast and abdomen, buffish white, broadly striped with dark brown; the remainder of the under surface, white; bill, black; irides, yellow; legs, yellowish olive, becoming darker on the feet.

Length, 23 inches; wing, 11½; tail, 7½; bill, 2; tarsus, 5½; mid-toe, 2.

This large and conspicuous species is found in all parts of Australia, except, perhaps, the most northern portions (unless those found there are identical, of which there seems to be some doubt, as they differ in several particulars), and is of frequent occurrence, being found in a great variety of situations—stony and ridgey country, flats and tea-tree swamps, and among the mangroves bordering rivers, associating in numbers from two to ten. It is shy in disposition, and not easily approached, yet, confident in its peculiar disguise, will sometimes almost suffer itself to be trodden upon before taking wing. Like many other birds, it employs the stratagem of feigning to be wounded to entice the intruder from the vicinity of its nest. Its note is an extremely mournful whistling wail, which is uttered in the evening and during the night, and resembles the syllables "wee loo" drawn out and repeated several times. The eggs are deposited on the bare ground, and are two in number; they are variable, but generally buff, and much blotched with brown of different degrees of intensity; size 2½ by 1½ inches. It breeds from September to December. The food consists of insects and berries.

www.ingramcontent.com/pod-product-compliance
Lightning Source LLC
Chambersburg PA
CBHW032302280326
41932CB00009B/671